THE
BOOK OF
CATHOLIC AUTHORS

(Third Series)

*Informal self-portraits of famous
modern Catholic writers, edited
with preface and notes*

by

WALTER ROMIG

fully illustrated by portraits

WALTER ROMIG, Publisher
979 LAKEPOINTE ROAD
GROSSE POINTE 30, MICHIGAN

COPYRIGHT, 1945
BY
WALTER ROMIG & COMPANY

Publishers of
The Guide to Catholic Literature
The American Catholic Who's Who
The Book of Catholic Authors
American Catholic Convert Authors
Negro Catholic Writers

TYPOGRAPHY, PRINTING, AND BINDING IN THE U. S. A. BY
KINGSPORT PRESS, INC., KINGSPORT, TENNESSEE

To

BROTHER GEORGE N. SCHUSTER, S.M.

An Apostle of Catholic Literature

PREFACE

Noblesse oblige! A person of character is obliging, and a Master of Ceremonies could hardly walk out on his audience while they display the enthusiasm that readers of this series are showing for it. And so, the fourth series is not merely in preparation; it is just about ready for press. What is more important, it maintains the same high level of value and of interest that is making the entire series so widely popular. The secret of its popularity doubtless lies largely in the fact that, being autobiographical, it brings you both the personality of each author as well as a specimen of his writing style.

Too, by now it has been well proven that the principal purpose of the series is being excellently attained, namely, that these genial, informal but informative autobiographies of distinguished Catholic writers are leading more and more readers from an author's sketch to his books.

Those who desire greater detail in factual biographical data are referred to the volumes of *The American Catholic Who's Who,* and those who wish for more material on any or all of the authors' books are referred to *The Guide to Catholic Literature, 1888–1940,* and its first permanent supplement, *The Guide . . . , 1940–1944.*

To all who have shared in the making of this series, in particular my wife, I express my thanks.

WALTER ROMIG

CONTENTS

of the first three series of *The Book of Catholic Authors,* with the number preceding the name indicating in which series the author's chapter is to be found

CONTENTS

CONTENTS

LUCILLE PAPIN BORDEN

HALF FRENCH, half British by descent, my forbears came to this country from Brittany and Cornwall in the early 1600's. A Crusader ancestor, Sir John Trenowyth, lies buried in Falmouth's little church of Saint Michael Penkivil, across the river Fal from the beautiful Cornish city. My paternal great-great-grandfather was the Marquis Pierre Liguest de Laclede, commissioned by Louis XV to come to America and found a city to be named for the King. This he did, but he named it for another King Louis of France, Louis IX, and called it Saint Louis.

It was there that I was born, and for the most part educated at the Sacred Heart Convent, Maryville, now a college affiliated with the Saint Louis University, which, a few years ago, gave me the degree of Bachelor of Literature.

In 1898 I married Gerald Borden. We have travelled all over the United States, Canada, and Europe, living for months at a time in Rome, Assisi, Florence, Venice, London and the English country, Ireland, Scotland, Wales, France, Switzerland. We stayed often in Bavaria, in Oberammergau, in the happy days of the Passion Play. And sometimes when there was no play, living in the house of Anton Lang, Christus of the play for three decades.

We disliked the rest of Germany; went to it, to see it, but rarely returned to any one place.

In Maine, up on Mount Desert Island, at the edge of Frenchman's Bay, so close to the water that when the tide is in I can drop a pebble from my balcony into the splashing waves, lies "Anchorhold," our summer home, named for the Anchorholds so exquisitely described by Enid Dinnis in several of her medieval stories. In her book called *Anchorhold* Miss Dinnis might have been describing our cottage. It lies in an acre of land, a white house at the rim of the sea. It is trimmed in green, and has a light shining in a window for ships. Alas, the light is darkened now and the window is dim, and more than one poor little fisherman's boat around the great bend that touches the open ocean, has made surrender its catch to an undersea monster without mercy.

"In the house there is a room for the Lord God." Anchorhold's little chapel is always ready to receive those who come to the early blessed Sacrifice. Beside it is a room always kept sacrosanct for whatever chaplain may come. While we have had a Provincial of the Franciscan Capuchin Order from England, on his visitation to the English foundation in this country, a Bishop, a Rector of Saint Patrick's Cathedral in New York, and a number of secular priests, those who come for the most part are the Capuchin Friars of the English Province, situated in Providence, Rhode Island. Their monastery is called Saint Francis Friary. Incidentally, we are both members of the Third Order of Saint Francis.

My husband was created Private Chamberlain of Cape and Sword, by his Holiness, Pope Pius X. Through his services, we grew to know the Pope better than most, and loved him devotedly. He gave me his own little silver pencil, one he had used for many years. I have always felt it to be a great help in the writing I have done. All the books I have written up to 1938 are in the Vatican

Library. Once Pope Pius XI said to me, apropos of my books: "sempre meglio—toujours mieux—always better." And he added: "You must continue the Apostolate." Later on, when the present Holy Father was Cardinal Secretary of State, myself and my husband, who had been made a Knight of Malta, were dining at a lovely Roman villa, on the eightieth birthday of Cardinal Gasparri, former Secretary of State. Obviously Papal timbre, Cardinal Pacelli was interesting, and interested, delighted, like all the rest at sight of the beautiful picture made by the old Cardinal bending over the big solitary candle on the first American birthday cake he had ever seen.

A few years later, Cardinal Pacelli, who had become Pius XII, sent me the Pontifical decoration "Pro Ecclesia et Pontifice."

My first three attempts at being the literary lion I had been led to believe I might be, were dismal failures. The first had to do with the Mississippi River. My father, a writer of great ability, had presented me with a diary in the hope something worthwhile might be evolved, between Saint Louis and New Orleans. Now there was much that might have been done with the material at hand. A first journey down the mightiest stream in our country, the old Anchor Liner, "City of Saint Louis," with its swashbuckling paddle wheel at the stern, roustabouts on the lowest deck, glad and ready to "rag" for pennies tossed from above. There was the little house on the bridge where the pilot spun stories for hours and told that a phantom ship had passed in the night, there was a genuine Show Boat with which the "Saint Louis" almost collided, searchlights from both vessels illuminating a group of actors in the bow as well as the little party of close friends on the City, gathered to watch them and to toss cigarettes across the nearby railings. There was a flood, the worst that had been for forty years, with little houses floating down the river, a small family picked off one of the roofs, a whole forest of trees showing only tops above the swirling waters. There was a landing at the third story of a warehouse in Vicksburg, and a terrified Negro who fell off the gangplank and was so frightened he turned a strange shade of white. Then, the plantations, and wheelbar-

rows filled with flowers rolled on to the boat by current beaux,
and rose-wreathed cottages, levees kept from flooding by sand-
bags, and a New Orleans with Joseph Jefferson playing Rip Van
Winkle as he had never played it before.

All that. And yet, I have been curiously allergic to the keeping
of a diary. I do it, even now, but it is the only writing I find
forced and a task. And yet—with every day of living and everything that happens absorbingly interesting, I would not give it
up. But the book turned out to be a hopeless botch. My father
said nothing, made no comment. Years later, long years, after
I had married, and after the publication of my first two romances,
my mother said one day: "When you came back after your first
trip to New Orleans and gave your father the diary, he read it,
sighed, and told me it was a great disappointment: She will never
be a writer."

Then there was the little episode of the "Centurion," a romance
of the time of Christ written by Sir Adolphe Routhier of Quebec.
I made a translation, fair, far from perfect. There was one phrase
I could not master. In spite of explanations on the part of the
old gentleman, in spite of being entirely familiar with French,
the sense of it did not come to me. My husband and I at the time
were staying at "Hauterive" summer residence of the Routhiers
on the Saint Lawrence River. One night I went to bed utterly
discouraged. At two o'clock in the morning, like a flash of light-
ning, the bewildering phrase cleared in my sleep. I woke, went
to my desk and wrote it down for fear of losing it by morning.
A little before eight, I started to the chapel for Mass, as Sir
Adolphe came slowly down the stairway, sad and discouraged.
I went to him and repeated the phrase as it had come to me. He
was so delighted that he beamed and kissed me on both cheeks.
So that failure slipped into the past.

When I wrote *The Gates of Olivet* it was refused. "Too much
war." "Oh, that's simple enough," answered the writer of this
first book, "I'll change it." So the actual destruction of a French
hospital in 1914 was changed to an airplane accident along the
perilous Cotes de Saufterre, where my husband and I with the

friend whose plane it was, were wrecked the Spring before on our way down to the Eucharistic Congress in Lourdes. The book was returned to Macmillan, published, and has had reprintings almost every year since it appeared in 1920.

It was during 1914–1918 World War that I wrote my first short story to console those who had suffered through the flail and the pain of conflict. I had seen the anguish of France, the tragic sorrow of England. My husband and I had stood for hours on the "Islands" of the boulevards of Paris, watching those brave little poilus march by in their red and blue baggy trousers, coats that did not know the first meaning of adjustment to the shoulders that carried them. After weeks of war work in Paris, a difficult crossing to England and strenuous service on the then Prince of Wales' committee for the families of men in the armed forces, my husband and I returned to America. While running a club for soldiers and sailors, working on a plan given me by Major General Leonard Wood for activities in the camps, I wrote "The Road to Christmas Night." It was returned with thanks. Whereupon I changed the name and sent it hurtling back to the magazine that had refused it. It was accepted at once published, and copied in a number of smaller publications as the years rolled by. It was starred by O'Brien in the *Best Short Stories* of that year. A Boston publisher seeing it, wrote asking if I had an available novel ready. I had never thought of writing a novel, but answered that the book would be in shape in about six months.

It took a little longer than that, the company failed and closed its doors. At the advice of an old friend, Winston Churchill, whose books Macmillan had always published, I took *The Gates of Olivet* to them. They have remained my only publishers through all the years.

That threatened fiasco overcome, I flung myself into a story of the Rome I had loved all my life—just as all my life I have loved Lourdes. *The Candlestick Makers* begins in New York, and goes on to Italy where many of the characters are real people in disguise. One of these, Diana Travers, so pleased one of the publishers that he asked me to bring her back in another book. So she appears again in *From Out Magdala*. With the experience of many other writers of romance, I have found it is better to create my background, then let the characters assume their own parts. All I have to do is to watch them, and record what they do.

Gentleman Riches, a story of the Cornish country for the most part, is founded on the actual life history of an old friend.

Sing to the Sun is the result of long and happy days, year after year spent on the hilltops of the most beautiful valley in all the world, the Umbrian Valley, sanctified by the undying romance of God's troubadour, "the little poor man of Assisi."

In 1925, Pope Pius XI being on the throne, Rome was crowded with White Russians. The Bolsheviks had established an Embassy there that somehow filled one with horror when passing the doors that concealed so much that was antagonistic to the Christian mind.

On a day in Spring the Holy Father said Mass at Saint Peter's for the refugees—Catholic and Orthodox alike. I was taken ill there, and for a month was allowed to see only three people besides my husband. The three were Cardinal Ceretti, former Nuncio from the Vatican to Paris, Father McGarigle, secretary to Monsignor D'Herbigny on whose head the Red Russians had put a price, and an old friend, grand-daughter of General William Tecumseh Sherman, Eleanor Fitch.

Easter came, and I was allowed to be taken for Mass to a small chapel in the Oriental Institute, chapel that had formerly belonged to the Russian Orthodox Church, but, like the Institute was converted to Catholicity. There, somehow, during the Mass, the story of Russia came crowding about me from all four windowless walls—like arms, or a sort of suffocation. *Silver Trumpets Calling* was the result of this Springtime in Rome.

In the Starforth Trilogy, the first book of the series, *White Hawthorn* hovers about the doctrines of sin and grace. The scene is laid in the Italy of Petrarch and Boccaccio, the heroine Fiorenza. The second volume, *Starforth,* is an attempt to paint a correct picture of Mary Tudor, whose life is woven into a romance concerned with what Father Robert Hugh Benson calls the Deformation period in England. *King's Highway,* last of the series is a story of the early formation of the southern states of America—with a short incursion into Canada—and a great deal about the Indians.

Once—In Palestine was written as a simple prelude to Christmas and Holy Week. The first, an intimate little account of Our Lady and the tender drama of Bethlehem. The second, the triumphant tragedy of Calvary. In writing the preface to this book, Father Cuthbert, the famous Franciscan Capuchin historian writes; "An artistic fantasy, an imaginative reconstruction, gathering up and enveloping at once the Scriptural story and its mystical implications . . . the fantasy reveals and does not distort the truth and beauty of the authentic story itself."

The next book published, *The Shining Tree,* is just a Christmas tale showing that even the New York the world considers cold and unfeeling, has a heart sufficiently warm to take unto itself all types of men and women from heights to depths, provided sympathetic understanding is given opportunity to bring the blossom of human kindness up to the sunlight.

From the Morning Watch is a series of rather wandering thought, not unlike the meditations of *Once—In Palestine.*

As possible suggestions to young Catholic writers, there might be about three. Study the best authors. My closest friends in my youth were Charles Dickens, Louisa Alcott, William Makepeace Thackeray, Agnes Repplier. The last especially for perfect English. A little later, there were Father Robert Hugh Benson's wonderful Catholic books. A second suggestion is—and it is more than a suggestion—never write a word that could injure an immortal soul. Remember the "millstone." Then—write, write, write. And keep your sense of humor vitally alive in your own heart and before your public. If you like fantasies, and fairies, read Enid Dinnis. She is an incomparable artist, a faithful and devoted friend. R. I. P.

EDITOR'S NOTE: Mrs. Borden's stories, all issued by Macmillan, include *Gates of Olivet,* 1932; *Silver Trumpets Calling,* 1931; *Sing to the Sun,* 1934; *Starforth,* 1937; *The King's Highway,* 1941; *The Shining Tree,* 1942; and the biography, *Francesca Cabrini,* 1945.

REVEREND JACOB R. BUCK

LIKE UNTO THE LITTLE BOY who was sent home to get data for his age and his mother wrote out the date of his birth, and he came back, drawing the note from his pocket and remarking: "Here, teacher, is my excuse for being born," I can vouch that I was born on the ninth of February, 1870. But there are times when I wonder what excuse I can give for that event.

My parents were Presbyterian, and my youthful days were various and mixed with the usual capers of youth. I was sent to the public schools where I learned my ABC's and in time the three R's and something of music. Later, a kind lady taught me to do some drawing and painting in oils.

Of course my religious training was Calvinistic and strict, which made everything pleasurable to youth sinful. Not being old or experienced enough to understand its inconsistency, I did not see its doing away with free will, and the throwing all blame upon God. Its principle is not "Am I offending God?" but rather, "What will people say?" Dancing, card playing and even mumbletypeg, especially on Sunday, were heinous. Every morning there was family prayer and reading of Holy Scripture. One morning, unthinkingly, I ate some green gooseberries. "That's what you get for picking and eating them on Sunday," I was told.

As a lad, I did any odd job to turn an honest penny, and thought I had reached man's estate when I secured a certificate to teach school. School teaching followed in Minnesota and North Dakota. I was a favorite with my pupils, enjoying many of their sports.

One morning in Sheldon, North Dakota, the school-bell was muffled. The face of every pupil was stolid and wore a shocked look. That evening I went for a sleigh-ride with the older pupils. "My," I said to Frank Mougey as we rode along, "were you not frightened to climb that icy roof to muffle the bell?" "Who told you?" he exclaimed in surprise. The cat was out of the bag.

My first contact with Catholicism was while teaching a country school near Georgetown, Minnesota. The oldest pupil (C. P. as he was called), was a devout Catholic, and I boarded with his parents. He and I have been the closest of friends and pals ever since. C. P. was very instrumental in my becoming a Catholic. I determined to learn something about the doctrines and dogmas so I could refute the many abominable stories which floated about continually.

Next, I worked for a time for the Security Trust Company in Fargo, North Dakota. There I joined the Masonic Lodge. Mr. W. A. Scott—a veritable David Harum type of man—was Past Grand Master of the Lodge, and manager of the company. I had chosen as my instructor a kindly old priest of Moorhead, Minnesota.

Mr. Scott, always chewing tobacco, surprised me one day by aiming at the cuspidor in the corner, hitting the bull's eye, and asking: "Buck, I hear you are studying Catholicity. Is it true?" I admitted it was. "I am a Unitarian," continued Mr. Scott, "and do not believe in the Trinity. But if you believe in Christ's divinity, you gotta be a Catholic. Going to be a Catholic?"

"The study is interesting, but I have made no decision, as yet,"

I returned. I began to think I might be mistaken about so-called Catholic superstitions. Through C. P. and his parents I had learned better about many things for which I had felt great repugnance.

I commenced my writings while I taught school. Sending articles to school journals, I grew quite proficient in expressing myself. I tried other publications too. I laugh now at my first effort about two young men who started a mercantile business in the backwoods. It was returned to me "with thanks." We had few story papers in those days from which to glean ideas, and though I tried to work in the calf-love sort in mine, they were not lurid.

The first story for which I was paid (two dollars) was short and indifferent, though amusing. I tried poetry also, but evidently my ditties were worthless and received little notice. I even tried detective stories in which I thought the main thing was to have the villain masked. But still no success.

I kept right on with my instructions in Catholicism. And they were long and strenuous. I think my instructor considered me insincere. But I finally yielded and was baptized on June 29, 1902, the feast of Saints Peter and Paul. C. P. was my Godfather, and my baptism was public. It was in Moorhead just across the river from Fargo where I was known as a Mason. Perhaps Father Augustine was acute. He announced it at Mass in the morning and the church was well filled. C. P. and I crossed the river over a railroad bridge through a pasture. Something jumped in the bushes which startled me.

"What's that?" I exclaimed.

"Just the devil getting out of your way," returned my friend.

My diligent study had engendered the thought of the priesthood. But I felt unworthy and hesitated. It seemed the very apogee of my former worldly ambitions, so I prayed and took much time to consider it. And finally I went to Saint John's University, in Minnesota, where I entered the seminary.

I had a fight with myself over my vocation, feeling I was too old. Consequently I went at my studies with such vim that I used up much of my nervous energy. I was deficient in Latin, scarcely knowing how to assist in hearing Mass, and serving Mass was a bugaboo.

Before the summer vacation I had broken down. I went to Regina, Canada, where my friends were then living. Two physicians advised my giving up studying and recommended a change of climate. I took this as a direct sign from God that I had presumed in thinking of becoming a priest.

One morning C. P.'s mother prepared a special dish of delicious fried chicken for me. I partook of it heartily. Asking why none of the others shared in it, I was informed by C. P., "O none of the rest of us have been to the seminary and learned that the mere laws of the Church count for nothing. This is Friday."

I decided to come west, and went to the Benedictine seminary at Mount Angel, Oregon. There I consulted a good old monk who told me my difficulties were but a trial which God had sent me to try me out, that it was God's way of testing me. So I went at it again, and this time made rapid progress. Through the Abbot, I applied to the Archbishop of Oregon City (now Baker City). Archbishop Christie, a man of very pleasing personality, accepted me at once. Then I made preparation for ordination.

I was ordained in Portland on the fifth of June, 1909, and was assigned to Forest Grove to establish a church with the missions of Cornelius and Gaston attached. I had kept up my writing and continued to do so, for it was being accepted now.

On one of my vacations I went to Florida to visit my nephew, Frank Goodman. While there an incident happened which amused the Archbishop greatly. I had said Mass and given Benediction, and Frank and I were sitting under the trees. Suddenly Frank remarked, "Uncle, I have about a hundred Negroes working for me. They have their own church, and it might be interesting to you to attend, this evening. What do you say?" I responded, "If I did not fear giving scandal, I should like very much to go."

"Ah," said he, "they do not know what a Catholic is, much less a priest." So he, Mrs. Goodman and I went. As we entered the small oblong building having a platform and a box used as a pulpit on which rested a Bible, the old preacher eying me curiously said, "De speaka will please take his seat on the platform." I hesitated but finally went up, taking my place among the others on the platform. He then offered a prayer, announced a hymn which was sung most beautifully. Then he turned to me saying: "We sure would be glad if de white brudder would say a few words to us." It was all done so kindly that I did not refuse, reading a passage or two from the Bible and then told a simple story. At its conclusion the congregation stamped their feet and clapped their hands. I told them I was a Catholic priest. The preacher said, "Well, that's the first time I ever heard of a Catholic priest talking in a Baptist meetin' house."

I remarked to Frank on our way home, "It is the first time I ever heard of it either." When I told my Archbishop, he laughingly said he would have to establish a church for the colored folk in Portland and make me the pastor. I repeated the story many times at the instigation of the Archbishop, which always gave him great pleasure.

After eight years in Forest Grove, I was transferred to St. Joseph's Church in Salem, where I remained until August 15, 1934.

In retrospect, I think I have done some fairly good work. I am still writing and giving instructions, so perhaps after all there may be "some excuse for my having been born."

EDITOR'S NOTE: Father Buck's books include *A Convert Pastor Explains*, 2d revised ed., 1929, Bruce; *The Sage of Exeter*, 1938, Bruce; *Why Do Catholics—?*, 1931, and *A Convert Pastor's Autobiography*, 1942, Our Sunday Visitor.

KATHERINE BURTON

IN MY FAMILY, when I was a small girl, there was just one rule regarding religion: I had to go to Sunday school every Sunday. There was no especial insistence on any one place and so I roved about, sipping the honey of faith wherever I wanted to. I had an aunt who was also rovingly religious and she took me to various churches with her. We went to an Episcopal church and to a Christian Scientist sometimes. We went to a Jewish synogogue where I heard of Dickens for the first time: they read, why I don't know at this late day, excerpts from Oliver Twist there one evening and the next day I began drawing this fascinating author from the public library. We went to the small Catholic church in our Cleveland suburb because she liked the music there. Also she used to help with the yearly fairs, and I did too sometimes; I remember that the year I was eleven I had charge of collecting fares for the merry-go-round. That was my earliest effort in behalf of Catholicism.

The Sunday school I selected myself, my special preference

being the Methodist, where the hymns were wonderful and you were encouraged to sing good and loud and the Christmas candy was the best in any of the churches. Then suddenly my aunt hauled me out of that sect and made a Lutheran of me, confirmed and all. I mainly recall that entire incident because of the minister, who was named Roentgen and had a brother who had invented a thing called the x-ray, about which the minister talked as much as ever he did the Scripture.

There was a later interval of going to a Presbyterian college and teaching in a Baptist School and getting married in an Episcopalian church. Then for a considerable time no sect at all saw me.

When I came back to a church it was with real faith. I had experienced serious trouble and it was the sort I felt I could not share with people I knew. I wanted impersonal help. A friend of mine took me one day into the lovely Church of Saint Mary the Virgin in New York City, where I was then living, and the thought came to me that I might consult one of the clergy there. Before a week had passed I had met the rector, talked with him and got the help I needed. Eventually I brought myself and my children to the church and there for at least four years I remained content, absorbing much of the Catholic faith and writing poetry so Catholic in content that it still surprises me when I read it over. The Catholic Church, however, seemed to me something of no great importance. We were the via media, we High Churchers, and that was the important thing.

It was not until I listened to some lectures by the rector emeritus of the church that I began to feel uneasy. He spoke on Rome and its church and he certainly landed on Rome with both feet each time he spoke. But Rome I knew was Catholic too, and it seemed, from my reading, to have at least a few correct ideas. Yet here was a man who also called himself a Catholic, saying pretty terrible things about the whole papal system and its later works. He ran Rome down so hard that I began to want to defend the Roman Catholics, and began reading more about them. Then one evening he said that we were the only true Catholic church for we were the followers of the early, primitive church, and we did not hold with the later innovations of Rome. Yet only that day I had read about Benediction being the invention of a Jesuit some three hundred years ago. St. Mary's had Benediction—and it was certainly no primitive devotion.

It was the beginning of the end for me. The real end came when the rector, Dr. Selden Delany, left his church of thirty-five years and became a Catholic—a real one. I had been uneasy for some time, but I felt that if he, who knew so much more on the subject than I did, could stay where he was I could do so too. Now he was gone and I knew he was right and St. Mary's had been wrong all the time.

There was an interval where I felt I belonged no where at all, and was very desolate. Then one day I went to see the white haired priest whom I had first seen when he officiated at Dr. Delany's reception into the Church. I told him my troubles and he advised me to go for a while to whichever church I felt I wanted to, not to worry and he gave me *The Difficulty of Anglicans* to read. Six months later I was a real Catholic.

My first surprise as a Catholic was to find how many intelligent and brilliant ones there were around. I had the feeling—inherited from what I had heard people say I suppose through the years—that some Catholics were good and some were kind but that they didn't have much education and not too many brains. Now through Mgr. McMahon I met such people as Fr. Bede Jarret and Bishop Francis Clement Kelley and read their books and those of other Catholics. I did some articles for *Commonweal* and met Mr. Williams and his clever staff. I wrote for the *Sign* and was asked to begin a woman's page on that magazine. I met the staff of the *Catholic World*. I was an amazed and delighted woman. Here I had not only found the true faith but I had fallen also into a wonderful literary company.

It was, in fact, through the editor of the *Catholic World*, Father Gillis, that I began to write books. I had done for him an article on Rose Hawthorne and her father, and he asked me why I did not do a book on the girl who had become Mother Alphonsa of the Dominicans. I began one and the first thing I knew it was finished and had a publisher. Since then I have just kept on writing books and the subjects I want to write on are still too many for me to have time to do them all.

I have kept almost entirely to the convert field and mainly to those who came from New England origins, men and women who were basically and definitely American in birth and in upbringing. I have wanted to show how these good Americans became also good Catholics and remained good Americans. From the beginning I have taken issue with Van Wyck Brooks who has built up his entire series of fascinating books on a misconception, so it seems to me: he claims that philosophy is responsible for New England's flowering and its fading. He ignores the fact of religion entirely or dwells on it very lightly. Yet it seems to me from my research that it was the harshness of the Puritan faith that drove men and women from it, out to something that had love and kindness and fellow feeling in it. Many of the best of their day—Emerson, Hawthorne, Longfellow, Thoreau—left the harsh sects for something better. Catholicism they did not consider as a living faith for to them it was only something dead though still lovely in a far away land. They could not see that it was living and that it was the necessity they lacked. So they became Unitarians and Universalists and kindly pagans, for there they thought they would find their basic needs—brotherhood and fraternity.

Some went on until they found the Faith, and it is of these that I have written—Kent Stone and Rose Hawthorne and Elizabeth Seton and Isaac Hecker and Sophia Ripley and John Tabb and Joseph Dutton—good Americans all and good Catholics, too, when once grace had set their feet on the right way.

The method in which I write, though now fairly an accepted one, is sometimes held up to ridicule. It is known as the fictional method of biography and that is definitely a misnomer. When a new book of mine comes out there are always a few reviewers who say disagreeably that it sounds like a novel. If by novel they mean that I am making things up they are mistaken. For,

save for small bits of talk that are only feed lines for another remark, every word I put into quotation marks had been said by
the person quoted—either in conversation or in a book by him
or in letters or diaries. The oddest review I ever had was by a
writer in the *Saturday Review* who complained that in my book
on Isaac Hecker I made Emerson, the Pope, Thoreau and Hecker
all talk alike. So much the better, I said, for Emerson and
Thoreau!

However, the reason for this form of biography is mainly that
more people will read it than would the more formal biography,
and so will get acquainted with the examples of our great converts, many of them hitherto sunk in the pages of too scholarly
and often too pious works. It has always seemed to me that there
ought to be two books on every important man and woman—one
for the scholarly, where all known facts are set down accurately,
and which may be consulted for information and research. And
there should be the light readable life, such as I write. For most
people are not scholars, and many of these converts, who are
such fine examples for the rest of us, would just stay unread in
the pages of the heavy lives that have been written about them,
often by really great writers. So it is the lesser writers like myself
who must write about them for the less scholarly readers like
myself.

EDITOR'S NOTE: Mrs. Burton's books, published by Longmans, include *His
Dear Persuasion*, 1940, a life of Elizabeth Ann Seton; *Paradise Planters*, 1939,
the story of Brook Farm; *Sorrow Built a Bridge*, 1937, a life of Rose Hawthorne Lathrop, who became Mother Alphonsa; *Celestial Homespun*, 1943,
a life of Isaac Thomas Hecker, a founder of the Paulists; *In No Strange Land*,
1942, sketches of some American Catholic converts; and *No Shadow of Turning*, 1944, a life of James Kent Stone, who became Father Fidelis of the Cross,
C.P. Ave Maria Press issued her *Brother Andre of Mount Royal*, in 1943.

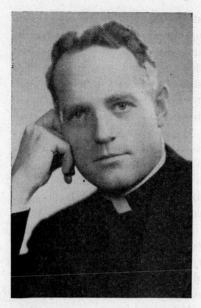

REVEREND PAUL BUSSARD

I HAVE FREQUENTLY THOUGHT that one of the punishments of Purgatory must be the task of writing one's biography. When invited to write some fifteen hundred words I was dismayed because one hundred would have been more than enough.

Anyhow, I was born. Some say it was in 1904; others, 1903. Personally it doesn't matter and history can have either date, or none. But it was on St. Cecelia's day, which is more important.

The family I joined had the distinction of being the only Catholics (I was No. 6 and there were two to come) in the town (Essex in Iowa). All the others were Swedish Lutherans, but when we left the Chamber of Commerce (pop. 500) gave my father a gold watch. The Lutherans put up with us and I cannot even recall ever being taunted about my religion, even when (in the third grade) I fell in love with the minister's daughter.

We walked four miles from the farm to the school. There was a road but I usually preferred the fields because the mud would often be knee deep in them.

My first encounter with learning was something of a set back. I learned that Henry VIII had seven wives and that one of them was Catherine Howard. I also learned that was my mother's maiden name. So with the family at the dinner table I launched out, "Well, I understand that Catherine Howard was the 6th wife of Henry VIII." My mother glanced at the upstart and dead panned just two words, "The fifth."

In spite of that I kept on going to school. The year after ordination one of my class mates, Father Edward F. Jennings, came over to the Cathedral where I was an assistant. He wanted to start a *Leaflet Missal* like the one Pius Parsch had going in Austria. I had written an article for *Orate Fratres* while in the seminary, so I was looked on as an authority on the liturgical movement. I didn't choose to run, but he kept pestering me until I at last agreed. He would manage it and I would edit it.

I took the first issue down to the post office in my little yellow Ford, but I had no more returned to the rectory when the post office phoned for me to come back and get them. I had violated just about every regulation in the P. L. & R. I have since learned that means Postal Laws and Regulations and that it is quite a large book. That was fifteen years ago and the poor *Leaflet Missal* is still being published.

After a year Archbishop Dowling discovered how little I knew and sent me to school again. I came back with a Ph.D. in education and was at once sent out to Nazareth Hall to teach Latin. Archbishop Murray wanted me to teach Greek, also, until I proved to him I didn't know the capital letters of the Greek alphabet.

After a month of that Father Gales wrote me a letter. He had heard I had been to school again, so he wanted me to help him on his 1001st venture—a thing he thought might be called the *Catholic Digest*. I went to see him and said, "That sounds good. You be managing editor, I'll be editor, and Father Jennings be business manager." He said, "O.K.," and that was that.

People are funny. About eight years later Father Jennings and I were eating spaghetti over in the Roman Cafe. All three of us had been talking of a Spanish edition for a couple of years, but only talking. Between mouthfuls (I often wonder why anyone eats spaghetti) I said, "Why don't you go to Rio and start the thing. Rio is a big town. You go down there and I'll do your work while you are gone." He said, "That's a deal. I'll go to see the Archbishop in the morning. Pass me some more of that cheese, will you?"

So he went to Rio and ended up in Buenos Aires and he is not back after nearly two years, and I really got stuck this time.

That just about brings me up to date. I don't write any more. I only read others' writings. My chief distinction is that I am the oldest assistant in the diocese, and that the Archbishop of it is very wise. He lets the three of us go along pretty much as we wish. He figures we haven't done much harm yet, and that, perhaps, we will some day do some good. I hope so.

I also hope this is fifteen hundred words because I have achieved the ambition of every one who writes a dissertation: I have exhausted my subject.

EDITOR'S NOTE: Father Bussard's books include *If I Be Lifted Up*, new ed., 1944, Catechetical Guild; *The Living Source*, reissued as *The Better Wine*, 1944, id.; *Staircase to a Star*, 1938, Kenedy; and *The Meaning of the Mass*, which Father Kirsch, O.F.M. Cap., edited for use in schools and study clubs, 1942, Kenedy.

BARBARA BARCLAY
CARTER

THE OTHER DAY I turned up an old exercise-book belonging to my twelfth year, and was amused to find an essay: "How I would earn my living if I had to," (the conditional clause representing a polite fiction, current till well beyond the end of the last war, that "nice" little girls did not expect to earn their livings as a matter of course). It is a business-like account of how a large fortune could be amassed by breeding dogs, but at the end comes the revealing after-thought: "If I did not breed dogs I might breed cats or be a writer." I remember still the uncomfortable feeling that all that had gone before was insincere and worthless; it was on writing that my will was fixed, as it had long been. I had written almost as soon as I could form my letters, first poems (in the childhood of the individual as of the peoples, verse-forms come before prose), then tales, and finally a "novel" of fifty whole foolscap pages, all of them carefully preserved by maternal pride. But how could eleven-years-old explain that inner compulsion—

or how it could be turned to the earning of a living? It was simpler to talk about dogs. . . .

We were then living in Richmond, a few miles from London. Of Santa Barbara, California, where I was born, I have alas! no direct memory, for my Anglo-Irish mother brought me to England before I was two years old. Only through her eyes and those of my much loved Welsh nurse, who came back with her, could I see the sun-lit orange-trees, the glittering blue of the Pacific, the sheer rise of the great mountains, but so vivid were their pictures that they form part of the texture of my childhood. I was not allowed to forget that I was an American. One day, when I was very small, an American flag appeared unexpectedly in a little shop in our neighborhood, and my old nurse led me to it with real excitement, "Kiss it, baby," she said, "That's the Star Spangled Banner. It's your flag." For many years after, it hung over my cot.

So, too, when I began to appreciate poetry, my mother would read to me for preference from an American anthology—Little Orphan Annie, and Paul Revere's Ride, and the Battle Hymn of the Republic. I soon knew by heart, though in regard to the last she would impress upon me that since my father came from Georgia I must not identify myself with the cause of the North.

Though living in England, my "second country" was not England but Wales—my old nurse's land, whither she took me for holidays that were the highlights of each year, to share the life of her kin—her brother the blacksmith, her sister-in-law who kept a baker's shop, her innumerable cousins who farmed the rich, mountain-guarded lands of the Usk valley, till I grew as passionately attached to the land itself as if it had been my own. Of all this I have written in *Old Nurse*. By a coincidence, one of the reviewers of my earlier book on Dante, *Ship Without Sails,* had to deal at the same time with two books on Wales, and bridged the transition by saying: "It is a very long way from twentieth century Wales to the fourteenth century Florence of Miss Barclay Carter's book." Actually, it was through the intense local attachment of the Welsh and the spell of Wales that

I was able to understand the aching nostalgia for Florence of the exile whom an American writer has described as "the most home-sick man in this home-sick world."

My school was run by an able Swiss woman, so that we special-ised in French. It was thus that my first appearance in print (otherwise than in the school magazine, where I wrote under the pseudonym of "Californian Poppy") was what may be by courtesy be called a French poem in honour of King Albert of Belgium, in *L'Independance Belge,* which was published in London dur-ing the last war. I was then fourteen. The war ended soon after I had left school for a secretarial training college. Many of us who had grown up with the thought of war-service as soon as we were of age for it, felt the need to find some other high cause to claim our allegiance. I found it in insurgent Ireland. The seeds had been sown by the parish priest in Wales, where, after my mother's death, my old nurse's house seemed my real home. Acquaintance with the poems of Pearse and Plunkett and MacDonagh ripened them. Had not my own grand-father been an Irishman? (That he, poor man, an Anglican Bishop of Je-rusalem and a strong conservative, might well have turned in his grave at the thought of a Sinn Feiner grand-daughter was no matter.) I joined the Gaelic League, started learning Irish, and, under the inspiration of the Celtic Twilight wrote two short stories set in the Ireland I had never seen, with sufficient verisi-militude to win publication in Irish papers. This was the first money I earned by my pen—something to tell in triumph to my aunts in England, my guardian in America, who had even fewer illusions than myself at eleven on writing as a means of earning a living. I felt I had made a beginning. Unfortunately, however, I have never been one of those who are able to write at odd mo-ments, in time squeezed from other work. And I felt more and more that for such writing as should be mine I needed the uni-versity training that had been denied me.

For three years I did secretarial work—in London, in Geneva with the International Labour Office, and with the Irish Lega-tion in Rome. In the meantime, on a visit to my ever-dear old nurse in 1921, I had been received into the Catholic Church. (The parish-priest had sown other seeds than those of Sinn Fein, but my decision—at Geneva, of all places—had a far earlier impulse at its origin, for my mother had had a great reverence for Catholicism and had shown clearly a wish to encourage me in a direction she herself shrank from taking as a forsaking of the church of her fathers.)

Then, I was twenty-one. I came into what seemed the large sum of a hundred and fifty pounds ($750). I took it to go to Paris, to study at the Sorbonne. With a Faustian thirst for knowledge for its own sake, rejecting all utilitarian considerations, I proclaimed grandiloquently that I wished simply to "apprendre pour comprendre," and for the four courses requisite for a degree chose Mediaeval History, History of Art, Ancient History, and French Literature. To these I added Italian Literature, for already Dante exercised on me a supreme attraction. For a year, too, I studied Scholastic Philosophy at the Catholic Institute.

I had taken the cheapest room that I could find, on the seventh floor of the Hotel Lhomond, behind the Pantheon, cooking my own meals—into which that friend of man, the horse entered largely—on a spirit stove. Even with such strict economy, my $750 would not have lasted long, had not Providence taken a hand. The hostel of the Catholic Institute gave yearly scholarships to Irish and American students. The Directress—she was a nun of the order of St. Ursula, though this was kept an open secret since the laws against religious congregations were still nominally in force—gave me one of the American scholarships one year, and an Irish one the next. It was thus that I was able to take my degree of Licenciee-es-Lettres (with the distinction of having been placed first in Mediaeval History), and at the same time the "auditorat" of Scholastic Philosophy.

While in Paris, I came into touch with the Christian Democratic movement, through Marc Sangnier and his "Jeune Republique," and thus heard of the work Don Sturzo was doing in Italy as leader of a great Christian-Democratic party. I had been back in London only a few months when I heard of his arrival in England. I was then living precariously as a free-lance journalist (supplemented by keeping the accounts for a private hotel), and wrote to ask if I might interview him. This was the beginning of a collaboration that lasted till his departure for the States in 1940, and which indeed still continues. I became his interpreter while he still knew no English, then the translator of his books and articles, his associate in various enterprises of which I shall speak later. Contact with such a mind was in itself an education, but I owe to him also a constant and precious guidance in my own work. It was with his encouragement, assisted by his criticism, that I produced my own first book, the reconstruction of the later life of Dante in the form of a novel, *Ship Without Sails.*

I had learned Italian in my last year at school, and at once the *Divine Comedy* seized my imagination, together with the figure of Dante himself. For years, without and often against my will, a story that centered round him wove itself in my mind, and whenever chance offered I had read what I could find about him and his times. For long, however, the task of writing on so great a theme seemed beyond my powers. When at last I addressed myself to it, I was confirmed in my leaning towards the form of a novel by the consideration that most of his biographers, presenting conjecture as fact, had written but fiction in disguise, and by the belief that through the novelist's imaginative approach it might be possible to reconcile apparently conflicting texts, and, paradoxically, to reach a truer picture of him than by analytical research. (In this I was justified: my conclusions as to the sequence of events in his exile and his up till recently much questioned sojourn in Paris, have since been independently put forward by one of the leading Italian Dante scholars of the day.)

In all, the book was the work of seven years, interrupted indeed by translations and articles. Each year my summer vacation was spent in tracing Dante's wandering steps across Italy, climbing to the almost inaccessible castles that had harboured him, visiting the lovely cities associated with his name—Florence,

Verona, Rome, Ravenna. The name *Ship Without Sails* has a
two-fold reference. Dante speaks of himself as "a ship without
sails, without rudder, driven to divers ports and gulfs and shores,"
and it was in such a ship that Lancelot (in whom Dante seems
to have seen a symbol of himself) came to such vision as might
fall to sinful man in the mystical quest of the Holy Grail.

The news that *Ship Without Sails* had been accepted by a
leading British publisher (Constable & Co.) was cabled to me
when I was staying in New Jersey, on my first visit to my native
country since I had left it as a baby. (It was in 1929—still the
Henry Ford era. Be it confessed that I then felt a stranger. My
discovery of the real America was yet to come.)

My second book, *Old Nurse,* appeared in 1936, published by
Jonathan Cape. Translations (Soderini's Leo XIII, Fanfani's
Catholicism, Protestantism and Capitalism, Don Sturzo's *Cycle
of Creation*), lectures and review-articles occupied the intervening
years. Dante remained my special theme. A collection of "New
Dante Studies," indeed, lost its hope of present publication
through the outbreak of war, and a like fate befell my play,
"Abelard" on which both Mr. Robert Speaight and Mr. Martin
Brown looked with favour, promising production when a propi-
tious moment came.

In the meantime, my association with Don Sturzo had brought
me ever more closely in touch with the Christian Democratic
movement. Towards the end of 1936 I was one of the founders
of the "People & Freedom" group in London (taking its name
from the mediaeval slogan, revived by Savonarola's followers),
with Mrs. Virginia Crawford as Chairman. (She had been a
favorite disciple of Cardinal Manning.) In 1938, we founded a
paper, *People & Freedom,* first a quarterly, then a monthly, of
which I am still editor, and in 1939, with Don Sturzo's help, we
brought out a book *For Democracy,* with Burns, Oates & Washbourne, in which leading Catholic sociologists of six countries
trace the growth and basic principles of democracy from Greece
and Rome to the problems of to-day and the immediate to-mor-
row. My own share was the Introduction: "What we Mean by

Democracy.") It has been recognised by competent critics as a really important Catholic contribution to sound political thought.

Such and kindred activities (such as the organisation of the British Committee for Civil and Religious Peace in Spain, and of the International Christian Democratic Union), which have become more exacting since the war, have limited my literary output. But a writer cannot live in an ivory tower without spiritual impoverishment, and I believe that this varied and practical experience will bear fruit when—as I hope—a time comes for me to turn single-heartedly to creative work.

EDITOR'S NOTE: Miss Carter's books include *Old Nurse*, 1936, Jonathan Cape; *Ship Without Sails*: *Dante in Exile*, 1931, Constable. She also wrote the introductory chapter and edited *For Democracy*, 1940, Burns, Oates.

CARLOS E. CASTANEDA
Historian

THE OLD MAIN BUILDING of the University of Texas stood out in broad relief that late September afternoon, its Gothic towers piercing the blue sky, tipped by the gold of the sunset. For four years I had dreamed of this moment. It was not until my second year in high school that I had begun to think of it, but when I graduated I had to work a year to get enough money to begin to realize my dream.

Mother died when I began high school and father died the next year. With four sisters, two older and two younger than myself, it was hard sleighing. I worked after school hours and studied nights. Then came graduation. But taxes were in arrears on the old homestead. I had to wait a year to help pay off the debt. As a teacher with only a second grade certificate, I taught in an ungraded rural school—six grades by myself, children as old or older than the teacher. In self defense I allowed my mustache to grow. Horrors! It came out flaming red. Imagine the combination: black hair, hazel green eyes, and a red mustache. I never allowed it to grow out again.

The year's teaching netted a very modest sum after other obligations were paid. But off to the University I went, full of hope and ambition. There I was at last, before the castle of my dreams, the main building of the University.

Late that afternoon I called on the pastor of St. Austin's Chapel, the chaplain of the Newman Club. I had not met him before. He was a man in his early thirties. Understanding and sympathy radiated from his eyes. His voice was rich and resonant, with a note of warmth in it. Father J. Elliot Ross was a man who invited and inspired confidence. I told him my situation. I had little money; I needed to find a room; I was willing to work to help pay the rent. I wanted to get a college education at any cost.

He listened with interest. Then he took me over to the chapel, up the back steps, to a small room in the garret. It had a cot; no water, no heat. We improvised a washstand, got an old table and a couple of chairs, and there I was.

For four years I lived in that room while at the University. I studied in my bathrobe, and sometimes in my overcoat. In the spring of my senior year, late one evening, Father Ross came to my room. He had a knowing smile that played about his mouth as he stood in the open door. "I want to be the first to tell you and to congratulate you on your election to Phi Beta Kappa."

Frankly, I had not even given a thought to the possibility of such a thing. I had studied hard and I had made good grades in most of my subjects, but I had never dared to dream that my record was good enough for this coveted academic distinction.

As Providence would have it, three years later I went to teach at the old College of William and Mary in Virginia, where Phi Beta Kappa was founded, and in December, 1926, when the sesquicentennial of the Society was celebrated, I had the rare privilege of being on the official program to read a paper on

"Modern Language Instruction in American Colleges, 1776–1800." On that program, attended by President Coolidge and John D. Rockefeller, were Henry Van Dyke, John Erskine, and many other distinguished scholars from the outstanding universities of this country, Canada, and England. Rockefeller became deeply interested in the old College of William and Mary and the old city of Williamsburg. His interest aroused at that time has made available to all America a reconstructed colonial capital, where Patrick Henry had delivered his famous oration in the House of Burgesses.

But Father Ross, dear to so many students of the University of Texas, did more than give me a room over the chapel. He was the first to suggest that I write and the first to encourage me in this pursuit. My interest in history dated back to high school days. At the University, in working my way through school, I was thrown into close contact with Dr. Eugene C. Barker, foremost Texas historian. I began to try my hand at historical writing. "The Indian Problem in Mexico" was my maiden effort, published in *America* in 1921. Next I wrote a longer article on "The Earliest Missionary Activity in Texas," published by *The Missionary,* in Washington. I had definitely launched my frail bark on the endless stream of historical writing. My field was to be Texas, Mexico, and Latin America.

I am not what you call a professional writer. My writing has been a sideline, a hobby I indulge in after my day's work is done. As a teacher and librarian I earn my living during the day. At night, on holidays, during vacations, and in spare time, I read and write history. At different times I have done research in the rich archival collections of the University of Texas, the University of California, the Library of Congress, the New York Public Library, the Newberry Library, the National Archives of Mexico, and numerous state archives in this country, Mexico, Cuba, and Central America. The old musty records, covered with dust frequently, are not as dry or as uninteresting as they appear. They are full of human interest, countless and unexpected details that help to revive the past, to live again the days gone by.

In this fashion I have gathered materials for my books on the history of Texas, the Southwest, and Mexico, from sources scattered far and wide.

Only those who have had a book published know the thrill of having the first child of one's mind, the fruit of endless nights of vigil, at last appear in print. My first book was *The Mexican Side of the Texan Revolution,* published in 1928 by the Southwest Press of Dallas, Texas. I shall never forget seeing the first copy of the finished book.

Since 1928 I have written fifteen books on historical and educational subjects in addition to numerous articles. Which of them do I consider my best, or the most important? It is like asking a father which is his favorite son. Yet, if I had to say which, in my opinion, has made the greatest contribution to the history of the Southwest, I would name *Our Catholic Heritage in Texas,* of which five volumes have been published to date. In these I have traced in detail the history of Texas in all its aspects from the time its shores were first explored and mapped by Pineda in 1519 to 1810. I began writing this work in 1935, but I had put more than ten years of research in this country and Mexico in preparation, besides the countless hours I spent still finding new materials. The work was undertaken under the auspices of the Knights of Columbus of Texas, who planned this publication as part of the Catholic contribution to the Texas Centennial in 1936. There remains one more volume for me to write in the series to bring the story up to 1845, from where an abler pen will undertake the modern era.

It was the writing of the first four volumes that I believe brought me the highest honor I have received. On October 12, 1941, in Gregory Gymnasium, at the University of Texas, I was made a Knight of the Holy Sepulchre of Jerusalem by Bishop Kelley of Oklahoma and Tulsa in a solemn ceremony I shall never forget. Election to membership in this, the oldest Order of Christian knighthood, is one of the high honors which the Pope may confer.

Almost twenty-four years to the day from that afternoon in

September, 1917, when I first arrived at the University of Texas, within the very shadows of St. Austin's Chapel in whose garret I had lived four years, I was dubbed Knight of the Holy Sepulchre of Jerusalem in a solemn Pontifical High Mass.

EDITOR'S NOTE: Dr. Castaneda is Latin American Librarian and Associate Professor of History at the University of Texas. His monumental work, *Our Catholic Heritage in Texas* is published by the Von Boeckmann-Jones Co., Austin, Texas.

ISABEL C. CLARKE

"Something of Myself"

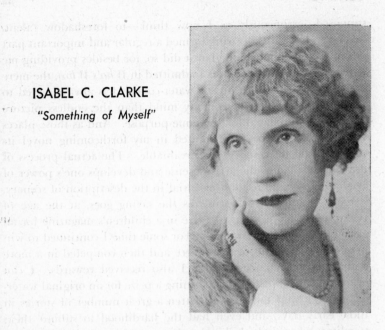

WITH DUE DEFERENCE to the late Rudyard Kipling I have ventured to borrow the title of his all-too-brief autobiography for this little account of my writing life. It is never an easy task to write about oneself; there is so much to say and so little one can tell.

Some years ago I wrote an article for *America* entitled "The Apostolate of the Novel," it being one of a series to which Catholic writers were invited to contribute. Although very diverse in form and matter they one and all set forth something of the ideals at which they were aiming, for now that the urge to Catholic Action among laymen is being stressed the writer has a deeper responsibility towards the Church. In his own special vocation he must further her work.

When did one begin? What prompted one to be a writer? In my case I certainly began to write as soon as I could scrawl a few pencilled phrases on a sheet of paper. These early stories were all illustrated, for drawing is really instinctive in most children. A little sketch of a house drawn at the age of seven was supposed—erroneously as I now think—to foreshadow talent, and ever afterwards drawing formed a regular and important part of our curriculum. I am glad it did so, for besides providing me with a favorite recreation (as I admitted in *Who's Who*), the mere sketching of a place in oils or water-colours has always served to impress it more forcibly on my mind than the endless picture postcards I purchased for the same purpose. And as those places were destined to be incorporated in my forthcoming novel its use as an aid to memory was invaluable. The actual process of drawing stimulates the artistic sense and develops one's power of accurate observation, most essential in the description of scenery.

I first saw myself in print, as the saying goes, at the age of twelve when I won the first prize in a children's magazine for an essay on Kindness to Animals. For some time I continued to win prizes and medals from this source and then competed in a more ambitious journal from which I also received rewards. I can even remember with pride obtaining a prize for an original water-colour sketch. I must have written a great number of stories in those early days, and even had the hardihood to submit them to editors who wisely declined to have anything to do with them.

A turning point was reached some years later when I encountered a well-known author at a dinner party. His name and books were familiar to me which may have been a passport to his favour, but for whatever reason on learning that I was anxious to write he invited me to submit some samples of my work to him. I told him I would do so on one condition, that he would seriously dissuade me from continuing if he thought it were useless for me to do so. It was a noble and generous offer on his part for he was a busy man, and I know now how the author shrinks from examining the works of literary aspirants. I took him at his word and sent him some stories. One of these met with his whole-hearted approval and he said had he still been editing a paper he would have used it. He told me where to send it and he was right, for it met with ready acceptance. Thus I earned my first honorarium for literary work.

But his further advice to me was invaluable. "Write a great

deal," he said. "You are bound to have refusals—everyone does —but the more you write the more you will place." I laid this to heart, and continued to write a great deal with varying success. I published short stories, essays, articles, poems, but the novels met with no success at all. Now and then a more kindly— or may I suggest a more far-seeing?—publisher would send me an appreciative letter, intimating he would be interested in future work, but as a rule the devastating printed slip was all that I received. I worked on quite unbaffled for had I not always intended to be a writer of novels?

In the early days of this century my future career was largely influenced by certain novels. These were *One Poor Scruple* by Mrs. Wilfrid Ward with its charming picture of intimate Catholic life, and *The School for Saints,* and its still more brilliant sequel *Robert Orange* by "John Oliver Hobbs" (Mrs. Craigie). They were the first I had ever read with a definitely Catholic *motif,* and they taught me the immense and far-reaching influence of the novel, showing me as I have said elsewhere its definite apostolate. For it penetrates perhaps where no ostensibly Catholic book would ever be found, and thus may bring the Faith to the notice of many who are completely ignorant of it. In short it may arrest attention, as I have learned from my own experience and the often pathetic letters I have received from my readers asking me, a stranger to them, what they should do next. I am aware that propaganda fiction has an unpleasing sound to many, but considering the vast number of 'isms' that are inculcated in the modern novel, I fail to see why this medium should not be used in the service of the Catholic Church. For religion plays an important part in the make-up of countless human beings and cannot be omitted by the student of psychology. There are naturally many problems which are peculiar to the Catholic. Occasions arise—as in *One Poor Scruple*—when human passions find themselves in direct conflict with the laws of the Catholic Church. Such situations are frequently imbued with a very profound interest. They are, in the language of the Church, "cases of conscience."

At the same time it was a matter of deep distress to me to read so much in current literature that was definitely anti-Catholic, and tended to portray the Church as the insidious enemy rather than the divinely-appointed friend and support of mankind. With the examples of Mrs. Wilfrid Ward and Mrs. Craigie before me I resolved that my pen should be devoted as theirs had been to the service of the Church. For the Church does not despise such imperfect instruments—have we not the ancient legend of Our Lady's Juggler to confirm this?

Fortunately for me, this class of fiction was no longer looked askance upon by publishers. Where Mrs. Wilfrid Ward and Mrs. Craigie had paved the way, the late Monsignor Robert Hugh Benson was most enthusiastically to follow. And it was not I think without significance that the first of my long series of Catholic novels, *Prisoners' Years,* was accepted within a fortnight of its completion by a firm of London publishers, and very shortly afterwards by one in New York. From that winter's day in 1912 (is it really more than thirty years ago?) there has been for me no looking back. Gone were the printed slips, the bulky packages awaiting me in the hall on my return to the house. Gone too was the sense of disappointment which had however been accompanied by no discouragement.

After the publication of my next book *By the Blue River,* which appeared more than a year later and was the result of a long visit to friends in Algeria, I was invited to an afternoon party at the London house of my publisher, the late Sir George Hutchinson. He was delighted with the success of this book, the first he had published for me, and which he had advertised in the most generous manner. And then what did he say to me? He repeated the advice of my author-friend given so many years before by saying: "I want you to write a great deal." Never did advice fall upon the ears of one more eager to receive it. I have now published between fifty and sixty books including three slim volumes of verse. Novels followed one another in rapid succession, and I have even seen myself reviewed under the caption of the "Industrious Novelist!"

After publishing four books I reverted to my "sepulchre," as I used to call that treasury of former failures, and exhumed *Only Anne*. Anne had been refused by eighteen publishers including Sir George himself. Reading it very carefully I came to the conclusion that here was a story with quite credible characters. But it was insufficiently developed, and, what was worse, was far too short for trade purposes. I need not remind my readers that novels by unknown hands must conform to a certain length. The minimum is usually eighty thousand words. It may be much longer but it must not be shorter, and *Anne* fell far short of the requisite length. And how well I now understood and even sympathised with those publishers who had refused to take it up in the past! So I set to work and re-wrote the book from beginning to end, my present experience showing me exactly what was wrong with it. It was published by one of those houses which had formerly refused it, as I was not slow to indicate to them.

During the years that followed I did indeed write a great deal, producing two books a year and finding an ever-increasing pleasure in my trade. But after a dozen years or more of fiction-writing I became aware of the need for a change and turned my thoughts to biography. *Haworth Parsonage*: *A Picture of the Bronte Family,* was my first attempt and proved a successful one, for in its cheap editions it has sold many thousands of copies. The tragic story of the three sisters immured in that dismal Yorkshire parsonage had always fascinated me. It was succeeded by *Elizabeth Barret Browning*: *A Portrait*. During my long residence in Italy I had the opportunity of visiting the various homes of the Brownings at Pisa, Florence, Rome and Siena. This topographical knowledge was also an advantage to me when some years later I wrote my most ambitious biography, *Shelley and Byron*: *A Tragic Friendship,* which dealt with the years when their respective lives were intertwined in Switzerland and especially Italy, and which saw the severance of their always uneasy friendship. This book was translated into French by Madame Barrante d'Estensan who received the prize annually awarded in

France for the best translation of a biography published during the year.

But to write a biography is a far more difficult task than to write a novel, involving as it does the most careful research. The result may read like a novel but on the other hand every word must be scrupulously true. The late Edmund Gosse once declared that only novelists should write biographies, and it is certain that they bring an imaginative insight to their task which as fiction-writers they are bound to possess.

I suppose all writers have listened to that exasperating question: Do you think it all out beforehand or do you make it up as you go along? I can answer both these questions at least partly in the affirmative. No author could sit down to write a novel without some definite plan or purpose. There must always be that initial flash of inspiration that determines the matter of the book. Some authors have called it the "germ," others the "gleam." Whence it comes it is often difficult to say. One hears perhaps of a situation or reads of one in a book of memoirs which might have developed very differently and thus becomes the nucleus of a story. A passing face in the street may equally suggest it, or it may flash into the author's mind so suddenly and unexpectedly that he himself cannot tell you whence it comes. But once that germ is established and has matured in the author's brain "the pen takes charge," to quote once more from Kipling. This at least is how it has been with me, though I have known authors who prepared the most careful and detailed syllabus of each chapter before beginning the actual task of writing. I am sure it is an excellent plan but my wayward and often wilful pen would never submit to be thus "cribb'd, cabin'd and confin'd." It must be free to wander where it will down unexpected byways and into fresh regions lured by beauty or sadness, comedy or tragedy. My note-books contain the barest sketch of any story and a few details of the leading characters.

My many years residence in Rome provided me with the scenery for numerous novels. The best known of these are I think *Carina, It Happened in Rome, Strangers of Rome,* and *Roman*

Year. Venice gave me the background for *The Light on the Lagoon* and Amalfi for the *Altar of Sacrifice.* Some of the scenes of a more recent novel *The Custody of the Children* are also laid in Rome, though the earlier chapters open in Ceylon. And now that I am living in Jamaica, having lost through stress of war my home of so many years, I hope that my novel *Welcome,* recently published, gives an adequate picture of this beautiful island.

EDITOR'S NOTE: Miss Clarke's more recent novels, all issued by Longmans, include *Custody of the Children,* 1940; *Welcome,* 1943; and *Where the Apple Reddens,* 1944.

CYRIL CLEMENS

"This is not a geography; it is a biography.
A geography is about maps; a biography's about chaps"
E. C. Bentley

I WAS BORN July 14, 1902, in St. Louis, Missouri, where my great grandfather, James Clemens, had arrived from Virginia about 1800. Reared an Episcopalian, he had become a Catholic upon his marriage to Anne, the daughter of John Mullanphy, behind whose bales of Europe-bound cotton General Andrew Jackson's men had fought and won the battle of New Orleans.

My father was James Ross Clemens whose illness in London was the innocent cause of Mark Twain's most famous saying, "The report of my death is greatly exaggerated." For the newsmen had confused the two Clemenses and had Mark not merely ill but actually dead! My mother, the daughter of John L. Boland, for many years St. Louis' leading bookseller, has written numerous articles and an autobiography, *Gardens and Books.*

I early taught myself to read and was soon enjoying such books as *Swiss Family Robinson,* Froissart's *Chronicles,* Hakluyt's *Voyages,* and novels of Scott and Cooper. A book that made an especial impression upon me was Selma Lagerlof's *Little Nils* which presents such a matchless picture of Sweden as seen through the eyes of the little dwarf who travels on the back of a wild duck. This work introduced me to the wealth and the glories of the Old World as no amount of poring over histories and geographies could have done.

And then *David Copperfield!* My dear mother, who has a voice of "incomparable sweetness and effect," read it to my sister and myself. This early taught me that one's unhappy experiences can be transmuted, as it were, into the gold of literature— as witness David's drudgery at Murdstone and Grimby's. The difficulties David had in learning shorthand weighed not a little in deciding me against the commercial course at preparatory school, I determined to take all the literature classes possible. Copperfield, in fact, was the first fiction hero I had encountered who didn't wind up by becoming a dashing soldier, eloquent statesman, powerful ruler, big business man, or sport champion— but was content to adopt the comparatively unexciting profession of writing. His example undoubtedly played its part in directing me towards authorship—for I grew very fond of David who, as we all know, was really young Dickens.

I was ten before I started to school at Barat Hall conducted by the Madames of the Sacred Heart. I recall in particular one nun who possessed the unusual pedagogical gift of making even prosaic rules of grammar somehow fascinating. At thirteen I became a boarder at Canterbury School, New Milford, Connecticut, established that same year of 1915 by a Catholic layman, Nelson Hune, the elder brother of Cyril Hume the novelist. The boys were encouraged to go on long hikes and I got to know the hilly, rather rugged, stone-fenced country exceedingly well. Walking has ever since remained my favorite sport. I believe with Thomas Jefferson that of all exercises walking is the best. There was a fine library through which we were urged to browse at will. My parents donated to the school Mark Twain's thirty odd volumes which I proceeded to read from start to finish. Perhaps the book that made the most impression on me was Twain's *Joan of Arc*. I remember that while reading this I kept thinking how wonderful it would be if I could grow up to write biographies myself and create between the covers of a book a living, breathing personality such as Joan's. I began to devour every biography within reach, including Roper's *Thomas More,* Lockhart's *Scott,* Southey's *Lord Nelson,* and Irving's *Columbus.*

After finishing at Canterbury, I enrolled for the classical course at Georgetown University where my father had studied in the mid-eighties. The University is beautifully situated on the high bluffs overlooking the Potomac. My dormitory was in the attic of an old red brick Colonial building where the United States Congress had held its sessions when burnt out of the Capitol at Washington during the War of 1812. All the Jesuits were stimulating men of parts and nearly all had a sense of humor. One in particular I recall who had a keen enthusiasm for old Father Prout whose inimitable *Reliques* was soon occupying my spare hours. At present I am engaged on the first biography of the neglected Irishman for which another enthusiast, Mr. Shane Leslie, is writing the introduction.

Early in 1923 I helped to found the first literary society in Georgetown's long history. It began to meet each week for the discussion of books and authors. One lad assigned to speak on George Meredith was slightly confused: for he gave all his details on Owen Meredith, although he wound up by saying, "Now, I have told you everything that one should know about George Meredith whose masterpiece was *Lucille!*"

I hadn't been in Washington long before I "discovered" the Library of Congress to which I enjoyed walking the four or five miles that separated it from the University—not infrequently I returned also on foot. Being in the library made me feel infinitely rich: merely by scribbling its name on a slip of paper and handing it in at the huge circular desk, one could get within a few minutes any book that had ever been published—if not the first edition, then at least a reprint! The power of Aladdin's lamp was nothing to it! I recall several pleasant chats with Theodore Maynard during research for one of his colorful biographies. I also got to know genial Chief Justice William Howard Taft whose frequent quoting of Josh Billings led to my writing the humorist's first biography, *Josh Billings, Yankee Humorist,* 1932.

Towards the end of my third Georgetown year, a spell of illness necessitated my return to St. Louis where in 1928 I obtained my A.B. degree from Washington University, after specializing in American literature. I found the English department still dominated by John Livingston Lowes who had left there a few years before to begin his brilliant career at Harvard. Lowes' *Road to Xanadu* proved extremely stimulating and was reread several times.

I was then invited to go West to gather Mark Twain lore. Just outside of Angels Camp, I found Twain's old mining partner Bill Gillis who recounted so many fascinating anecdotes that in 1930 I was able to bring out *Gold Rush Days with Mark Twain.* At Angels Camp I also served as judge for the Contest held annually to commemorate the *Jumping Frog of Calaveras County.* Tens of thousands of people had come from all sections of the country to witness the forty odd frogs jump. Everything had been arranged with all the formality of a horse race, and the excitement of the spectators proved every bit as intense. In San Francisco I had numerous talks with a most interesting old lady named Mrs. Mary Tingley Lawrence who had known General William Walker the Nicaraguan fillibuster and had assisted Bret Harte in the preparation of his first book. I also discovered in his quiet retreat the prototype of Twain's "Connecticut Yankee," James Marvin, whom I describe in *My Cousin Mark Twain,* 1939. Then living peacefully in San Francisco was Julian Hawthorne with colorful stories to tell of his famous father, Thoreau, Emerson and the other New England worthies. When I told him of my hope to devote my life to literature, the eighty-year old man laid his hand upon my shoulder and said, "Do so by all means but realize that writing, as Emerson somewhere says, is about the hardest work in the world. I have never once regretted embracing it as my life profession. I like to reflect that even while I sleep my biography of my father is being read and influencing people."

The spring of 1930 found me going to Europe accompanied by my mother. On the steamer across I amused myself writing sketches of the people I expected to meet abroad. In *Mark Twain and Mussolini,* 1934, I described them after meeting them in the flesh. I was invited to address the Paris Rotary Club. After telling my best jokes for some minutes, I sat down with every countenance serious. Then the translator got busy, and I had the uncanny experience of seeing my audience laugh *some five minutes after* I had told a humorous anecdote! While in Paris I called on Rene Bazin, Paul Bourget, Henri Bordeaux, Abbe Ernest Dimnet, Andre Maurois. They one and all proved exceedingly courteous and most encouraging to a young American interested in writing. They had numerous questions about America regarding which their ideas were sometimes erroneous.

When I began to address numerous clubs in England on Mark Twain, I was pleasantly surprised to find his humor even more keenly appreciated there than in America. My travels soon taught me to disbelieve most of the easy generalizations about various nationalities: the English manifested no slowness seeing a joke nor were the Italians always eating spaghetti, nor the Irish potatoes, nor the French frog-legs!

In the course of a pleasant chat Hilaire Belloc suggested that a useful and interesting biography of a man could be written by presenting the opinions entertained about him by his contemporaries. The idea appealed to me and I chose Chesterton. Thereafter when visiting my English literary friends I usually managed to ask them their opinion of the genial G. K. C. In 1939 I produced my *Chesterton as Seen by his Contemporaries,* of which Mr. E. C. Bentley, the author of *Trent's Last Case,* says in his introduction, "Mr. Clemens has assembled a vast number of other people's memories and appreciations which show the attitude of Chesterton's contemporaries towards him better than any individual critic could describe it."

The highlight of a summer-school course at ancient Cambridge was several meetings with A. E. Housman of *Shropshire Lad* fame which inspired my *Evening with A. E. Housman*. I quote Padraic Colum's foreword to this book because Boswell's *Johnson* has always been one of my favorites—a small edition of which I usually have in my pocket: "As I read about A. E. Housman I had a feeling that a new Boswell had come amongst us. For the author has Boswell's power of bringing us into his hero's company; he has Boswell's literalness, too. He records literally, too, one is convinced, Housman's table-talk."

During my year of European travels I had heard much of Shakespeare, Browning, and Dante societies. Strolling on deck while returning to New York, I came to the conclusion that America's best known author deserved a society named in his honor. Upon my return to St. Louis I founded the International Mark Twain Society among whose charter members were Hilaire Belloc, G. K. Chesterton, Alfred Noyes, Maurice Baring, Shane Leslie, Rt. Rev. Ronald A. Knox, Agnes Repplier, Rene Bazin, Giovanni Papini. In 1936 the *Mark Twain Quarterly* was established with myself as editor. When a distinguished member dies, a whole quarterly is often devoted to his memory. This was done in the case of Chesterton with many of his friends participating. Each memorial number thus constitutes a unique biographic record invaluable for future biographers. The *Quarterly* also enables our members to know what their colleagues are doing, for at the start of the war, we numbered some two thousand members—mostly men-of-letters scattered throughout some thirty nations.

Late in 1942 appeared my *Young Sam Clemens* dedicated to my little son Sammy Clemens whose charming mother, a direct descendant of George Washington's adopted daughter Nellie Custis, I married on October 18, 1933. This book dealing with "Clemens before Twain" as the London *Times* says in its review, is based on material obtained during tramps through the regions associated with Mark Twain in Missouri, California, and Nevada. Since so much had already been written (Twain is almost as bad as Shakespeare in this respect) my endeavor was always to present *new* material. The noted novelist, August Derleth says in a recent review, "The author has told the story of Young Sam in such a way that it can be enjoyed by young and old alike. The story carries through from Twain's days as a mischievous schoolboy to his beginning authorship—the formative years out of which grew some of America's greatest literary classics."

I hope to cover Mark's whole life in a series of volumes based on fresh information.

EDITOR'S NOTE: Mr. Clemens has written appreciations of Chesterton, Housman, Santayana, F. D. Roosevelt, P. V. Nasby, Josh Billings, Frost, and Strachey, as well as a series of volumes on his cousin, Mark Twain. Most of these are issued by the International Mark Twain Society, Webster Groves, Mo.

URSULA CLINTON

IT IS A STORY of childhood, this tale of my first love for literature and first original song. I hope, on that account, that you will not think it too childish, too trivial.

It really goes back many years before I was born for its introduction. Heredity played some part in it. My love for poetry and music was partly an inheritance. So also was the urge to compose. Environment fostered both, and I came to love and create literature. To God's inspiration and protection I owe the rest.

Probably some of my ancestors shouted their own war songs at the Battle of Hastings, and others, on whom I prefer to dwell, plucked Irish harps in the ancient bardic days as they made up their songs of Finn McCuill and Deirdre of the Sorrows. But I can only trace the singing gift surely back to the pioneering days of Australia when my grandmother, Hannah Lynch, a young Limerick woman who had lost her material inheritance through family disaster, came out to live with cousins in Geelong, Victoria, and married an Irish gold miner, Peter Mackin Clinton, who, in the romantic fashion of the 1850's, had left his uncle's ship, on which he was being trained for a sea career, in order to try his luck at world-famed Ballarat. They went to dwell at Illabarook on the gold diggings south of Ballarat.

She took with her a sweet soprano voice which soon became the admiration of the newly-settled district. It had worn out before I was of an age to remember it, but I have often been told of its beauty by old residents of my native township, Illa-barook. Her songs, however, were the songs of others. The pioneering experience did not fan in her the creative fire of song. Instead, it passed it on to her fourth child, my father, Stephen Clinton.

He did not exercise his gift till manhood years, and then he did so secretly. I was twelve or thirteen years of age and had been writing prose and verse openly and confidently for a few years before his initials were discovered by an alert friend in a Victorian magazine. Taxed with the authorship of a poem, he confessed to it, and to others, and soon an amazed family learnt his secret. He continued, however, to use initials or pen names. He did not publish any book.

Always a lover of beautiful sounds and sights, when he married, he surrounded his home with an infant forest of a few acres. The place already had growing on it stunted sheokes, black-woods and other Australian trees which the stock running over it, when it was part of the local common, had eaten down.

Rejoicing at my father's kindness in protecting them with a fence, they soon regained their primal beauty and size. To them were added, as the years went on, little trees of many different species. Most of these were Australians—about fifty different kinds of wattles, blue, sugar, crimson flowering and lemon-scented gums (eucalypts), wild cherries and others. There were also some beautiful foreigners—pines, cedars, tree lucernes and holies—and the trees and human children grew up together, the former soon leaving the latter well behind. The little wildflowers, too, became braver when released from fear of cattle and horses. In the spring they rioted everywhere in the forest paddock, and the grasses grew tall spears to further protect their little colorful friends. It was a very Australian place. The garden flowers were almost outcasts.

The winds came with their aeolian harps in the sheokes and pines, and the wild Australian birds came to sing part songs to their accompaniment, and to dance when the boughs danced. Green and golden honey-eaters there were, hanging upside down after the flowers that climbed in our windows, and magpies warbling at dawn and moonlit midnight. The harmonious and grey thrushes honoured us, and the pallid cuckoo repeated his chromatics all the spring day. Blue wrens vied with the wild-flowers and parrots with the crimson flowering gums. Rich sunsets glowed between dark trunks and moonlight gave blue mystery. Stars hung in the branches of tall, slim trees, and rain brought out the sweet faint bush scents.

In this exquisite Eden my brother and I and, later, my sister grew up. Small wonder that we were children of fancy and faerie. When we played at school with other children our games were the conventional community games, but when we entered our own little world, imagination was the predominating force. The forest acres were inhabited by folk of our own creation.

When it rained and indoors we must remain, we danced and acted impromptu plays. And we read—how we read!—children's books by the dozen, among them my favorite, *Gum Tree Brownie,* a collection of Australian fairy tales by Tarella Quin, illustrated by the well-known Australian fairy artist, Ida Rentoul, and Ethel Turner's more human Australian children's stories. There were also the breath-taking books of my father's library of which we were given the freedom. There were no books in it to injure us. My father was a school-master—and a Catholic—and knew how to nourish the child mind. Being a poet also, he knew how to nourish the poet's mind. I fell in love with Shelley and Keats, Coleridge and Shakespeare, Tennyson and that mediaeval who sang:

> "Sumer is i-comen in,
> Gaily sing cuckoo."

And I was very responsive to the Australians, Kendall especially. His "Bell-birds" and "September in Australia" sang through my mind for days at a time. Kendall's world was so like our world.

When I was seven, I began to learn the piano. As soon as I had gained a little musical skill, rhythm and melody captivated me and my mind created imagery which the music suggested.

Dancing was another beloved recreation. On moonlight summer nights before going to bed, we loved to sing and dance out on the grass in our magic garden. Our parents were only too glad to encourage our artistic trends. My mother (she was born Mary Cogan, a New Zealander) loved dancing and all the bright and happy things of life, and my father was hoping for us to show signs of literary talent. On one entrancing night the moon so bewitched one little ten year old dancer that she slipped into metre and rhyme spontaneously—and realized with a thrill what she had done. She had composed her first poem.

It was followed by others composed in a similar way, and soon her brother Leo was following her example. (His poetic urge, however, seems to have been lost since his University years.) Her sister Veronica, then a babe, grew up with a like devotion to verse-making and reading, but later, when a life of illness was sent her by God, she deliberately put aside her literary activities to concentrate on spiritual perfection. She died in her twenties, the nearest being to a saint that I have ever known, and she always was, and will be, one of my dearest inspirations and helps.

The child Ursula soon began to experiment in prose. Short stories were written and illustrated with fearsome drawings, that showed imagination if no beauty of line. Later, in about her fifteenth year, came a more ambitious project, a novel with a sociological bias—"Saved from the Slums." It now provides amusing reading, but was taken very seriously by school-girl friends at the time of its composition. It had a definite religious note in it, as had many of my childhood poems though in some other ways I was, as you may have thought, inclined to the pagan.

My first appearance in print, apart from letters to children's pages of newspapers, was when, in my fifteenth year, I sent a poem to Mary Gilmore, an outstanding Sydney poet, for criticism. She published it in the Women's Page of *The Australian Worker* (*her* page), commented on it favourably and wrote me a special letter of encouragement for which I shall always have reason to thank her.

About this time a great break occurred in my life which entered a very important formative phase. I was sent to board at a convent, Loreto Abbey, Mary's Mount, Ballarat, a beautiful place with a reputation for genuine Catholic culture. My four years there influenced my literary and spiritual development very much. The true significance of my religion began to dawn on me. The sensitive influence of understanding nun teachers and the spiritual graces from daily Communion made of me a new personality. My English teacher, an Australian, Mother Mary Michael Gibson (God rest her soul!) took me through entrancing worlds of literature. She also gave me a firm and logical grounding in Christian doctrine and Scripture. With a day divided into definite, inescapable tasks, there was no time for verse-making. What little was done was stolen from sleep time. But I was absorbing impressions most necessary to me, observing and contemplating, and from my school days I took treasures invaluable and never-ending.

I passed on to the University of Melbourne to study for an Arts degree. At St. Mary's Hall, the Catholic Women's hostel of Newman College, I came under the influence of another great nun of the same order, an Irishwoman, Mother Mary Patrick, I.B.V.M., herself a writer well known to many Catholic circles of Melbourne, an artist also, and an ardent Sinn Feiner. (These were the early 1920's.) She introduced me to the wonders of Irish literature, including the works of the Sinn Fein poets. At the Hall, Newman College (the Catholic College) and the University proper, I also met several students, Catholic and non-Catholic, with whom I naturally became friendly. I won a prize offered by the *Newman College Magazine* for a poem "Sursum Corda." (It appears in my book.) Archibald Strong, lecturer in English and well-known Australian poet, was the adjudicator.

This achievement confirmed my resolution to continue with creative writing, and when P. I. O'Leary, literary editor of the Melbourne *Advocate* showed an interest in my work, I began to feel my literary feet. His keen criticism and kindly advice have always been appreciated by me.

On graduation, I took up a teaching career, and most of my life has been spent in various secondary schools of the Victorian Education Department. For some time, however, I was on the staff of the Department's Publications Branch, writing for *The School Paper,* a children's monthly magazine produced for the various grades of primary school. Apart from that experience, my writing has been done in my leisure.

In my early twenties, I joined the editorial committee of *The Horizon,* the monthly organ of the Catholic Women's Social Guild. With this I have been associated ever since, first as a children's page editress; later, when I was in country districts, as contributor, and then, when I returned to the metropolis, as general editress. For fourteen years I have edited this little paper through lean years and fat, but I really think that I am now due to be retired. The work has all been honorary—and arduous—though interesting, and necessary. Often it has meant putting aside my verse-making, and I have been tempted to desert it, but when the workers in the vineyard are scarce, what is one to do?

Since my childhood days it had always been my dream to publish my poems in book form. Because I was poor, the dream had to wait till 1931 when I braved the depression itself with my volume, *Read in a Fire.* I was happy to have as my publisher Frank Wilmot who, under his pen name "Furnley Maurice," had published several books of verse himself. He died in 1942 nationally acclaimed as a great Australian poet. Nettie Palmer, one of our foremost Australian literary critics and essayists, gave me sage advice and help in preparing my book.

There is material in my note-book for another book of verse —two or three books—but their publication is still a future dream. Shall I brave the rigours of war as I braved the depression? Perhaps! But where find time to prepare these books? To my *Horizon* duties I have added another duty—leadership of the Writers' Guild of the Paraclete Arts Group, a Melbourne Catholic Action Society. Perhaps there is needed someone to drag me off to a hermit's cave and leave me there to publish a volume of verse or starve.

And now my message to the young Catholic writers of the world. The Church needs you, maybe as never before. You must dedicate your talents to God's service and hers and lean back on prayer and the Sacraments to strengthen your resolution. And you must fit yourselves technically for your writing. Your noble thoughts are of little use unless you can express them artistically and clearly to attract your readers' attention, appeal to their reason and inflame their hearts. And do not be afraid to give yourselves wholly to the service of your Leader, Christ. There are too many people of our time trying to bargain with Him. They will give Him so much of their time, no more. Place all at His disposal. He may give some of it back to you, but He may not. In either case, however, He will give you a spiritual peace that the world cannot give and would you not prefer to co-operate with Him in saving millions of souls rather than be a best-seller writer who has helped to destroy millions?

EDITOR'S NOTE: Miss Clinton's book of poems, *Read in a Fire,* was published by the Univ. of Melbourne Press in 1931 and reissued in 1940.

REVEREND ALEXANDER J.
CODY, S.J.

IT IS HARD for me to go back to the first time when I started writing, but I can quite vividly recall a thick red-covered composition book. I was somewhere about the age of ten. The pages of that book were filled with my big, boyish, vertical, and not always vertical, penmanship that ran in a series of Western episodes that threatened to be endless. All vestiges of any plot have long since been forgotten, but the heroine, I remember, was always given the name of my favorite aunt, and the villains, unblushingly, were given the names of my boyhood enemies. The number of villains waxed and waned according to the neighborhood sessions of peace or war. Most generally there were sessions of war.

A long interval comes after this until my entrance into freshman class at Santa Clara College. There I learned the art of composition and literary appreciation by the hard way of analysis and imitation. It was drudgery, as any apprenticeship to a worthwhile perfected achievement must be, and a drudgery long drawn out, with so many revisions and so many re-writings laid upon my original text that the craftiest of literary sleuths could not ferret the original out. Some of those multi-corrected papers I have used in the earlier days of my own teaching, that the would-be writers of my own English classes would know that their final clarity of thought and their final filing of phrases had not yet been reached. One or two of those authors from my college freshman days I have not dared to look in the face since, not so much for what they did to me as for what I did to them. However, Addison and I still meet, via the Roger de Coverly papers, in an annual friendly ceremony for auld lang syne. And Milton, also, in his L'Allegro and Il Penseroso and his masque of Comus. These poems gave joy, then as now, in their matchless cameos and their rich tapestry of the Renaissance. Though I wrote a little at verses, almost lisping in numbers for the numbers came, I toted about with me for a long time a college imitation of Comus as my first ambitious attempt at authorship. At this late date, I can admit, unabashed and quite understandingly, that nothing came of it.

Aside from random verses in college magazines the first publication came in a series of short essays on the American poets that appeared in the *Northwest Progress*. They were very copy-cattish in their criticism, had but a transitory value, and died an early literary death. The one personal gain was a cherished first acquaintanceship with Madison Cawein.

The real impetus came later with the encouragement and aid of four persons in particular. To these four, any later literary success that may be mine, is mostly due. First, Father Edward Garesché, S.J. At the time he was busy with a little *Sodality Bulletin* in nowise as pretentious as the *Queen's Work* and he invited me to make contribution. Twelve five-hundred-word articles were contributed in all, which taught me economy and value of words and stern selection of salient details. Father John Corbett, S.J., comes next. At that time he was editor of the *Messenger of the Sacred Heart* and when his tenure of office ceased he graciously handed my cause on to his successor Father Charles

Mullaly, S.J. The kindly interviews of one summer expanded into a gracious correspondence over many years that resulted in a series of stories appearing in the *Messenger* under his editorship and the editorship of Father Mullaly. The stories evidently pleased, for appreciative letters came to me from all parts of the country, mostly from the rank-and-file Catholic homes, with questions on description that fitted bits of their own neighborhood, and questions on character delineation that (flatteringly) could have been patterned on themselves or on the person next door. With the arrival of these letters came the further compliment of syndication through the various Catholic newspapers of the United States. One story even found its way into a book on practical aids for Catholic teachers. All of this was but a verification of what Father Mullaly had written in one of his many notes of commendation, "You have the touch that will please."

I found a great joy in the writing of those stories. They sharpened my observation of persons and scenes, made me in some instances almost photographic though ever with the saving grace of light dispelling shadows and silhouettes of spirit above the too, too solid flesh. They held the joy, too, of my first imaginative character walking off an independent old man. Roscrans in those stories began as a mere type, a marionette where I pulled all the strings and, as ventriloquist, did all the talking. There came the story where he walked out on me, slammed the door in my face, took the street turning of his own choosing and said as he went what *he* wanted to say. It was my great moment of storydom. Dickens, I recalled in my brief exultation, used to slink down the London streets shadowed by his literary progeny. Some of those *Messenger* stories I later salvaged in a slim volume entitled *The City Dusk*.

During this same period, too, I branched out into other types of writing. Some articles on the religious brotherhood having run serially in *Our Sunday Visitor* were gathered into a brochure under the original title *They Also Serve*. The brochure filled an evident and nationwide need, for sincere appreciation came from the reverend Provincials of the various Orders, but the most flattering appreciation came from Europe in authorized Flemish and French versions. Articles on American Indian themes, too, began to appear in the *Indian Sentinel* whose managing editor, Miss Inno McGill came forward as another sponsor for my literary advance. For a number of years many letters passed between us with helpful criticism, tidbits of literary lore and much enthusiasm for my verse that appeared over my own name and over a nom de plume in many of the Catholic magazines.

It was my poems that brought me the fourth person to help me forward in my literary quest. That person was Sister M. Ignatia of the Sisters of Mercy at Manchester, N. H., the editor of the *Magnificat*. Sister M. Ignatia was not only a constructive critic but far more a fairy and a cloistered godmother to myself and to many others more known than I in the realms of American Catholic letters. Most of these poems have since been gathered together and put out in book form. Children of a writer's brain just as children of a parent's flesh have their own individualities and endearments. So have these four books. *Our Lady Courtesy* contains the prize winning poem in the Fourth Marian Poetry Contest sponsored by the *Queen's Work* in 1920, and a sonnet on Sergeant Joyce Kilmer that in its first printing elicited a letter from the soldier poet's mother. "There have been almost countless poems . . . to his memory, but none have touched me as yours has done, and from the depths of a sad but proud heart I thank you again." With that prized letter began a long friendship with the elder Kilmer household. *God's Looking-Glass* brought contacts with Ednah Aitkens and Charles D. South. *Enchanted Casements* took care of other contacts and garnered a veritable sheaf of magazine and newspaper appreciation so laudatory that I was embarrassed at the high names of those mentioned as my literary kin. It was all very nice and I was very thankful, but I knew that blood relationship was out and adoption questionable. *Peddler of Beauty* found further appreciation and much encomium in the poetry magazine *Spirit,* particularly for a section of a Rondeau sequence. This fourth book, too, furthered a literary, and much more than a literary friendship, with Brother Leo, F.S.C., of St. Mary's College, Sister M. Madeleva, C.S.C., Mr. Frank Spearman and that fine Catholic actress of the cinema, Una O'Connor. The poems in some shape or other have continued to find favor down a decade of years, for hardly an anthology season goes by but some letter arrives with a request to re-print. The last in a growing procession of anthologies is that by Rev. James M. Hayes, *In Praise of Nuns*. It is a glorious company to be in and compensates for the occasional less glorious company in the literary caravan, where, at times, I have unwittingly found myself.

But sister M. Ignatia gave me other valued assistance beside the valued first assistance to my verse. She admitted into her magazine three of my one-act plays and a whole phalanx of familiar essays. The essays ultimately found their way into two volumes entitled *Gardens* and *Grottos* and *Tarts and Cheese Cake*. Sister M. Madeleva, at the time stationed at St-Mary-on-the-Wasatch, near Salt Lake City, hastily wrote that she brought them to her English classes "with a particular first hand pride," and later in a letter concluded, "I want God to make your soul daring to think, your heart dauntless to experience, and your pen strong for superlative work in His Name." Brother Leo commented in a note to a mutual friend: "*Tarts and Cheese Cake* affords me perfect diet; thereon I laugh and grow fat: and perhaps, even, I shall grow wise. It's a bully little book and I don't mean maybe." That title of *Tarts and Cheese Cake* (a phrase taken from one of Dryden's plays) has always provoked gales of refreshing laughter from the very first day when the heavy burdened expressman arrived at the University of San Francisco and looked in vain for a large and very pretentious kitchen to dispose of his load of cook books. Reviews uniformly were most favorable, as of essays 'in the fine tradition of English letters.' I began to feel, that, perhaps, I could—distantly—bow to Charles Lamb, and—momentarily, and tentatively, and dubiously—hobnob with E. V. Lucas.

Later writings of a more religious nature took place in the shape of three volumes, one of occasional sermons, the other two of occasional conferences. At present the editing of Sodality pamphlets, now stretched into seven bound volumes and given over in great part to the American high school boy's literary and, principally spiritual self-expression, consumes much of the leisure that could otherwise go into one's own literary creation. However, all writing on a strictly belle letters basis has not been given over entirely: one or other manuscript is in formation and awaiting the propitious hour of a reading public's serenity and a printer. For Father Talbot, S.J., has been so gracious as to put my name on his list of American Catholic Authors, and I am holding on tenaciously, even if it be in a lower place.

Writing for Catholic magazines is an excellent training for the aspiring Catholic author. Whatever it may have been in our grandfathers' time, the writing for Catholic magazines today will not pickle to piety. A high standard of technique, clear thinking and elevated thinking are required, that, in a like proportion, or even in any proportion at all, will not be demanded anywhere else.

EDITOR'S NOTE: Father Cody's books, available from him at the University of San Francisco, include (poems) *Enchanted Casements, God's Looking Glass,* and *Our Lady Courtesy;* (prose) *Gardens and Grottos, Paths of Peace,* and *Vessels of Election.*

PADRAIC COLUM

I WAS BORN in the eighteen and eighties and belong to the same generation of Irish writers as James Joyce, James Stephens, and Thomas MacDonagh. My childhood was spent in the Ireland of the countryside and the small market town, of the street-singers and an odd storyteller; the first verses I knew were from ballads I heard sung. My schooldays were in a town outside Dublin, Kingstown, now gone back to its ancient name, Dunleary, a town between the hills and the sea, around which there were grand opportunities for rambling. In my development as a writer an important event happened to me here: as I was turning twenty I found in the public library Ibsen's *Master Builder* and *Hedda Gabler*. The reading of these plays gave my mind a dramatic cast, led me to think in dialogue and action, and this while I had a very slight acquaintance with the theatre.

Just at that time what has been called the Irish Renaissance, the Celtic Revival, was a very vital movement. As we ordinary young men and women knew it, it was a strongly nationalist movement tinged with mysticism and romanticism; it led us to give our time to learning the Irish language in little comradely groups; it gave us an interest in the old traditions and the old pastimes and made us look to the country people as the keepers of what was national and racial; it also prepared the way for an armed revolution in which my contemporaries were leaders. And so when in my twenties I went to live in Dublin there was much to give the spirit of a young man exaltation. An Irish Theatre was being promoted by William Butler Yeats. George Moore who, at the time, was regarded as the most modern, the most exciting novelist in English was to be met on the streets and occasionally heard from a platform. Arthur Griffith, the founder of the militant nationalist movement, was running his weekly journal. A. E. kept open house on Sunday evenings, and those who went there heard talk about poetry and painting and the idealistic side of politics. People were looking for a manifestation of the national spirit in literature.

I wrote my first poems for Arthur Griffith's and A. E.'s journals and was immediately welcomed by people who took trouble to show a young writer how to form himself. And there were young men around who could discuss poetry and prose in a luminous way: James Joyce was one of them. I entered the group in which Yeats, "A. E.," Lady Gregory, John Millington Synge, the Fay brothers, were engaged in creating what was to become a national theatre, and picked up dramatic technique watching rehearsals and taking small parts in plays. In my twenties I wrote three plays for the Irish Theatre,—*The Land, The Fiddler's House,* and *Thomas Muskerry*.

After this early one, another group arose which included James Stephens and Thomas MacDonagh, one of the poets who was executed after the insurrection of 1916. With them I edited *The Irish Review*. The idealism of the Irish Revival was embodied in two schools which Padraic Pearse, a poet who wrote in Gaelic, who was one of the leaders of the insurrection of 1916 and was executed after it, now set up. I taught in them. I entered journalism as a profession, writing for the Dublin and some of the London liberal dailies. Then the European war of 1914 broke out. I was just married at the time; a relative in America invited my wife and me to visit her, and I came over.

The first literary opportunity that came to me in America was the writing of stories for a children's page in the Sunday edition of a newspaper. I drew from the Irish folk traditions for the material of these stories. I put them together as my first book for children, *The King of Ireland's Son,* which was illustrated by Willy Pogany. Its publication made me in the minds of New York publishers a writer of children's stories, and Macmillan then commissioned me to take over the Iliad and the Odyssey as a book for children. I did this, and then made over more Greek stories with the Norse and the Welsh and wrote other books for children. My name became known for this sort of work and in 1923, on the invitation of the Legislature, I went to Hawaii to make over the native traditions into a book for children. *Legends of Hawaii* represents the work I did there.

And I went on writing poems. After my Irish poems, published as *Wild Earth, Dramatic Legends,* and *Old Pastures,* I wrote poems about birds and beasts, published as *Creatures.* (but all four volumes have been included in my *Collected Poems*). I wrote an Irish romance, *Castle Conquer,* and started a long novel that I am still working on and which will be published with the title *The Hen Wife's Son.* I also wrote plays. One of them will be produced, it seems, in 1945. Its title is *Balloon,* and it is a play wholly different from any I have had produced or published; it is a comedy in which I attempt to revive and place in modern circumstances the types of the Commedia dell' Arte. At present my wife and I (she is the author of *From These Roots*: the ideas that have made modern literature) are attached to the Philosophy Department of Columbia University.

EDITOR'S NOTE: Mr. Colum's books include *The Frenzied Prince,* 1943, McKay, heroic tales of ancient Ireland; *Where the Winds Never Blew and the Cocks Never Crew,* 1940, Macmillan, a folk-tale for children; *Road Round Ireland,* 1934, McBride; *Legends of Hawaii,* 1937, Yale University Press; *Story of Lowry Maen,* 1937, Macmillan, an Irish heroic narrative poem; and *Collected Poems,* 1932, Macmillan. Mrs. Colum's *From These Roots,* Columbia U. Press.

JAMES BRENDAN CONNOLLY

A SON OF JOHN and Mary (O'Donnell) Connolly, I was born in South Boston, Massachusetts, on October 28, 1868. My parents were natives of the Aran Islands in Galway Bay, were married over there, and while still young came to South Boston to live.

I was the sixth of John and Mary Connolly's ten sons. All the Connolly boys like to rove. One of the older boys, Michael, went South on a government job, settled in Georgia, studied law nights, and was admitted to the Georgia Bar. He specialized in Maritime law, and was named Admiralty Commissioner for the port of Savannah.

When I got the family itch to rove, brother Mike got me a job with the U. S. Engineer Corps then at the work of improving the rivers and harbors of the south east Atlantic coast. While with the Engineer Corps, I saved a dredge hand from drowning. *The Savannah Morning News* gave two columns to the account of the rescue.

I left the Engineer Corps for a special engineering course at

Harvard College. I left Harvard when I was refused leave of absence to compete in the revival of the Ancient Olympic Games at Athens. I had been the American amateur hop-step-and-jump champion and record holder before that. I won this event at Athens, being first of all to win, and so became the first Olympic Victor in 1500 years.

I came home a hero, but I had also come home broke, having paid my own expenses for the Olympic trip, and now I had to start making a living again! I had begun writing while still in grammar school. At an annual examination I filled sixteen foolscap pages with a paper on the Declaration of Independence; which paper was sent by my proud teacher to a convention of school superintendents as a sample of what a twelve year old Boston public school boy could do.

I began my writing for a living by doing space things for two Boston daily papers and two monthly sports magazines. I was making a local name for myself as a special writer when the Spanish War broke out. I enlisted with the Ninth Massachusetts Infantry, the famous Fighting Ninth of Civil War fame. The regiment served through the campaign of '98 in Cuba. During the siege of Santiago I carried rations to isolated comrades after being three times ordered back by my battalion commander, Major Michael O'Connor. While in Cuba I wrote letters to a friend about Army life. The friend turned them over to the Boston *Globe* which played them up heavily. I was told I would be court martialed for some of the things I said in my letters; but I wasn't court martialed.

Bad food, bad water, bad sanitation, and meagre medical service played havoc with that little army in that terrible summer in Cuba. After the Spanish troops in Cuba surrendered, the Ninth was sent home and mustered out. By that time every man in it was down with some form of fever—malaria, typhoid-malaria, yellow fever and what not. And yellow fever was not at all the worst of them.

When I began to feel half way good again I shipped as hand on a cattle boat to England. I went broke in London, tramped my way back to Liverpool, where I had free passage on a cattle boat home. I did an article on the cattle trip for the Boston *Transcript*.

While still twenty-five pounds underweight from tropic fever, I took a job as physical director of the Gloucester Athletic Club. I played football on the Athletic Club eleven, spent the fall and winter (1899–1900) there, chucked that job in the spring, took a steerage trip to England, looked the London slums over, and went on to Paris, to take in the Paris Exposition, and, incidentally, compete in the Second Olympic Games. I lived on twenty cents a day for my first week in Paris, meantime training for the Olympic Games by walking countless miles around the city. On the day of my competition I had a breakfast of one egg, one roll, one cup of cafe au lait. That morning I walked seven miles to the athletic park, lunched on the good air of the Bois de Boulougne, and got second place in the event.

While wondering what I would do for my next meal, I ran across Bob Garrett, a wealthy friend from Olympic days in Athens. Garrett staked me to my room rent, some nourishing meals and a steerage passage home. Arriving home I wrote my first short story, an athletic story for a boys' weekly, to repay Garrett. I then did several newspaper and a magazine article on my steerage experiences.

My next move was to make fishing trips with the captains I had come to know while in Gloucester with the Athletic Club. I had no intention of writing them up, but at this stage of my development I was able to appraise men fairly well. Here were great men, and all the greater because they did not know that they were great. I began by writing of actual experiences with the Gloucestermen, continued with them as the heroic men they were in short stories. My first stories were sent to *Scribner's Magazine*, and immediately accepted.

My first half dozen stories were brought out in the volume, *Out of Gloucester*, by Charles Scribner's Sons; and immediately republished in England. Eight subsequent volumes of my short stories, one book of personal experiences, and three novels were republished in England.

These volumes were written between times. Editors had been getting after me early to do special work for them. *Scribner* and *Harper* magazines both commissioned me to make Arctic trips. I fished with Finnish fishermen over by the White Sea on the Siberian coast; and the Lapp fishermen out of Hammerfest. I went on a whaling voyage to seventy-six degrees north, with the famous Norwegian Captain Morgan Ingrebrystken. I sailed with English fishermen in the North Sea, with German fishermen in the Baltic Sea. There was a mission to the Russian border to study immigration matters. I put in a trip for the Boston *Transcript* to the Consistory at Rome in 1911. I made a mission to Europe for *Collier's* in 1908, I revisited Greece in 1906 to polish off a short novel, "An Olympic Victor," for *Scribner's*.

President Theodore Roosevelt gave me authority to go aboard any American navy ship any time anywhere and stay as long as it suited me. I saw navy life from ward rooms and admiral's cabins as a guest; and from the fo'c's'le end as an enlisted man. I was with the American naval rescue party after the disastrous Kingston Jamaica earthquake; the commanding American Admiral Davis mentioned me in his dispatches for meritorious service in Jamaica.

I was with the Battle Fleet of Theodore Roosevelt's day when it made the passage of Magellan Straits at cruising speed in fleet formation, in a thick fog—that greatest of all fleet passages in maritime history. Eventually, I had battleship, cruiser, destroyer, collier, airplane, dirigible balloon, submarine and hospital ship experience. I was on the steamer Republic (1909) when she was rammed off Nantucket—(she sank later) the time radio (wireless then) was first used for signalling distress from a ship to sea. There was also an oil tanker trip to the Gulf of Mexico; and a run on a Mississippi River steamboat, and a trans-Atlantic race on a ninety-ton schooner for the Kaiser cup.

I ran for Congress on the Bull Moose ticket in 1913. I was defeated, but ran 2500 votes ahead of my ticket.

In 1914, I was *Collier's* correspondent in Mexico, that time we landed troops at Vera Cruz. That same year I entered a story in the *Collier* short story competition. Eight thousand manuscripts were submitted anonymously in that competition. My story, "The Trawler," won first place.

During the first World War I was *Collier's* naval correspondent for European waters. I saw service with our U-Boat hunting destroyer fleet out of Queenstown in 1917. I came home for Christmas with pneumonia; got over it and went back as correspondent in Brest—Bay of Biscay air and surface patrol in 1918, came home from there after the war with the flu.

In 1921, I was named Commissioner for the American Committee for the Relief of Ireland, my mission being to visit Ireland and report on the story put out by London that American Relief money was being spent for arms and munitions for the Irish Republican Army. I was able to nail that London report as a canard. The Black and Tan War was at its height while I was in Ireland. I had various interesting experiences while there, met with prominent Irish leaders on both sides, including De Valera while on the run, and the British Commander-in-Chief Macready in Dublin Castle. On my return I severely indicted the British conduct of the war in a series of articles for the Hearst Press.

That fall I was one of the crew of the Gloucester schooner Esperanto when she won the International Fishermen Championship off the coast of Nova Scotia.

Altogether I have written nineteen volumes of short stories, novels, personal experiences, and several hundred newspaper and magazine articles on widely varying subjects.

I write mornings after breakfast—a three hour stretch usually, with now and then a lay-off.

After more than forty years of writing for a living, my advice to younger men is to write of the things that they know something about. For equipment: a gift for writing is a great asset; but a greater asset is sympathy for all kinds, any kind of people. Sympathy makes for understanding.

I am a member of the Army of Santiago de Cuba, a Spanish War veteran, a member of the National Institute of Arts and Letters, a Knight of Columbus and a Gloucester Master Mariner. I live at 9 Braemore Road, Boston, with the wife I married forty years ago and a daughter, Brenda.

EDITOR'S NOTE: Mr. Connolly's more recent books include *Canton Captain*, 1941, Doubleday; *American Fishermen*, 1940, Norton; *Master Mariner*, 1943, Doubleday; and his autobiography, *Sea-Borne*, 1944, Doubleday.

REVEREND TERENCE L.
CONNOLLY, S.J.

AS A BOY AGED ELEVEN, I once asked the New England school-maam who was my sixth grade teacher: "What are Jesuits, please?" Her usually amiable countenance grew stern, her thin lips moved slowly and she answered: "Jesuits are members of a Society named after Jesus, but they are not much like Him." It was a curious incident, in view of my subsequent vocation. But it is not for that reason I mention it here, but as an example of suppressed bigotry, only occasionally articulate, in New England nearly half a century ago. In my youth it was a blight upon the complete knowledge and appreciation of my Faith in all spheres except that of moral conduct. In later life, the memory of it was my chief inspiration to explore the manifestations of the Catholic faith in history and literature, so that the young men in my classes might never suffer from the deprivation I had known.

When I graduated from high-school, I was as unaware of the heritage of Catholic literature as I was of Hebrew. A few years later, as a young Jesuit studying poetry, the discovery of that heritage dulled forever my reaction to Keats' lines, "On First Looking into Chapman's Homer." The demesne I had discovered was so much more expansive and its serene source, so much purer!

First it was Dante that attracted me as the Catholic expression of what I found imperfectly conveyed in Milton. After a comparative study of the two poets, I set down a fragment of it in an essay. For correction I brought it to the late Richard H. Tierney, S.J., then editor of *America,* the only real genius I have ever known. In the midst of his incredible labors, Father Tierney read and corrected the paper in my presence and when he had finished, said: "Why don't you publish it? If you don't publish now, you'll never do it." Shortly afterwards, "Faith in Milton and Dante" was printed in the *Catholic Mind.*

It happened that at this time Long's *History of English Literature* was the prescribed text-book in a course I was giving at Fordham. The obvious bias of its historical background forced me to prepare corrective notes for my classes, and later Fordham University Press published them in two small volumes: *An Introduction to Chaucer and Langland,* and *The English Renaissance and the Age of Elizabeth.*

About this time, while teaching modern poetry, I was seriously handicapped by the lack of satisfactory commentaries on our great Catholic poets. My attempt to meet this need in the case of Francis Thompson, finally resulted in the publication of his *Poems* with notes and commentary. Study of Thompson led, quite naturally, to the study of Coventry Patmore, the chief influence in Thompson's later life and poetry. Comparison of Patmore's early work, before he became a Catholic, with his later work in the *Odes,* revealed that the poet no less than the man, under the inspiration of the Catholic faith, attained heights previously beyond him. This, I knew from experience in the classroom, would make the study of Patmore productive of immeasurable good for Catholic students with a flare for literature. Too often they incline to the view that to be artistic one must be "arty" or "daring." A sure antidote is Patmore's authentic mysticism, his apotheosis of woman, and his theme of conjugal love, expressed with masterful and original technique and with passion as intense as it is pure. The result was the publication of *Mystical Odes of Nuptial Love,* including Patmore's "Wedding Sermon" and *Odes,* with notes and commentary.

The work on Patmore led me to make a new and original translation from the Latin of Saint Bernard's *On the Love of God,* chief source-book of the *Odes.* A partial translation of the work, begun by Patmore's first wife and finished by the poet himself after her death, was out of print, and a new translation was badly needed by students of the *Odes.*

Through my interest in Thompson I met Mr. Seymour Adelman, a young man who for more than ten years had been collecting Thompson manuscripts and volumes. Shortly after our meeting, young Adelman brought his collection to Boston College for a public exhibition. Later, the entire collection was purchased and presented to the College, and it was my privilege to prepare it for permanent exhibition and edit the catalog, *An Account of Books and Manuscripts of Francis Thompson.*

In 1938 an unexpected opportunity sent me to Ireland to attend the Abbey Theatre Festival, and to England to continue my Thompson studies. It was the newspapers' "Silly Season" when I arrived in Dublin and I soon found myself the centre of a terrific controversy, precipitated by asking the meaning of Yeats' one-act play, *Purgatory,* which was given its premiere during the Abbey Festival. The incident greatly hampered my study of Irish playrights and poets. But other happier experiences in Ireland are among my life's loveliest memories. One day I hope to set them down for the enjoyment of others.

In England I visited the places most closely associated with Thompson—Ushaw, Storrington, Pantasaph, London—and from his sister, Mother Austin; from Archbishop Kenealy, his "Friend, Philosopher and Guide;" from his class-mate, Father Adam Wilkinson, and others, I learned much not found in books, about the poet and his work. But as the guest of Mr. Wilfrid Meynell who saved Thompson, body and soul, man and poet, I gathered priceless information and was given an opportunity to study the poet's manuscripts under the sure and kindly guidance of his "Father, Brother, Friend." Through the over-whelming generosity of Mr. Meynell, I returned to Boston with Thompson notebooks, manuscripts and volumes many times more numerous and precious than those already in the Boston College Collection. After many months of labor the new treasures were added to the permanent exhibit of Thompsoniana in the Boston College Library, and now I am trying to prepare a new catalog of the enlarged collection. The story of my Thompson pilgrimage is the subject of my recent volume, *Francis Thompson: In His Paths.*

As must be evident, the chief inspiration of the little I have published has been a desire to help other students and teachers to know and appreciate Catholic literature. If education is the harmonious development of all the faculties, education in literature should not result in discord and disagreement of intellect and will, with the imagination and emotions. A Catholic student who is taught chiefly the poems of Shelley, Keats and Byron, for instance, is being trained to react emotionally and imaginatively to literature that often expresses a philosophy of life that he has been taught to abhor! But in the appreciation of great Catholic poets such as Thompson and Patmore, all faculties of the soul sound in one great harmony of aesthetic delight and spiritual exaltation. This I personally experienced in my work of many years. The sharing of it with others has been my chief reward. *Deo volenti,* it will be the inspiration of much that still remains to be done this side "the nurseries of Heaven."

EDITOR'S NOTE: Father Connolly's works include annotated editions of Coventry Patmore's *Mystic Poems of Nuptial Love,* 1938, Bruce Humphries, and Francis Thompson's *Poems,* revised edition, 1941, Appleton. His most recent book is *Francis Thompson: In His Paths,* 1944, Bruce.

VERY REVEREND JOHN J. CONSIDINE, M.M.

A GIRL IN A BOARDING SCHOOL in Kansas wrote to me recently that her teacher told her to ask me what reading I liked during high school days. I recognized the letter immediately as an item in that program of forced labor which teachers are required to impose upon the reluctant young, one of those hurdles along the highway to matriculation that every girl must gracefully leap to grasp her sheepskin.

Could I truthfully answer Mary Ellen, I asked myself, and yet tell her something which Sister would regard as helpful? There was that *Graustark* and *Beverley* of Graustark period when I feverishly read two novels a week from the public library. Perhaps I had better not mention that, though I have a suspicion that it accomplished something for me, entirely unrealized at the time. It provided an era of muchness in the book field, like meeting many, many new people every day. The kaleidoscope of scenes and characters which rapidly bowed in and out of my mind probably whetted my imagination and gave me a fullness of ideas,

thin and tawdry though they were, which led me to undertake un-
hesitatingly to scribble off with the greatest of ease a fat weekly
column in a local newspaper.

"Are you the author of that column in the News?" asked Sister
Rose, one of my teachers at Holy Family High.

"Oh, I guess so," I replied, squirming and uncomfortably anxious to move along, since I realized that while there was quantity
in the column there was little of quality that would draw a *placet*
from a teacher.

I decided to tell Mary Ellen about more careful periods, marked
by two activities which probably did me some good.

One was the period of the abstracts. The abstracts were a piece
of drudgery imposed in school, but which, secretly and without
confessing the terrible fact to a soul, I enjoyed immensely. We
were required to read such books as *Ivanhoe, Kenilworth, Oliver
Twist, David Copperfield* and prepare a plot summary and character analysis as we went along, with a selection of choice passages
and a recording of whatever reflections came into our youngish
heads.

As I say, I enjoyed this immensely. Without realizing it at the
time, the deep absorption in each volume led me to think less of
plots and more and more of the author's power of expression.
One of the books which caught me completely in its toils was
Lorna Doone and as I look back on it, it was the beauty of atmosphere that it created which meant the most to me. Thirty
years later, I find that the memory of Lorna or of John Ridd do
not mean much to me; rather it is the charm of the Doone country, which, through Blackmore's hypnotic use of words, drew me
so absorbingly and reflectingly into its recesses.

Then there was the poetry period. It began when one day I
discovered a huge volume in my lap, *Bartlett's Quotations.*
Whole poems had never caught me, but here now was an infinite
series of choice nuggets. I took a book of linen writing paper,
made a booklet of it with cardboard covers and a candy box cord,
and for quite some time took pleasure in discovering in Bartlett
single lines and couplets that I liked. I think the practice was

very helpful in giving me an appreciation of words, though I never became a poet. During my poetry year in English class, I took to the woods and sat by babbling brooks a number of times to turn out products for Sister Ricardia. I felt much more satisfaction, however, in reading poetry than writing it. Perhaps Mary Ellen will take up the Bartlett habit and get much farther with it.

At Maryknoll, the late Bishop James Anthony Walsh exercised great influence on all of us in the college English class. He was a sensitive man but an eminently practical one and his great theme was simplicity, frugality and selectivity in the use of words. Our assignment was usually the writing of a two hundred word descriptive item or editorial and under the impetus of his searching criticisms we found ourselves chiseling these pieces with all the devotion of a sculptor working his marble. Sometimes we kept for weeks on a single morsel, in the hope that at the end there would be the reward of seeing it accepted for a place in The *Field Afar*. It was Bishop Walsh's high standards that won his magazine so much esteem among many who were not particularly devoted to missions but greatly devoted to good writing.

Writing, however, is a hollow, puny activity without interior experiences to give it substance. I found that I had no particular gift for words, that I had no faculty for weaving gossamer webs of delicate beauty out of thin air. Unless something happened in my life my writing was finished.

But I was in a field in which things were almost bound to happen. Missionary circles carry on in terms of continents and lo! I suddenly found myself catapulted from the gentle, smiling hill country of the Hudson Valley to Rome, the heart of Christendom. The urge to write came back as throngs from every corner of the earth surged through the corridors of the Vatican Missionary Exposition of 1925. The result was a book published by Macmillan, *The Vatican Missionary Exposition, a Window on the World*.

At the close of the Holy Year, the authorities of the Sacred Congregation of the Propaganda in their hunt for workers for their research department hit upon me and for twelve months or so I partook of the concentrated essence of missionary data. I dealt in particular with statistics, a providential thing because it transferred me from the field of fanciful flights to the dry-as-bones realities of exact analysis. I came to know the name and location of practically every one of the five hundred and more mission territories throughout the earth and could give a passingly good description of the outstanding characteristics of each as known to the Holy See. At the end of the year my collection of figures was published by the Vatican Press as a routine volume in Latin, *Missiones Catholicae*. For the next ten years I had a part time assignment to help prepare Propaganda statistics for publication. Our most ambitious project appeared in 1935, under the Italian title, *Guida delle Missioni Cattoliche,* a volume of over a thousand pages.

In 1927 a novel project for Rome came into being, a missionary news service. Since I was conveniently at hand, I was given the task of organizing it. Advice came from many sources including American friends in the Associated Press, Mr. Thomas B. Morgan of the United Press, and counsellors in Rome, Paris, Munich, London, and the United States. Mr. Justin McGrath, Frank Hall's predecessor of the N.C.W.C. News Service in Washington, was particularly kind.

Fides Service—for this was the organization's name—soon had spread its tentacles over Asia, Africa, and the far corners of the earth. We received our material principally by mail, supplemented by a small wire service from the leading cities of Asia. While we never attained perfect coverage of the world field, we strove desperately to achieve this ideal and certainly received billowing rivers of data over which we had to labor tirelessly from eight each morning until sometimes late at night extracting pay dirt.

Writing at Fides Service became a matter of yardage. We were divided into five departments according to language, English, French, German, Italian, Spanish, and we were separately responsible to each country in the world where our particular language was current. Thus to the English language department fell the United States, English Canada, England, Ireland, Scotland, Australia, New Zealand, the Philippines, India, South Africa, and the British colonies. Much of the material was useful in all countries but every week there were stories which required treatment according to the special interests of one or other nation.

Under the pressure of meeting deadlines, fine writing was usually out of the question. I experienced constantly a sense of failure in this regard. There was the handicap of working in an atmosphere of foreign languages because very few missioners were English-speaking and it was a question of using French, Italian, Spanish, and German manuscripts, of talking most of the day in Italian or French and then sitting down to a typewriter to strike off copy in English.

But there was the thrill and inspiration of great happenings which constantly stirred us. At Fides Service we really lived; we felt the pulse of great events, both in Rome and throughout the outer world. The years with Fides Service were a very satisfying experience.

There were a number of journeys, some in Europe and some to other continents. I went with the Papal Mission to Ethiopia and in the 1930's I was sent by Fides Service on a voyage of about a year and a half across Asia from Palestine to Japan, then to the East Indies and finally across Central Africa from the East Coast to the West and thence back across the Sahara to North Africa and Rome. The expenses of this expedition were paid by a series of articles which I prepared as I journeyed for agencies in seven different countries.

Upon returning to Rome I was quite dismayed to realize how poorly these stories were written. It was only after returning to the United States that I was able to arrange for a few tranquil hours each week to cast my huge gatherings of material into a book. This became *Across a World*. Tom Kernan was the mentor of this work and under his disciplined guidance I was required to avoid the slovenliness of haste.

Since returning to America I was also required to prepare a biography of Maryknoll's bandit victim, Father Jerry Donovan.

This has appeared under the title *When the Sorghum was High*. In this case I chose Katherine Burton as mentor. I can speak from experience of the value of such a manuscript umpire, a warden to protect the writer from the pitfalls of subjectivism.

Writing, I can assure Mary Ellen and all other members of high school English classes, is for most mortals an arduous and disillusioning task. It means patient years spent seeking to draw from the treasuries of the literary great. Most of us, however hard we try, acquire lamentably little from the masters. It means, further, meeting up with rich and moving experiences of life, the great teacher. Even with more than an ordinary share of good fortune, we end by concluding that we have proven decidedly unprofitable servants.

EDITOR'S NOTE: Father Considine was born in New Bedford, Mass., in 1897, entered Maryknoll in 1915, and was ordained in 1923. He became Vicar General of Maryknoll in 1943. His books include *The Vatican Mission Exposition*, 1925, Macmillan; *When the Sorghum was High*, 1940, Longmans; *Across a World*, 1942, Longmans; *March into Tomorrow*, 1942, Field Afar Press.

MILDRED CRISS
(Mrs. G. L. Catlin)

BOOKS! With all the books in my background I certainly should write far better ones than I do. My mother wrote books, her mother wrote books, and when my father, Thomas Ball Criss married my mother, Helen Huntington Gates, who is a niece of Collis P. Huntington, my father did a great deal toward cataloging Mr. Huntington's famous New York library. My father's own library contained many treasures, such as the first volumes to be printed on the Caxton, Planti, Aldine and Elzivir presses, and a first edition of Samuel Johnson's *Dictionary*. My father's library in Orange, New Jersey, where I was born on October 6, 1890, was the only school room that I knew until after I was sixteen. Before I could read, I was allowed to dust the precious volumes and I learned my A B C's from Ainsworth's *Tower of London*, another first edition, illustrated by George Cruishank. My father also bound books, and in his third floor bindery of our home in Orange, my special privilege was to attend to the glue pot—an evil smelling, large iron pot in which special glue was boiled for very special purposes.

My education, in the strict sense of the word, began when I entered Hollins College, Virginia, a most memorable day for me *and* for the faculty. They did not know what to do with me. I was prepared for Sophomore classes in English, but alas, I was decidedly shaky in the multiplication table—and still am. Mr. Criss had his own convictions about education. He believed in teaching a child in a way that would stimulate a desire to learn and keep on learning, and he felt that forcing distasteful subjects on a pupil might crush a perfectly natural eagerness to understand more and more of what life was all about. I have only one objection to my father's theory and that is, I am woefully lacking in many things which the average child learns in the sixth and seventh grades, and I have to waste a good deal of time digging into a dictionary, an encyclopedia and an atlas.

There was much about Hollins to like, but the place troubled me. At the time I did not know why. I know now that I did not know how to study under pressure, and I am sure that I was not in the least inspired by the religious atmosphere which was anything but Catholic. Brought up as an Episcopalian—rather casually I fear, but with a sense that God was Love—I resented the idea that to please God, one had to be just a bit gloomy. Perhaps, my impressions were entirely wrong. Maybe I did not know how to adjust myself to much that was strange to me. However, thanks to a poem or two and the tireless interest of a Professor Cummings, I took the prize in literature, which pleased and fattened my inordinate ego.

Instead of returning to Hollins after my first year there, I went to *finish* my education at Mlle. La Salle's Pension in Geneva, Switzerland, where I learned to speak French and to love the French people.

In 1911 I married Benjamin Floyn McGuckin, whose father was Professor of History and Mathematics at the City College of New York. More books! Professor McGuckin was one of the most delightful, gentle and cultured of men. I learned a great deal from him and we were always the dearest of friends. He had been born and bred in an atmosphere of agnosticism and his family had lived in no other, but Professor McGuckin died in the arms of our dear old Irish laundress, a devout Catholic, and his last words were, "Dear God."

Aside from slender volumes of poetry—one published by Mr. George Haven Putnam as a gracious way in which to show his gratitude to me for having rescued him from a mountainous surf on Long Island—my first books to be published were the result of spending many summers abroad with my son, William Criss McGuckin. His happy discovery that foreign children were not *foreign* at all, and the good that came from the relationship between them, made me eager to write books about *foreign* children for American boys and girls. *Betty Lee in Paris, Malou, Martine and Michel, The Red Caravan* and *Madeleine's Court* represent those early endeavors. As my son grew up, my books grew up too. The older ones are, *Mary Stuart* (Young Queen of Scots), *Isabella* (Young Queen of Spain), *Pocahontas* (Young American Princess). And now that I am a grandmother I seem to be writing an even older book, which includes the entire life of the Dom Pedro II of Brazil.

The first World War! As a result of its horrors, I began to take a very real interest in religion and took it upon myself to teach the Bible. Curiously enough little girls, big girls, poor girls, rich girls, hardworking women and society women came to my classes. In the dark a good deal about what I was teaching, I taught and taught. One evening, after my pupils had gone, when there had been questions which I had not been able to answer, I cried. In came the dear old ignorant, but all-knowing, Irish laundress, who put her arms about me and said, "Don't you be feeling bad. Faith'en just go to Father Casey and he'll be after tellin' you what to teach, and it'll be Truth." It was and I knew it.

It was about this time that I had the good fortune to meet Abbé Ernest Dimnet and Doctor Selden Delaney, Rector of St. Mary's Anglican Church in New York. Abbé Dimnet taught me how to study, what to study, Doctor Delany and I thrashed out the Anglicans' claim about Apostolic Succession and we dispensed with it. I joined the Catholic Church in the Christmas season of 1928 and Doctor Delany soon became a priest.

On July 17, 1929, my marriage was annulled on the grounds of Disparity of Worship, in the Diocese of Brooklyn, New York. My son became a Catholic during his Freshman year at Harvard. In 1934 I married George L. Catlin whose eleven-year-old daughter Carmelita had lost her Spanish mother, a Catholic and a great pianist.

And it must be said that in the work which I am doing at present, I am in need of the friendly guidance of my publishers, Messrs. Dodd, Mead and Company, especially that which Miss Dorothy Bryan offers. I count a great deal on the encouragement given to me by my son. He enlisted in the Army as a Private shortly after Pearl Harbor and is now a Lieutenant in the Mountain Infantry. I also depend on the kindly and extremely intelligent interest of my step-daughter Carmelita, who is hard at work in the services of transcontinental air line, and on the co-operation of my husband, now a Reserve Officer in the Navy, who tirelessly corrects idiotic mistakes in my manuscripts.

EDITOR'S NOTE: Miss Criss's books include *Isabella, Young Queen of Spain,* 1941, Dodd; *Pocahontas, Young American Princess,* 1943, Dodd, and *Mary Stuart, Young Queen of Scots,* reprinted, 1944, Dodd; *Dom Pedro of Brazil,* 1945, id.

EDWARD J. DOHERTY

AS I MAY HAVE HINTED in *Gall and Honey*, I don't mind writing about myself; though, if given my choice, I'd rather write about something more interesting. However, I can deal with the subject more sympathetically than any other biographer possibly could, or would. And that's something.

Gall and Honey was written after my wife, Mildred, was killed in Beverly Hills, California. It ran serially in *Liberty* magazine under the title, "Newspaperman." It was butchered, of course. I wrote about 80,000 words. The magazine printed 30,000.

I didn't mind the butchery. I've been a newspaperman most of my life, and copy-readers have slaughtered my stuff day after day for many years. I get even with them only by refusing to read anything of mine after it gets into print. So, of course, I don't mind, and—my stuff never bores me.

I was abroad when the story was published. *Liberty* had sent me flying the Atlantic to write stories of the German bombs falling on London. I had a great time in London, but no bombs fell.

I went all over England, but couldn't find anything exciting. I flew to France, but found no fight there. Bottles, yes; but no battles.

It was the period of the "sit-down war," the "bore war," the "phony war." Eventually my editor, Fulton Oursler, got the idea there was going to be no action at all, so he called me home. I cabled him that I was en route to New York, but I took a round-about course, by way of Amsterdam, Copenhagen, Stockholm, and Helsinki.

The Finns were having a real war with Russia, and I got a good look at it. Before I left Finland I had visited the western front, and spent several hours within half a mile of the Russian line.

I didn't want to return to New York. I was having the most exciting time of my more mature years, being bombed, machine-gunned, half-frozen, and constantly endangered by Finnish chauffeurs who insisted on traveling at one hundred kilometres an hour over the icy roads, constantly skidding and unskidding.

I refused to answer cables from the front office which asked "Why don't you come home?" or to heed those reading, in effect, "Come home or else!" But my visa permitted me just so long a visit; and when it terminated I was forced to leave.

It was with very bad grace that I returned to New York. The boss should have fired me for disobedience, or acting without orders, or something. But he didn't. He kept me on the magazine staff, and gave me assignments close to home, where he could watch me.

When the Germans started through Belgium and France and Norway and Denmark, I expected to be sent back to Europe. But, to my chagrin, I was merely sent to Harlem to get material for an article that was to be called "The Wickedest City in the World."

Me in Harlem! The great Eddie Doherty who should have been riding in the nose of bombers, or standing on the bridge with an admiral, or travelling with armies plunging into battle, was assigned the prosaic and distasteful job of writing about vice and crime in the streets and night clubs of New York's Negro

section. The man who should have been thrilling all America
with his accounts of heroic effort, epic suffering, and triumphs
hammered out of overwhelming defeats, was spending his days
and nights gathering trivial facts from cops, gin-mill managers,
street-walkers, and paid tipsters. Me, I! How had the mighty
fallen!

The Lord God Almighty was shaping my destiny; but I was too
blind and too picayune to realize it.

In Harlem, quite by accident, I met a Russian woman.

I had met lots of Russians in Finland. They lay in burned
tanks alongside the roads. They lay buried in the snow. They
filled the woods. Russian soldiers frozen months before.

But this Russian woman had nothing frozen about her. She
burned with the love of God. So great was the flame of that love
that it warmed and quickened all who came close to her.

This was the Baroness Catherine de Hueck, founder of Friendship House, a social settlement in 135th street, between Fifth and
Lenox avenues—a social settlement different than any I had ever
stumbled upon in all my hoodlum years.

Friendship House worked for and with the Negroes. It dispensed charity of all kinds, without asking questions, without
hesitation. It fought for interracial justice. It fostered study
clubs, credit unions, co-operative associations, and other advanced
ideas of self-help for the Negro poor. And it disseminated Catholicity in a thousand ways.

I became enamored with the place, with the young people who
worked under the direction of the Baroness, and with their mode
of life. And, eventually, of course, I fell in love with the foundress.

These young men and women were college graduates, mostly,
with the right to put letters after their names, if they wished.
They had left good jobs to enter Friendship House. They received no salaries. They were given second-hand clothes to wear.
They ate at a common table, and there were times when there
was nothing but stale bread and warmed-over tea on that table.
Yet they were the happiest group in New York. They loved

"holy poverty"—I had never heard that phrase used until I visited Friendship House—and they loved to talk about God.

Imagine that! A little band of saints in "the wickedest city in the world!"

I went to school to the Baroness and to her "children;" and for the first time in fifty years began to get some little insight into the warmth, the beauty, the majesty, the color, the infinite glory of the Catholic Church.

One day I brought to the Baroness the manuscript of "Newspaperman," which I had retitled "Gall and Honey."

"You used to be a literary agent," I said, "maybe you can sell this. No other agent has been able to do so. It has come back from every publisher. Maybe it's too 'Catholic' for them. You probably know a Catholic publisher or two."

"I'll read it," she answered. "If I like it, I'll sell it."

For the first time I felt a little queasy about the book. Millions of people had already read it in *Liberty,* and I hadn't minded that at all, though I had, in effect, made a general confession to those millions. But making the same confession to this particular woman—that was different. Reading the manuscript might alter her good opinion of me. And it was important to me—why, I couldn't have told anybody at the time—that she didn't think I was too big a heel.

She read the book, and the only reaction it seemed to have had on her was to make her curious about me. Which was wonderful. It gave me the opportunity to take her here and there, of an evening, and to talk to her for hours at a time in some quiet café or some out-of-the-way restaurant where the music played softly and the lights were not too bright.

There was no doubt about it. "Gall and Honey" drew us closer and closer together. Friends of mine began to make remarks. "I always knew you had the gall of a burglar, and I see you've got a new honey." Wise-cracks like that.

The new honey was sweet, after the bitter gall I had swallowed in the death of Mildred. But it would have been just as sweet, had I never tasted gall. And I was determined to keep that honey close to me all the rest of my life.

But Honey said "No."

She had two Friendship Houses now. The second one had opened in Chicago with Anne Harrigan and Ellen Tarry in charge. There were two dozen or more staff workers. It would be impossible, the Baroness said, to marry anybody. She must remain in the work of the lay apostolate.

Priests close to the work of Friendship House, and at least one bishop who knew the scope of its activities, had told her she could not marry. So she wasn't going to marry me. Uh-uh. Never.

It was like one of those love stories you read about. "I love you, I love you, I love you; but I can never marry you—never, never, never! There is a barrier between us that cannot be removed until I die."

A man can try to be light and funny, writing about it years afterwards. But at the time there was nothing to laugh about. The barrier was there, and there was no climbing it, no flanking it. It seemed to be the will of God that two people, though they were very much in love with each other, should go their separate ways and never see each other again—all for the greater honor and glory of God in the extending of His kingdom.

So we stayed away from each other for long intervals. And it was during these intervals that I began to write *Splendor of Sorrow.*

Ever since I was a child, and much concerned with the seven sorrows of Our Lady, I had wanted to write a book about her. The idea had died, apparently. But, through Friendship House, it had been resurrected. The Baroness and those crazy kids who couldn't talk about anything except God, brought the idea back to life and nourished it into an obsession.

I started to work on the first sorrow, and learned to my consternation, that I didn't know enough of my religion to write the book. I began asking questions. But I couldn't always get answers. I went to priests and nuns and bishops, but still the right answers would not come. I didn't realize I was asking questions that only theologians could answer—that is, theologians who had given their whole lives to the study.

Well, you know how newspapermen operate. When they want

to write a story with a banking angle they call up a banker, ask a lot of questions, and produce a story that is authentic. When they want to write of an operation, they question a surgeon as to his technique.

So, being compelled to write this book of Our Lady's sorrows, and being unable to get adequate information from authorities on this earth, I decided to call on the saints in heaven.

Lying in bed at night, half-asleep and half-awake, I would talk to the saints, ask them innumerable questions—and receive innumerable answers.

This was an extremely pleasant pastime, for I not only enjoyed the company of these celestial friends, but also, for the time being, I was not feeling sorry for myself and the woman I loved. It was pleasant, even though I came out of these interviews wide awake to grab a pencil and a pad of paper and to write, sitting up in bed and getting iced all over, for an hour or two or three, the things I was given to write.

I didn't see the saints. I had no visions of any kind. Nor did I hear voices. The answers came to me as silently as I issued the questions. The thing that amazed me was that the answers were so clear, so simple, so positive. Still, I thought, I don't know that these answers are right. Maybe I'm making them up myself. Any real Catholic who reads this stuff will tell me I'm ninety-nine percent wrong and one percent crazy.

But, one night, I was asking St. Joseph about the boy Jesus. He was lost, and St. Joseph and Mary were looking for Him, and could not find Him. I wanted to know what color His eyes were. St. Joseph said: "Why I don't know; I never noticed." That astonished me. No man had ever been so close to Jesus in His lifetime. He must have looked into those eyes thousands of times. I asked the question again, and St. Joseph answered: "What's the color of God's glory. That's the color of His eyes."

St. Joseph saw in his Foster Son, only the glory of God! That answer convinced me I really had interviewed the saints. And so I finished the book.

I was living in California when I wrote the last chapter. I was also writing the story of the Sullivans, for the movies. I had been away from the Baroness for many, many weeks. And I decided that enough was enough. I flew to New York and made this proposition:

"The time has come when you can leave the local Friendship Houses to the direction of others. You have Nancy Grenell in New York and Anne Harrigan in Chicago. Let's go to see our friend Bishop Sheil in Chicago. If he says we can't marry, then it's goodbye for the rest of our lives. It's all or nothing. If he changes his mind and allows us to marry—then we'll be married as soon as we can. What do you say?"

"The voice of the bishop," she answered, "is the voice of God, to me!"

It was a bit terrifying, waiting on the veranda of the Bishop's residence, to hear the verdict. A judgment pronounced by the voice of God! I wondered, how the soul feels—awaiting the blessing or the curse of Almighty God. And I wondered why my hands were sweating so.

"A long time ago," the Bishop said, after a long pause, glancing from me to the Baroness, "I made you promise me, Catherine, that you wouldn't marry."

It didn't sound very promising.

"Yes, your excellency, I promised."

The bishop nodded his benign head, and then he smiled.

"At that time your marriage would have wrecked Friendship House. But now—things have changed. Friendship House has grown up. It can stand on its own feet, both in New York and Chicago. It still needs your general supervision. But there is no longer any reason why you shouldn't marry."

So we were married and lived happily ever after.

And Friendship House and its crazy kids acquired a step-father who was very, very fond of them.

EDITOR'S NOTE: Mr. Doherty is on the editorial staff of the *Chicago Sun* and the *Friendship House News* as well as contributor to *The Torch, The Sign, Extension,* and other Catholic magazines. His books include his autobiography (which ends where his chapter in *The Book of Catholic Authors* begins), *Gall and Honey,* 1941, Sheed; *Splendor of Sorrow,* 1943, Sheed, and a life of Blessed Martin de Porres, O.P., 1945, Sheed.

REVEREND ALBERT H.
DOLAN, O.CARM.

I WAS BORN IN WISCONSIN, not in but near Oshkosh. At nine, I was moved from Fond du Lac, Wisconsin, to Syracuse, New York, and after grammar and high school days there, I attended Niagara University (and cherish happy memories of N. U. in general and of the R.E.V.R. in particular). I had my philosophy in Rome at the North American College (and could never adequately express how much I owe to my teachers, associates and associations there). I entered the Carmelite Order in 1918 and have been teaching, preaching, learning and writing ever since.

Even before ordination I owed much to the intercession of St. Thérèse. Consequently I undertook to propagate devotion to her in America first through the spoken and later through the written word. Thus there was developed an audience of Little Flower devotees to whose spiritual needs I undertook to minister in later years in such non-Theresian books as *A Modern Messenger of Purity, Enjoy the Mass, Happiness in Marriage* and the *Summa* pamphlets.

If my books and pamphlets have any merit, it is the simplicity of their style. I strive to speak and write so that no word will be over the head of the average Catholic, and the average Catholic, as statistics prove, has the vocabulary of a third year high school student. (Cf. O'Brien Atkinson's *How to Make Us Want Your Sermon.*)

For instance, I would not use in a book or sermon, the comparatively simple word "fidelity" but use instead "faithfulness" lest some one miss my meaning. Thus constantly to strive for simplicity involves labor and, from that standpoint, I find writing distasteful. But when the labor is over, I rejoice, as all writers do, at the fruit of the labor.

Being a Carmelite, I never preach nor write without a reference to Our Lady, and my greatest ambition is to complete a life of the Blessed Virgin which can be sold for ten cents and thus be assured of a wider reading public than a more pretentious and expensive work. That life, so urgently needed by thousands of Catholics who will not read a book about Our Lady, has been rewritten five times in the last ten years but I am not ready yet to release the manuscript for publication.

The writing of which I am proudest are my letters to my mother which she preserved and which I found after her death; letters from Niagara, Rome, and from the earlier scenes of my priestly labors in Chicago. With nothing else have I ever felt satisfied, although if asked which of my books I consider best, I would reply *Roses Fall Where Rivers Meet,* and, in second place, *St. Therese Returns.* Of any reader of this sketch I ask a prayer that my pamphlet on Our Lady may see the light and be not too unworthy of her.

EDITOR'S NOTE: Father Dolan's works, all issued by the Carmelite Press, include his *Collected Little Flower Works* (including eight books previously published separately), 1929; *Roses Fall Where Rivers Meet,* 1937; *St. Therese Returns,* 1933; and *Happiness in Marriage,* 1940.

REVEREND HILARION
DUERK, O.F.M.

I WAS BORN IN ST. LOUIS, Mo., Oct. 28, 1883, and am quite proud to be one of twelve children, the last. My immediate ancestors from both my father's and mother's side were thoroughly Catholic. Permit me to here recount the following:—When my mother was but a small child in Switzerland, she one day accidently poked a pointed knife into her left eye. The family doctor declared the eye hopelessly lost, but my mother's father refused to give up hope. He made a vow to the Mother of God and immediately undertook a pilgrimage to a not-too-distant shrine called, "the Holy Well" (of the Virgin Mary). At the place of pilgrimage, after fervent prayer, when the bandages were removed from my mother's eye, it was found that the wound had healed. Careful medical examination showed that she saw as perfectly with that eye as with the other. A blemish or scar remained in the eyeball, yet the eyesight was very good throughout her long life; even in her old age she never wore glasses.

In Switzerland, my mother's father was school teacher and

parish organist in the village of Blaua, Canton Bern. Anti-religious movements that had been smouldering for a long time gained strength. Laws had been made forbidding teaching of religion in the classroom. Grandfather, at that time in the full vigor of manhood, continued teaching religion to his pupils. He was reported, apprehended, brought before a judge, and released with the warning that if he ever attempted religious teaching again he would be doubly punished. After a short time, however, he did not hesitate to resume religious instructions. He was reported and apprehended a second time. The judge banished him, giving him sixty days to leave the country. Although I was a rather wild and carefree boy, these events, treasured as a sacred and most precious heirloom in my family, made a salutary and lasting impression upon my mind.

However, the wonderful religious example and teaching of my poor, but excellent parents, and the ardent zeal of Rev. Francis Albers, O.F.M., my parish priest, did more, a great deal more, to influence my whole life and my published writings which are a part of me. In spite of my boyish conduct, or perhaps on that account, all Fathers and Brothers of the Franciscan Monastery at St. Louis treated me very kindly; nevertheless, I often received a well deserved scolding. I served Holy Mass every day, sometimes in vacation as many as five or six Masses a day, and was delighted to be permitted to do so. At that time I decided, God willing, to some day myself be a Franciscan priest. Almost from the very start of my studies for the holy priesthood, I learned to carefully read the best books of English literature, copying gripping passages, pointed expressions, beautiful descriptions, and painstakingly trying to reproduce similar "scripta" in my various compositions for the classroom. It was thus that my interest in writing took its beginning. Rev. Maurice Brink, O.F.M., was my excellent, sympathetic teacher in English.

June 24, 1910, to my great joy I was ordained a priest. Cleveland, Ohio, from 1914 to 1920, proved to be my first place of literary activity in connection with the press. Two small but vigorous Cleveland fraternities of the Franciscan Third Order (about 300 members) were entrusted to me. They wanted "Franciscan literature" to help satisfy their thirst for things Franciscan. Alas, in those days handy Third Order Literature was scarce. In desperation, I decided to myself write the kind of literature I needed. Cautious friends told me: "Unless you have an honest and live publisher, writing for the press is an expensive and precarious affair. Many an enthusiast could not sell his writings and was left behind with an empty purse. In some cases the financial loss was great." I highly appreciated this advice and grew determined to be cool and careful. During the day, hospital and parochial duties, prayers in choir and other monastic exercises kept me busy. Evening hours and nights were used for my literary activities. Knowing that publishers are not interested in low priced literature that by its very nature has a limited sale, I went directly to a printer, agreed on the printing, binding and delivery cost, and then furnished my manuscripts. However, for Chalippe's *Life of St. Francis*, 1917, I procured a regular publisher. A little over five thousand copies of this book were sold the very first year and to this day sales continue to be excellent. My tertiary fraternities paid for the publication of a monthly bulletin that was eagerly read, and for six "de luxe" pamphlets having from twenty to forty pages. Each of these pamphlets, if I recall correctly, had a limited edition of 2000 copies; that is all we could use. We sold every one of them, lost no money and made no money. Did they do any good? They did. In those years I received at Cleveland 2765 persons into the Third Order, mostly daily communicants. The great majority of these new members developed into excellent tertiaries. Many of them were young persons. I ascribe some of this success to my publications.

In 1920 I was transferred to Chicago, there to line up the First National Third Order Convention for October, 1921, and to write the official report of the convention. Well, I fulfilled both consignments, generally meeting with spirited co-operation. Printing and binding of the First National Third Order Convention Report, 1922, 1500 copies, cost exactly $3,500. Getting out this report was almost incredible labor, but I like to think that if there

is anything I have ever written that benefited others it is that
report. Nor was there any financial loss. Thanks to co-operation
of Third Order members throughout the country, after all convention expenses were paid, including the report, we had still
$2,109.63 on hand.

In subsequent years I wrote a number of short articles for
various Catholic magazines and papers, including a two years
series of Monthly Patrons for Franciscan Tertiaries published
under the pen name Albert Blair in the *Franciscan Herald,* 1934
and 1935; likewise, a series of sermons on St. Anthony and St.
Elizabeth, 1931, printed in the *Third Order Forum,* a periodical,
established in 1921 by the First National Third Order Convention, ably edited ever since by Rev. James Meyer, O.F.M.

In 1934 I was sent to Memphis, Tenn. Among other important
duties, teaching nurses psychology and ethics was assigned to me.
Psychology was always one of my favorite branches of study. We
sorely needed a textbook that is short, clear, to the point, and yet
rather complete. In 1935 I published my psychology for nurses,
and, upon request, the following year I got out a similar psychology for other students. Both books met with a very kind reception and are still selling well. My most recent publications are
a parish history (1940), and a series of twenty-four historical
papers (1941) published serially, with the proper ecclesiastical
permission, in various newspapers of southern Minnesota.

Enough about these things. Now a few words to aspirant
writers. Do we need Catholic writers and authors? Yes, indeed.
Would that we had thousands of them in every branch of literature, history, science, art, and fiction. Publishers are anxious to
receive manuscripts; they are begging for them. Yet, not every
manuscript is accepted. When you write for the press, select
excellent matter that is apt to have a somewhat general appeal.
Master your subject. Write carefully and well. Do your very
best. Remember that writing in a sense is a trade. Learn the
trade well and try to make your book better than others of a similar nature already published. Then you will have no trouble in
finding a publisher. You may even succeed in writing lines that

will live on long after you are dead and that will continue to bring wholesome recreation or gratifying information, salutary thoughts, noble aspirations, to many poor human beings hungering for the better things of life.

EDITOR'S NOTE: Father Duerk's works include *Catechism of Psychology for Nurses*, 1935, Kenedy; *Psychology in Questions and Answers*, 1936, Kenedy; and pamphlets mostly on various canonized members of the Third Order of St. Francis.

REVEREND T. GAVAN DUFFY

(1888–1942)

By Paula Kurth

"HE WAS A GREAT MAN . . ." The words leap spontaneously to the lips when we speak of Father Gavan Duffy, author, educator, and missioner, who died in India in 1942. And the words are no platitude, but his true epitaph.

Born in 1888, in the south of France, Thomas Gavan Duffy was the son of Sir Charles Gavan Duffy, one of the brilliant patriot leaders of the Young Ireland Movement who was associated with Davis, Mitchel, Mangan and the mother of Oscar Wilde (Speranza of *The Nation*) and who later served as Prime Minister for Australia. The boy inherited his father's brilliance and originality, what might perhaps be called his genius. He early began his cosmopolitan existence, being educated at Stony-hurst, Thurles and in Paris. At eighteen he joined the Paris Foreign Mission Society, nursery of so many glorious martyrs, and was ordained in 1911. He went at once to India, and the little town of Tindivanam—"Tindy" he affectionately called it—in

South Arcot, not far from Madras and the equator, became his headquarters.

It was at Tindivanam that Father Gavan Duffy established his famous Training school for Catechists—five hundred in number —which Monsignor John J. Hunt of Detroit called "the ecclesiastical West Point of India." In fact when people thought of Father Duffy they automatically thought of catechists too; and that is exactly what he wanted. "More and better catechists" was his watchword for over a quarter of a century, and it was the idea in forming the delightful periodical *Hope* which he wrote at unpredictable intervals, when maybe he could snatch a few midnight hours from his busy round, and sent back to his helpers on the home front. In doggerel, in fine verse, in amusing anecdote, in characteristically clipped, lucid prose—it was all the same to him provided he got his idea over—, he sang the song of the catechist.

Father Gavan Duffy looked upon the catechist, the native lay missioner, as an invaluable means of multiplying the priest who, with all the zealous good will in the world, is not ubiquitous. The catechist, usually complete with wife and family, settles in some remote small village, melts into its background, and proceeds to Christianize it from the inside. As Father Gavan Duffy said, "The preaching of the priest is from the outside, and also it is too fleeting in character to produce the full result. But the catechist lives the life of the village, exemplifies Christian family life, chats with the people at their work and during their leisure hours, patiently teaches the children, gives neighborly help in time of trouble, and in every way makes Christianity the property of the people. . . . Without catechists a priest is a knight errant; with catechists he is an organized and far-reaching force." The "Catechist Idea" has the endorsement of bishops throughout the missionary world.

Catechists, however, are worse than useless unless they are well trained—ergo, the Training School at Tindivanam where students were taken as young lads and shepherded through a preparatory course carefully planned by Father Gavan Duffy. Pedagogical methods were stressed of course—the interested person may refer to *The Sower Went Out* for details as to their uniqueness and efficiency—but even more stressed was character formation. Father Duffy had faith in the potential goodness of "that sunbeam of mankind," the human boy, and spared no effort to make it a permanent actuality for the citizens of his Boystown. St. Tarcisius was a special favorite and in his poem honoring this young martyr of the Blessed Sacrament, he says, "Any real boy, if chance allowed, would be so slain." He early recognized the advantages of Boy Scouting as a factor in character training, and, choosing what was best and most suitable from the movement, he supplemented it by a high spirituality. The result was his Knights of the Blessed Sacrament at which we heirs of Catholic tradition can look with wondering admiration. He personally oversaw the details of the organization, made it a point to be present at the campfires, and even wrote a series of Scout Songs for use at them. The songs are mostly set to well-known airs, though a few were his own composition, and the Hindu moon must have had reason for astonishment as the troop of dark-skinned Tamilian youths enthusiastically struck up new versions of "Au Clair de la Lune," "The Stein Song," "Parigi o cara," or Gilbert and Sullivan favorites like "Tit Willow." Father Duffy found Gilbertian humor particularly congenial: he must have needed a good supply of it in that land where, as he hints in a characteristic essay on Chesterton, "Everything is either at sixes or at sevens." He believed in allowing idleness no quarter and interesting activities were ingeniously planned for recreation times. On his last begging trip to the United States he was jubilant over the purchase of a Charlie McCarthy dummy which he knew would thrill his boys, and a book on ventriloquism also went back to India with him, together with a box of dime-store treasures such as Tindy had never known.

Teacher extraordinary that he was, and driven by that thirst for souls which is the underlying theme of the most beautiful poems in his books *Wayfarer for Christ,* Father Gavan Duffy left nothing undone which he thought would help spread knowledge of the Kingdom. How literally he took the command to go and teach is seen in his "Mission Message in the Sunday Gospels"— incorporated in his volume *The Seven Last Words*—where God is found to say: "You have your orders 'Going, teach all nations.' I cannot make it any clearer; all right then, sonny, you just go." He served for years as Diocesan Inspector of Schools; and his great educational labor, the set of Catechism Folders, is "A complete course in religion, based on the unity of the Gospels, dogmas, and sacraments, and providing for the greatest freedom and originality in the teacher" for which, as Bishop Cushing points out, "he quarried the stones from within himself." If such quarrying is the hardest kind of work even in favorable circumstance, what must it be in 110° of humid heat.

No mere missionologist was Father Gavan Duffy but a dyed-in-the-wool practical man. On his four begging trips to America he contrived to visit other mission lands en route, and to study the methods used in them. So he passed through Annam, where Theophane Venard won his crown; through Korea where Just de Bretanieres suffered, and through China and Japan. And he made a pioneering trip in a motor truck four thousand miles across the heart of Africa although he had been told such a trip was absolutely impossible. His fascinating experiences can be found in *Let's Go,* illustrated by himself.

It is just because Father Duffy knew his missions so thoroughly that he could speak with authority on matters of mission importance. And that too, is why his books (there are sixteen of them in the *New Hope* Series) are, as one reviewer put it, "A whole library of mission lore." This Series covers many angles of mission work and should be represented in every Catholic library. Father James J. Daly said of them, "They contain the varied experience of an unusually talented man during twenty-five years of intensely hard work among the natives of Southern India. They sparkle with wit, wise reflection, interesting information and keen intelligence in touch with the world of books and men and expressing itself with a fine literary taste." Particularly to be recommended are *Fantastic Uncle, The Blind Spot,*

The Voyager and *The Sower Went Out,* which purport to be letters to a seminarian nephew from a veteran missioner relaying "the smell of powder from the front." Certainly they achieve their aim of reproducing the mission atmosphere—the spiritual oppression of surrounding paganism, the loneliness, the endless round, the dirt, the heat, the sustained self-sacrifice in small things that add up to heroism. Yet through them all runs an undercurrent of humor that reaches its glorious heroic peak in *The Voyager,* as poor Father Joly bumps along the dusty road on the pillion of his missioner friend's motorcycle.

Catechists have to be maintained at their stations as well as trained, and their humble salaries of five dollars a month have to be found regularly. Moreover the money "is not easy in the uptake" as Father Duffy soon discovered, and after 1929 it became almost napoo. His own private fortune had early gone into mission work. He could not afford to overlook any way of rousing interest among the home folk, so he turned movie producer. Most men would have been appalled by the stupendous job of producing a movie in the backwoods of India. But not for nothing had Father Duffy that red hair. A script was written in short order, a camera and photographer hired, an elephant borrowed, a cast assembled which proved quite as temperamental as some of our own stars, and the film miraculously kept from melting in the heat. The result was *The Catechist of Kilarni* (yes, the actual name of an Indian town—not made up) which subsequently brought American audiences face to face with the missioner's problems.

Father Gavan Duffy was not a good beggar; it would be hard to discover a man less fitted to the role. But it all came in the day's work. Nothing, however, would convert him to the snake stories school—he found it hard to believe that Catholics should need any other reason for helping the missions than a genuine desire to spread God's Kingdom. "We have the finest cause there is," he wrote. "It goes straight to the roots of faith. And it does not need to be bolstered up with fairy tales." Witness his Father Gus Butterworthy on a begging tour lugging those heavy bags of mission literature and lantern slides up steep steps while the sweat poured from his brow, trudging the winter streets sniffling with cold, being handed a cigar—and nothing more—by an old school-mate turned millionaire, sitting in clerical parlors during hungry noons while the pleasant odors of lunch in progress floated under the door—and all the time the home folks wondered that he could be spared so long from his work in India, while the people in India envied him his long delightful holiday.

Father Gavan Duffy's was not a character readily understood. Association with him for several months while he was arranging for the publication of his books gave me ample opportunity of observing him at close range. His love of truth was almost a passion; and, concentrated in purpose and absolutely sincere, he found it hard to be patient with petty subterfuges which his keen light blue eyes penetrated quickly. Mission life, he held, did not leave room for the pursuit of the amenities. Yet he was the sort of man who could have reveled in amenities. You would think, for instance what fun he would be on a house party. A certain Gaelic sense of fighting a losing cause was canceled out in him by the supernatural virtue of hope—or Hope rather; he spelled it with a capital.

Father Gavan Duffy was a prodigious worker. He knew how to manage time and get the most out of every minute. And he was order personified; his files were methodical, correct, and up-to-date, his handwriting was small, artistic, and neat, and the very pencil on his writing table was always sharpened and laid in readiness. "Tables" would have been the more correct word in that last sentence for his favorite idiosyncracy towards time saving was to have several tables on which to work, one for each particular job in hand with all the data and papers connected with that job together on it, ready for attention. He had unusual mental grasp of complicated situations, a foresight that often enabled him to forestall difficulties, and, perhaps most important, all the sticking power in the world. Big as was the task of managing the Training School, to say nothing of his educational and literary work and vast correspondence, not long before his death he was also acting as parish priest for two extensive areas. This huge stint is the more extraordinary when it is recalled that he had not had robust health for many years.

But no long last illness was to be his. Always expeditious, like some saint we read of, Father Gavan Duffy did quickly what had to be done. He was ill only twenty-four hours. We are fortunate in having a detailed account of exactly what happened. It was written by Father Michael Curtin, his great friend and loyal co-worker; and because his death was not without heroism, and because it was so of a piece with his life, we cannot do better than quote briefly from that account:

"Tom died of tetanus," writes Father Curtin, "physically not at all a pleasant death. He had the first touch of it Sunday morning (last September seventh) on rising. Previous evening nothing, only plenty of good humor. . . . By noon undisguisable pain had set in. . . . From then on and through Sunday night he did suffer considerably but cheerfully. . . . We did not want him to speak much but he did speak quite a little. He had the boys brought into the room in groups and spoke to them. His real desire in this connection was that the boys should see the Father Gavan Duffy, they so reverenced, in his last wrestlings with death, that they should realize what a humble weak thing the poor body is at its last end. He was the educator to the last and . . . appeared never so much his authentic self as 'at the breaking' of his body." Anti-tetanus injections had been given and the Archbishop made arrangements for him to be taken in an ambulance to the hospital in Pondicherry, and this was done early the next morning. At first the doctors were not unhopeful but, to go on with Father Curtin's account, "Our grand big-souled Tom died at twelve forty-five Monday, the Feast of Our Lady's Nativity." The date particularly touched Father Curtin who continues: "Our Blessed Mother Tom loved with a special love. With a boldness of Faith, I will say. Somebody wanted to give Her on Her birthday one of the fixed stars, one of the unblinking stars seen far below on this earth of ours." Very solemn and very beautiful were the words Father Gavan Duffy spoke to his friend their last evening together. Father Curtin tells of the charm they threw "over Tom's cruel death, a charm that got me and would certainly get each and everyone of you. It was on Sunday evening about five o'clock he made his general confession to me. He preluded it with a five or seven minutes' conversation. My bad memory will set it down as well as I can. He said, 'Michael, it is all but a certainty that I am going to die. I would like to make a simple act of Faith. I believe in the Catholic Church and her Divine Sacramental System. I love Christ and now offer my life utterly to Him. I know with a glance of His eye He can rub the slate clean. I call at this moment on my Mother Mary and I appeal to my Patron, St. Thomas. One thing I am very glad of here and now. I loved truth. And I think I have been loyal to it all my life. This can even now make me tremble with joy. As to death I am not merely resigned to it, I definitely prefer it to life. Yet let things be as God wills. I think I have done the work God meant to be done by both my hands.' "

Father Gavan Duffy is buried at Tindivanam in the school garden. As a rule Indian boys are not demonstrative: their hard lot in the native villages too often deadens their finer feelings and gives them that impassive attitude towards loss and calamity which is almost a national characteristic. But Father Curtin tells of the Tindy boys kneeling in relays at the grave and keeping it continually covered with flowers and green things though it was not the season for green things and flowers in that part of India —while their poverty stricken pockets provided the stipend for a sung Requiem Mass.

EDITOR'S NOTE: Through the courtesy of *The Magnificat* Miss Kurth's chapter on Father Duffy is presented here. Miss Kurth is also the editor of The New Hope Series of Mission Books by Father Duffy. The Series includes *Blind Spot, Fantastic Uncle, God-palaver White Man, God's Little Hope, Price of Dawning Day, Scout Songs, The Seven Last Words, A Sower Went Out, The Voyager, Wayfarer for Christ,* and *Yonder.* The Series is published by the Convent of the Sacred Heart, 334 N. Taylor Ave., St. Louis, Mo.

REVEREND PETER MASTEN DUNNE, S.J.

EVEN IF CANDOR is admirable, sincerity laudable, and realism desired, still it is with some diffidence that one approaches and autobiographical sketch, even if it be brief. That the sketch is to be confined to one's literary development makes it easier. Yet, only absolute sincerity, tinged with modesty, can make writing about oneself acceptable.

From the age of sixteen I enjoyed writing. A Jesuit novice at seventeen, my literary ambitions soared as soon as I had entered my studies, if one is to judge from notebooks full of elegant phrases culled from the finest beds of literature; or from efforts made to describe to myself or to others orally the smiles of California's nature as dispensed about the beautiful Los Gatos. Reciting choice bits from memory did much to further bore my companions.

The first time I wrote for publication was during my first year of teaching as a Jesuit scholastic in St. Ignatius high school in San Francisco. It was 1915, the year of the Panama-Pacific ex-

position. I was intrigued by the Chinese exhibit of the then infant republic and described it in an article which I sent to
America. It was rejected and an unsympathetic superior said
this would teach me a lesson. I suppose he thought I was being
too ambitious for so young a Jesuit. I remember vividly my,
perhaps pardonable, satisfaction when in the early summer of
1919 I first broke into the pages of *America*. It was while at our
summer camp at Manresa looking over the curving beaches of
Monterey Bay, there where Irving Cobb said Neptune spilt his
bluing pot. We were sitting under cypress trees after lunch
amidst the tents when the day's mail was delivered. The week's
issue of *America* was there. I had been waiting for it. Would it
have my article! Eagerly I reached for it; got it first and saw my
first published effort in a review which was for the general public.
—This was for me a good moment.

Four years of theology (1919–1923) were done in the French
seminary at Hastings in England. Anti-clerical troubles had sent
the Jesuits out of France. Here I continued my writing. I bored
my friends and perhaps my family with formal descriptions of
the charm of the English countryside at the changing seasons; I
kept a diary and put into it narratives of observed beauty that had
struck into my very soul; also, I wrote several articles for *America*
and for the *Teachers' Review* of Woodstock College. All but one
were accepted. This is probably the reason why, at the end of
tertianship, done in Cleveland, Ohio, I was ordered to return to
New York to become associate editor of *America*. That was in
1924.

Another development occurred in England which has borne
fruit for all these years, which bearing I hope will be continuous
until the end comes for me here.—On the threshold of my departure for England in 1919 I took a summer course in history
from the later Father Theodore Pockstaller. This stimulated an
already pretty strong liking for history and I decided to make of
history a career. Father Pockstaller had taken history at the University of California and received his doctor's degree under the
direction of that grand friend of all human beings and especially,

I think, of Jesuits, Herbert E. Bolton. The latter was just getting out his *Kino's Historical Memoir of Pimeria Alta*. Pockstaller took me over to the university for an introduction and an interview. Bolton spoke of his Kino, said it would be soon out. When that fall I (now in England) heard of its publication I sent for a copy of the two volumes. And I remember exactly what I wrote to Bolton in the fall of 1919: "If the Jesuits of old have done such fine things in Mexico and Lower California why should not their modern confreres know of them and write of them."

I determined to do both. Ore Place, the Hastings Jesuit theologate, was a reflection of the catholicity of Catholicism. All the nations were there. At least we counted twenty-three. Irishmen from all over the world, and, while French predominated, there were Spaniards, Belgians, English, Dutchmen, Chinese, Poles, Jugo-Slavs, Egyptians, and a Mesopotamian from Mosul in Iraq! One of the Egyptians, Nakhla, had huge black and popping eyes and a great hooked nose, crowned by a thick shock of coal-black curly hair. He surely must be a descendant of old King Tut or of Rameses II. I got hold of this vivacious, energetic individual of extraordinary vitality, who knew all the European languages. He graciously agreed, almost offered, to tutor me. I must become familiar with French for it was the language of the house; I must know Spanish if I intended later to write about Mexican missionaries; and German ought to be thrown in too. We carried out our program. At the end of the four years of theology I had acquired a reading knowledge of the three languages. I had learned my Spanish and could now be ready to do some study and make some researches into the brilliant career of the Jesuit missionaries of old Mexico.

Thus it was that in the second half of the year 1919 there began burning the flame of a modest ambition. The little flame is still burning, but the ambition had years to wait even for the beginning of fulfilment. Complete fulfilment must wait still for many years.

Editorial work on the staff of *America* now (1924–1925) engaged my literary energies, even though by the indulgence of Father

Richard Tierney, editor-in-chief, I was able to take some courses in history in the graduate school of Columbia University. I slugged away at book reviews, wrote the news for the Latin countries, turned out an occasional article, and helped in editing the *Catholic Mind.* Father Francis Talbot, later editor-in-chief, was my immediate boss as literary editor, and my contacts with him, with his engaging personality, were of the most pleasant kind. Once we both agreed to write an article for the Christmas number. Our colleagues would choose the better for publication. Frank Talbot won, of course. I was and have since remained unable to reach the luster of his golden pen.

Nor is that all.— I was a no-good journalist and a worse proof-reader. I was let out after a year! To Santa Clara then, teaching history, and after a year to Los Gatos to aid in giving the required literary formation to young Jesuits. This was my old home, the novitiate, and I loved it. I taught history too. My reading during theology and the Columbia graduate school had made me familiar with the Renaissance and the Reformation period, and I began to realize that many Catholic writers and not a few Catholic historians were disingenuous and unscientific in their presentation of the facts of this period. I now had lots of fun criticizing the timid and over-conservative school of Catholic historians. Articles were accepted by the *Historical Bulletin* (St. Louis University), the *Ecclesiastical Review,* the *Catholic School Journal.* I was forthright in telling of the corruption of the Church in administration and personnel. Criticism, even angry criticism, was aroused. The *Ecclesiastical Review* was fine, but the then editors of the *Historical Bulletin* rejected two other articles on the causes of the Protestant Revolt. They said I presented the Protestant point of view. But fifteen years later (1941–1942) these same two articles were published in the same review when it was under the direction of the late Father Raymond Corrigan! We *do* make progress.

Now comes a book, a very modest one. The San Francisco nuns, the Helpers of the Holy Souls, asked me in 1928 to write a biography of Mother Mary of St. Bernard, foundress of their San

Francisco house. This I consented to do, they furnishing the materials—letters, sketches of her early life, and the rest. The first draft of the eleven chapters was completed in eleven successive weekly holidays from teaching. In print these fill one hundred and forty-seven pages, title *Mother Mary of St. Bernard* (1929). But alas, on the very seventh line of the first chapter there is an historical blunder which neither censors, proof readers, nor the French nuns caught. I call Louis Napoleon president of the First Republic.

Eleven years and then a second book.— In 1930 I was sent to the University of San Francisco. Criticism, I feel, of my presentation of Reformation history was responsible for the move from Los Gatos. I had by now given up hope of satisfying the old ambition of achieving the doctor's degree in history. But in 1932 my Provincial superior, Father Zacheus Maher, desired that I become a doctor. The Jesuit General in Rome, the late Wlodimir Ledochowski, must approve because criticisms of my intellectualisms had been numerous and had gone to Rome. Father General did approve and I went to my old friend Bolton to guide me in the historical field I had looked wistfully upon from England thirteen years before, the early Jesuit missions of Mexico. I was Bolton's fourth Jesuit, and being the most recent I was a Benjamin at forty-five. He sent Father Jacobsen and me down to Mexico to inspect old documents and to breathe an ancient atmosphere. We did both. After my companion left for home, I went far into the mission country, rode out over wild trails on horseback, pierced deep into Jesuitland. Early in January, 1933, I went down alone from a mining camp, stripped, and tumbled into a deep, blue pool of the Fuerte River (rich in Jesuit lore) as it ran briskly through the foothills of the great Sierra Madre range. It was a glorious swim in a mission river.

From all of this resulted the second book and second of a series of works on early Mexican Jesuits. Under the chief editorship of Doctor Bolton, Father Jacobsen got out his *Educational Founda-tions of the Jesuits in Sixteenth-Century New Spain* (University of California Press, 1938). Then from the same press two years later issued my *Pioneer Black Robes on the West Coast*. My third, and third of the series, has become snagged in the press. War priorities and the rest. It was due the fall of 1942 and was listed in the California catalogue of publications as *The Tepehuán Revolt*.

There is a fourth and still a fifth. One is a biography of a missionary, the other is on a later group of Jesuit missions. These are completed and all ready for the press. I have laid them away in moth balls. Here they shall rest until the end of the war.

EDITOR'S NOTE: Father Dunne's books include: *Mother Mary of St. Bernard*, Kenedy, 1929; *Pioneer Black Robes on the West Coast*, University of California Press, 1940; *A Padre Views South America*, 1945, Bruce.

REVEREND JOHN A. ELBERT, S.M.

I WAS BORN IN BROOKLYN, New York, on March 15, 1895, the seventh child of Louis Constantin Elbert and Joanna Wagner. My father came from the village of Roellbach, near the town of Klingenberg, Bavaria. Mother was a native of Gabsheim near Woerstadt, Rheinhesse. They met in New York City, were married, established a home there, and later settled permanently in Brooklyn. There, in the Church of All Saints, the baptismal record reads: "John Aloysius Elbert, baptized March 24, 1895." And here in the parochial school I first entered upon the path of knowledge. In the summer of 1902, the family moved away from the more congested section of the city to what was then something of a suburb, in the Ridgewood section, and there my elementary education was completed under the tutelage of the Sisters of St. Dominic, at St. Barbara's Parochial School. In the fall of 1907, the Brothers of Mary took charge of the boys' school and for one year I was privileged to be under their direction.

In September of the same year, my good mother died at the early age of forty six years, worn out by her gallant struggle to raise a family of twelve children, four of whom had preceded her in death. She was called home to the reward exceeding great, bearing her torch of faith and leaving behind for all of us a memory of strength and sweetness.

By her death and previously by the marriage of the oldest sister, the family tie began to break up, and so it was not difficult for me to secure permission to leave home, in the summer of 1908, to become a candidate in the Society of Mary, which had its headquarters in Dayton, Ohio.

The years between 1908 and 1916 were spent in doing the regular high school and college program of studies of those days, which consisted of a straight academic schedule on both levels. In the spring of 1912, March 25, I was permitted to take my first profession of vows in the Society of Mary, and in the summer of 1918, the final and perpetual profession. I had already done some preliminary teaching in the parochial school of St. George, Cincinnati, Ohio, and in St. Mary parochial school, N.S. Pittsburgh, Pennsylvania. From 1916–1918 I taught in the newly-established West Philadelphia High School for Boys, and from 1918–1921, in the high school department of the University of Dayton, then known as St. Mary's College. It was during this period that my first attempts at writing for the public appeared in the pages of *America*.

In the summer of 1921, I was sent to the international seminary of the Society of Mary, located at Villa St. Jean, Fribourg, Switzerland, to pursue the course in Thomistic philosophy and sacred theology, at the University of Fribourg. Here it was my good fortune to spend five years in quiet study under the able guidance of the Dominican Fathers and other masters such as Steffens the paleographer, Kirsch the archaeologist and historian, and the distinguished Marianist authority, Emil Neubert.

In those university years between 1921 and 1926 I did some writing, principally on philosophical and literary subjects, which appeared in the pages of the *Columbia Review,* the official magazine of the American student colony at Fribourg. And besides the required studies in philosophy and theology, I delved into history and into languages,—French, German, Spanish. During the long summer vacations there was time for extensive reading in English, French and German literature. My favorite authors were Shakespeare, Newman, Browning; in German, Goethe, Schiller, and the modern novelists, such as Paul Keller; in French, the classic dramatists and the newer writers of fiction.

The long course of professional studies was crowned with the ordination to the holy priesthood, on March 20, 1926. The following July I returned to the United States.

During the next two years I taught philosophy and education at Mount St. John, Dayton, Ohio, the Motherhouse of the Cincinnati province of the Society of Mary. It was here that I wrote and delivered the Eucharistic conferences which were published later as a booklet entitled *Eternal Testament*.

In 1928, I took over the administration of Purcell High School, Cincinnati, and during the next three years teaching and writing ceased. In my last year as principal I attended some classes in the department of philosophy at the University of Cincinnati and was given the entire following year, without regular duty, to complete the work and the thesis required for a doctorate in philosophy. The degree, the first accorded to a Catholic priest in that department of the University, was conferred in June, 1932. The thesis was published in the following year as a slender volume, *Newman's Conception of Faith Prior to 1845*.

In the fall of 1932 I was appointed president of Trinity College, Sioux City, Iowa, and remained in that office until 1938. During this time, besides editing the two works above mentioned, I found time to write a book on the Seven Last Words, entitled *Three Hours' Agony of Our Lord Jesus Christ*, and a series of Lenten sermons under the heading *Greater Love*.

Thirty years after entering the high school of St. Mary College as a student, I returned to my alma mater, now the University of Dayton, as president of the institution. Here, too, the administrative duties left little time for literary effort. In 1940 I managed to turn out the small volume, *Devotion to Mary in the Twentieth Century*, and the following year a work entitled *Prayer in a Modern Age*.

After completing six years as president of the University of

Dayton, the opportunity is again mine of engaging in the teaching field of my first preference, namely that of philosophy. In time, the duties of a professor of philosophy at Trinity College, Sioux City, may give sufficient leisure for some literary pursuits. Such, at least, is my hope.

Writing has never been my primary occupation. Teaching is my profession by choice and administration has been my lot during the greater part of my time since the completion of my final studies. Writing has been an outlet, though a necessary and spontaneous one, for the ideas which emerge from the continued application and interest in the work of ruling and serving a community of religious educators.

The monetary return on publications has been less than secondary and only sufficient to supply me with more books and to keep my friends in free copies of my own. I do, however, hold that a book should at least carry its weight, that is, it should have enough general appeal to induce a reputable publisher to bring it out without expense to the author. If a proposed work cannot meet this preliminary test, it ought not to go into print. This rule may, in some instances, exclude a veritable masterpiece from the light of day, but in our times it works mostly for the general good of the author and the reader.

Ideas come to me readily. Putting the ideas into finished form is the difficult part of the labor. My desk and files are crammed with notes and jottings which will never appear in print, for lack of time and energy.

I take it that every man is necessarily influenced in the form and content of his writing by every author in whom he has read to any considerable extent. And every person who writes or even merely speaks the English language, is indebted to Shakespeare in some measure. Other than these factors, I am not conscious of more specific influences in the little writing I have done.

EDITOR'S NOTE: Father Elbert's later works include *Devotion to Mary in the Twentieth Century,* 1940, Bruce; *Greater Love,* 1937, Bruce; *Three Hours' Agony of Our Lord, Jesus Christ,* 1936, Bruce; *Eternal Testament,* 1933, Bruce; and *Prayer in a Modern Age,* 1941, Catholic Literary Guild, but now taken over by the Salvatorian Fathers, St. Nazianz, Wis.

BROTHER ERNEST, C.S.C.

I AM VERY HAPPY, my dear friends, to write this sketch for you, and that for two reasons: first, because of your interest; and secondly, because it has just been impossible to answer the hundreds of letters that have come to me for biographical information. Now I know that I will not disappoint any more of you, for all will be able to read this book. So you see I have reason to be happy!

Long before I started to school I could read and write, but as I look back over the years, it seems to me that my desire to write is older than my craving to read. I cannot recall the titles of any of my early literary attempts, but I can still see my mother softly crying over Father Finn's *Claude Lightfoot*. When she put the book down, I picked it up to try to find what it was that made her cry over a book! I don't think I found it, but so interested did I become in that story that I read every Father Finn book I could get my hands on. And of the hundreds of reviews I have seen of my books, none of them pleased me more than the one in the

Messenger of the Sacred Heart, the Jesuit magazine, which referred to me as "the modern Father Finn." Let me add, however, that I think it is just too good to be true!

During my grade school years at St. Mary's in Elyria, Ohio, my home town, I was always more interested in English than in anything else. When I entered high school I began to send little articles to the diocesan Catholic paper under a penname. I was indeed proud when I saw my first efforts in print.

On March 19, 1918, I became a Brother in the Congregation of Holy Cross and began my novitiate in the shadow of the world-famous golden dome of the University of Notre Dame. During that year I had the friendly advice and encouragement of Brother Alphonsus, a great student of Stevenson and Cardinal Newman. Shortly after I began my undergraduate course in the University, Brother Alphonsus insisted on turning in for publication in *The Scholastic,* the Notre Dame literary magazine in those days, a poem, and a short story I had written. Both of them were published, and from that day to this writing has been a joy.

While I was a student I had the opportunity to meet and talk with "John Ayscough," the famous English novelist and essayist, and the author of one of my favorite books, *San Celestino.* He was very encouraging to young writers, and expressed to me my own idea that, to become a writer get busy and write. I also met Father John Talbot Smith, author of *The Black Cardinal,* and other books; Dr. James J. Walsh, author of many volumes including *The Thirteenth, Greatest of Centuries;* Father Thomas N. Taylor, the English priest who had the honor of making the standard English translation of the *Autobiography of the Little Flower;* Charles Phillips, poet, novelist, and biographer, who was also one of my teachers. I enjoyed many half-hours in his study at the time he was working on his life of the greatest of modern pianists, Paderewski. Father Patrick Carroll, C.S.C., editor of the *Ave Maria,* and author of several fine novels, taught me the technique of the short story; but he charmed me by his reading. I could listen to him for hours.

I have listed some of the many authors I have met, but the one who influenced me most I did not meet in person—Mary T. Waggaman. I did, however, have the pleasure of a few letters from her. I have read all of her books, some of them many times. Plots of several of my books came to me while reading her stories. Today I am almost afraid to pick up one of her novels, for I know I'll think of at least two more plots, and I can't, for sheer lack of time, write all those I already have in my head!

The great priest-poet, Father Charles L. O'Donnell, C.S.C., encouraged me to publish my first novel. Today it is known as *Eddie of Jackson's Gang*. Hundreds of letters from happy boys and girls have come to me telling how they laughed and cried over young Eddie. Of course I don't want anyone to cry over my books!

With the instant success of my first book, and in spite of my heavy duties as a teacher at Cathedral High School, Indianapolis, Indiana, I began to collect material on all the Orders of Brothers in the United States. Scott, Foresman & Company published the volume under the title, *Our Brothers*. I have been told it has been instrumental in leading many into the religious life. One young man became a Trappist priest after reading it. What more reward could I expect!

Captain Johnny Ford followed, and is now in its third printing. With its appearance my readers increased to thousands, and orders came in even from far-away India. After all these years I still get scores of letters annually from delighted readers of this story.

After I received my bachelor degree in philosophy in the University of Notre Dame, and was graduated in library science in the Catholic University of America, Washington, D. C., I turned to write books that would make religion classes in high school more interesting. The first of these, *Religion and Living*, was well received, and I know it has aided hundreds of teachers from one end of the continent to the other. It was followed by *Equipping the Teacher of Religion*, which I got together while I was teaching in the Catholic University of America, and in which I gave others the benefits of my years of teaching Catholic boys.

Once again I turned to the novel, and in rapid succession appeared: *Dick of Copper Gap, Boys of the Covered Wagons,* which was put on the *List of Books for School Libraries of the State of Oregon,* and won for me an honorable membership in the Eugene Field Society, a national association of authors and journalists; and *Adventures of Tommy Blake.*

For years I had wanted to write biographies of the saints in such a way as to appeal to readers up through the high school. After taking my master degree in arts in the University of Portland, I made up my mind to begin this adventure. I insisted that these stories must be told in a fictional style, and be illustrated in the most modern manner. Conservative publishers could not be interested. But I went ahead, secured Brother Hilarion, C.S.C., a student of the famous Emil Jacques, and finally brought out *That Boy,* a story of St. Gabriel, C.P. As I had thought, the first printing sold in less than a year! It was followed by *The Boy Who Saw the World,* a story of St. Francis Xavier, done in the same manner, and again illustrated by Brother Hilarion; and *The Giant Saint,* a legend of St. Christopher, with drawings by Mr. Herbert Heywood, head of the Art Department in the University of Portland. I am very pleased with the reception given these books. I have in my possession more than a dozen letters from bishops and archbishops in praise of these books.

The war with its demand for more men, pulling them away from linotype and presses, has for the time being, made it quite impossible for my publishers to bring out books on schedule. Two manuscripts have been accepted: a novel, *And the Winds Blew,* and another book in the series of saints, *The Boy Who Threw Away His Gold,* the life of St. Francis of Assisi. And here's a little secret for thousands of boys and girls who have read my books: I have written and am waiting to publish the following novels: "Peanut Tony's Boy," "Forest Fire!", "That House is Haunted!", and the biographies: "Young Prince Gonzaga," a story of St. Aloysius; "The Boy Who Worked Wonders," a life of St. Anthony of Padua; "The Man Under the Stairs," a story of St.

Alexis; and "The Dragon Killer," a legend of St. George, universal
patron of Boy Scouts.

My last word is to those of you who might be thinking of writing. Just get your pencil and paper and begin. There's no use to wait. If you have a story to tell, and want to tell it keenly enough, no one can stop you. Don't think you must have hours at your disposal. I have written all of my books between classes, and I have frequently taught as many as six a day. And neither is special preparation necessary for you. Anyone familiar with the history of literature will know that. So there you are. Good luck!

EDITOR'S NOTE: In 1944 Brother Ernest was appointed first Editor of *Junior Books*, a national magazine devoted to reviews of books for Catholic youth. His own books include *The Adventures of Tommy Blake*, 1940, St. Anthony Guild; *St. Francis Xavier*, 1941, Dujarie Press; *The Boy Who Threw Away His Gold*, 1943, id.; *Eddie of Jackson's Gang*, 1941, St. Anthony Guild; *The Giant Saint: a Legend of St. Christopher*, 1942, Dujarie Press; and *That Boy! a Story of St. Gabriel, C.P.*, 1940, id.

CECIL JOHN EUSTACE

THE THOUGHT HAS OFTEN OCCURRED to me that a writer has a fore-taste of Judgement Day, since everything he has written stares him in the face, in black and white, and it is difficult to unsay what he has said. There it is, accusing, banal, startling, sometimes en-lightening sometimes appealing—but there it is, for the whole world to see, and to judge.

When I started to write, I had no idea of becoming a Catholic writer, for the simple reason that, in those days, I had no idea of becoming a Catholic. I have already told the story of my con-version, in my book *House of Bread: a Catholic Journey,* so I will not repeat it here. It is sufficient to say that the evolution of a Catholic writer is a difficult and exacting problem, which must be different for each person who traverses the road.

My first desire, twenty years ago, was to write for the screen. I started to learn how to do this by paying for a series of lessons on scenario technique and short-story writing. I believe that it is impossible to teach anyone to write, especially fiction, for this is a gift which one either has, or has not. But competent guidance in story-writing and in the technique of presentation of material is, I think, very useful. I have never regretted the time I spent on this course.

Most young writers start out by trying to be sensational in their writing. I was no exception to the rule. My first stories were highly bizarre romances, concocted after the pattern of horror-story writers, such as Bram Stoker and Edgar Allan Poe, or dangerous love stories, smart, sophisticated, and telling, after the style of Balzac or Michael Arlen, who was then very popular.

As I had read a good deal of Newman, when at school and even during my Anglican days, I found it hard, as one may imagine, to acquire the racy kind of literary style necessary to sell to the popular magazines. However, I did eventually start to interest some editors, and at last sold my first story—to *Breezy Stories,* of all magazines. This is a terrible confession to make, I know, in *The Book of Catholic Authors,* but I am speaking merely now of short story techniques, and the romance and weird-story type of magazines were those which appealed, in those days, to my vivid imagination.

After this I started to sell a few stories to scientific magazines, an article on how to write novel credit-letters to a business magazine, a yarn about a native girl and a white man in the Far East— a story of retribution to the white man—sold to an English magazine in London, and to a Negro magazine in Chicago.

I wrote exactly what I wanted to, with no thought of any definite market in mind. If I had been wise, I should have specialized in a certain type of story, for a certain class of magazines, but in my anxiety to write, I turned out a stream of stories as varied as they were novel. They found their places—when they did sell— in an extraordinary variety of magazines. I sold stories, at this time, to magazines ranging all the way in reader-appeal from *The English Review,* in London, England, which had been the vehicle for the best short stories written in the contemporary modern English literary scene, down to *Amazing Stories* and to a number of the "pulp and paper" magazines.

In 1927, at the age of twenty-three, I published my first novel *The Scarlet Gentleman,* which was an extremely romantic, over-verbose and amateurish attempt. It came out in London, and sold fairly well. It was not until 1931 that I became interested in more serious things, and this kind of writing started to pall on me. The question was—what to write? Or, rather, what to study?

I had always been a voracious reader, but my reading had been scattered. I had absorbed most of the classics of English literature, but had never delved much into philosophy, and was totally unfamiliar with theology as a science. Pere Alphonse Gratry's book *Les Sources* (in English translation *The Well Springs*) interested me actively in the idea of giving form and substance to my life. I still look back on the reading of this book as one of the milestones of my journey. The idea of dedicating my life to some ideal, to devoting some time to real study, and to planned reading, had never occurred to me before, but once explained, appealed very much to my roving and uncertain temperament.

Furthermore, I found Pere Gratry's book stimulating. He deals, in a brief manner, with the inter-relationship of knowledge, of the place and purpose of reading, of each science, of sleep, of regular habits, of prayer, and of meditation and contemplation. And as I drew near to the Catholic Church, I perceived, to my amazement, that these things actually had a place in this amazing organization, and that there were men and women who dedicated themselves to this ideal.

After my entry into the Church in 1929, I found myself in a peculiar emotional and artistic dilemma. I had acquired something of a reputation as a coming young short-story writer. My stories had sold in England, in the U. S. A., and in Canada, and had been translated into French, Scandinavian, and German. It is true that they were popular stories, but they brought me good money. And yet, after my reception into the Church, I discovered within myself the ferment of new interests.

It was not fiction which interested me at that time, but the thirst for new knowledge—for specific Catholic knowledge, which had for so many years been denied me. I threw myself into the study of Catholic literature. I read St. Thomas, St. Augustine, Newman, Father Garrigou-Lagrange, and many other great Catholic theologians and philosophers. I have described all this in *House of Bread,* and of how I was fortunate enough to read Jacques Maritain's books, and to find, in him, a kindred soul to my own. I read everything he wrote. I studied, I made notes, I ranged far and wide in my reading, and I was lucky enough to find some good learned priests who were willing to guide me, and to explain away my difficulties.

In 1933 I published *Romewards.* This manuscript was turned down by one publisher, but Benzigers took a chance on it, and much to my surprise it became the Catholic Book Club's selection of February, 1933. It was also published in England and Canada, and still sells in small quantities each year, eleven years after publication. *Romewards,* of course, was not a great book. But it was reviewed well, and sold in reasonably large quantities.

Between writing *Romewards* and *Mind and the Mystery: A Catholic Explanation,* which was published in 1937, I adapted into novel form the scenario of *Damaged Lives,* a Columbia motion picture dealing with the health-problems of social diseases. Quite frankly I did this work for the little bit of money it brought me, as I needed money badly at that time. But I enjoyed making the adaptation also, and thus fulfilled my old dream—not of writing a scenario—but of writing a novel from a scenario. The resulting novel was published by Putnam, in New York and London.

Mind and the Mystery was reviewed well, but it was published before the present popular interest in scholastic philosophy. I did a great deal of thinking over this book, and although it is, in the main, too closely written and too scholastic in its terminology for the average reader, it did serve to clear my own mind of a lot of my difficulties. Its sale was small, but it brought me letters from several distinguished professors and teachers, congratulating me on my "popularisation" of a difficult subject.

In 1938 I published *Catholicism, Communism and Dictatorship,* largely from notes made during five or six years of study club work. The book was reviewed well, but did not take on—in my opinion—as it deserved to do. By this time I commenced to realize that the Catholic book buying public is a small one—albeit a growing one—and that one must not expect to make either fame or fortune by being a Catholic writer—or, rather, by being a writer on Catholic matters.

The chief point I wish to emphasize in this description of my evolution as a writer of Catholic things, and as a convert, is that I was unable, during all this period, to write any good fiction. It is true that I did write some short stories, and that these sold largely to a few American newspapers and magazines which offered a market for short-short stories, but my interest was not in fiction any longer, but in philosophy, and in theology.

During this time I wrote three novels, I have the manuscripts of all three of them with me now—all unpublished. None of them was as good as the work I had done before in the fiction field. All of them lacked the inspiration that must underlie all true creative work, because all of them were didactic, or almost apologetical in tone. In other words, I was merely using characters to try to preach some kind of moral lesson, or to make a philosophical point.

Between 1938 and 1942 I wrote a 780 page exposition of the growth of western life, (which I called *The Promise of the West*), and of what I consider to be the gradual decline of Christianity as a force in temporal affairs. The scope of this vast manuscript was too diffused, hitting upon too many fronts, to make it a publishable venture. I sent it to an English publisher, who had the famous English poet T. S. Eliot read it for me. He expressed sympathy for my views, but suggested that I turn it into six or seven books. And this I am going to do, in due time.

In 1944 I published a brief autobiography, *House of Bread: a Catholic Journey*. I was surprised that the reviewers, although they were all very kind to the book, some of them highly laudatory, nearly all missed the point I was trying to make—namely the importance of the interior life of grace in the soul of the individual Catholic, and especially its appeal to the would-be convert.

I also wrote a brief book dealing, through the lives of five women, with the relation between poetry, art, and mysticism. I hope this will be published some day soon. In the meanwhile, I am finishing a short book on Canada, as a world laboratory, wherein the conflicting universal forces of London, Rome, and Moscow, compete for the souls of the people. It will be a psychological study of the French and English speaking Canadians, and their two differing ways of life, one Catholic and Latin, the other Protestant and Anglo-Saxon.

And one day soon I am going to write my Catholic novel. I have written, for fourteen years, book-reviewing, articles, stories, for a variety of magazines. The field for Catholic journalism is varied, but not particularly encouraging for a specifically Catholic writer. Yet it seems to me that the Catholic writer has a tremendous opportunity before him.

The whole world is now being transformed by the devastating forces of world revolution and chaos. The Catholic way of life, its hidden principles, and the secrets of its interior life, must be made palpable and known to the non-Catholic world. This can be done, not alone by apologetics and reasoning, by Catholic treatises, for non-Catholic people will not read them. It seems to me that there is room for a great novel by a Catholic, in which the deep things of the way of the Cross, and of Christ's way of love, can be shown through the lives of real people. There is room for biographies of Catholic saints and heroes, and for Catholic plays. But the Catholic writer, like any other writer, must first learn the technique of writing, the art of literature.

I have never been totally dependent upon my writing for my income. Any writing I have done has been done in spare time, and this exacts a toll, both mental and physical. But writing is, for a Catholic also a means of apostolate. Who can tell what influence a good book will have upon an unprejudiced mind? It has been my own good fortune to hear from many people who have read my own books. In this way I have made many new friends, and some dear ones.

The rewards of a Catholic writer are less financial or monetary rewards, than spiritual and social ones. In my humble opinion, it is well worthwhile. But I think I speak the mind of all Catholic authors, when I say that our task would be made easier, and publishers themselves would be much more inclined to sponser Catholic books, if more Catholic people read them. We Catholics are not good book buyers or readers. It is true that we are improving, and this is encouraging. And it is upon this note that I will end. The Catholic writer, above all, must be true to his Faith, and true to truth. Only in this way will he reap the fullest rewards of his art, which is to help bring souls to God.

EDITOR'S NOTE: Mr. Eustace's books include *House of Bread*, 1943, Longmans; *Mind and the Mystery*, 1937, id.; and *Romewards*, 1933, Benziger.

REVEREND PAUL J. GLENN

WHEN A WRITER of textbooks whose place is in the gallery with compilers, anthologists, and low fellows who make "digests," shoulders his way to the stage and takes a place among the star performers,—that is, among real authors,—there is need of explanation. To adapt a line from the Declaration of Independence, "a decent respect to the opinions of mankind requires that he should declare the causes which impel him to the indiscretion."

Well, I came in on a pass. I was invited by the management. I am a guest of the house. The editor of this noble volume was once, in a far time, my pupil. We did not pluck the rowans fine, but we managed some sailing, however skimming, upon the wide seas of philosophy. He recalls those days, does the editor, and, splendid chap that he is, he retains no cherished rancours. He has honored me by inviting me, and with insistence, to take the place I here occupy.

I was born in the town of Scottdale in southwestern Pennsyl-

vania, on May 3, 1893. For the place of my birth I entertain a
deep and enduring affection. To me it would be the loveliest
village of the plain but for the fact that it is a town of valleys
and hills. It is by no means a deserted village, although the
great "depression" did harsh things to it. I may not offer here
the long list of reasons which must compel any person of fair
mind to acknowledge the excellences of my old home town. Let
me only say of it (with real appreciation, and not at all jokingly)
what Proctor Knott said of Duluth, "It stands so exactly in the
center of the visible universe that the sky comes down at the same
distance all around it."

Scottdale has claim to many a distinction, but to none more
notable than the fact that for more than fifty years it was the
home and the field of labor for that splendid man and most excellent of pastors, Father Michael A. Lambing, gone now to his
great reward. I am to say what gave impulse and direction to my
writing; I must name Father Lambing as the earliest and most
powerful of such influences. For all that, he never suggested
authorship to me, nor did he set themes for my youthful pen,
except upon one occasion when he proposed that I write on
a subject of which I knew nothing and in promotion of a
movement with which I had but languid sympathy, and that
I enter the paper in an "essay contest." I obediently prepared
and submitted a manuscript. I have not heard of it since. I do
not know who won the prize, nor indeed what prize was offered.
I only know that my first pebble cast into the sea of literature
was singularly unproductive of those rippling circles which are
supposed in time to reach the farthest shores. But Father Lambing was master of a clear and virile expression which caught
my early fancy and won my lasting admiration. He never wrote
much for publication, but all that he wrote, even his casual letters,
said unmistakably what he had to say in the most straightforward
English, and yet had a balance and a turn of phrase that
amounted to true literary art without a trace of artiness.

Let me dwell a moment upon Father Lambing, for I am to
offer advice in this brief sketch, and he serves perfectly as instance

and example. He was a close and loving student of two great thinkers and writers. I mean no irreverence in linking their names as though they were equals. They were Cardinal Newman and Saint Paul. No young man or woman with the fine urge for writing could do better than follow my old pastor and friend in the choice of models.

Most of my schooling in "the grades" was done in St. John's, Scottdale, under the direction of the Mother Seton Sisters of Charity. It would be more than indelicate of me to propose myself as a specimen of the sort of work these Sisters do. I cannot qualify as a "sample." But a good part of my life has been spent among teachers; I may claim a rather intimate knowledge of classroom methods and abilities. And it is in no spirit of idle compliment that I say that the Mother Seton Sisters are teachers of the first quality.

From St. John's school, and alas, from the joy of life at home, I crossed some twenty miles of hill and dale to become a boarding pupil at St. Vincent, the famous Benedictine institution on the hills above Latrobe. I had done a good deal of Englmann's Latin grammer under the stern tutelage of Father Lambing, and thus I was able to pass the entrance examinations for the second year of the preparatory course, known in those days as "second academic." For the next eleven years I was a pupil at St. Vincent, and passed through the "prep," the college, and the theological seminary. I was ordained in December of 1918. Later, I returned to St. Vincent for a year's graduate study in preparation for a doctor's degree.

In college, and indeed throughout the days of seminary training, I did much writing. For one proud year I was editor-in-chief of the college magazine, and I served on the staff of this publication for more than seven years. Our faculty mentor, this lengthy while, was Father Gerard Bridge, O.S.B. I owe to him, far more than to any other, such adequacy of literary expression as I have come to possess. Father Gerard was always the kind friend, but he was an exacting master. He was not to be pleased or fooled by the facile flippancies which young collegians are likely to regard as clever writing. Looking back, I marvel at the patience of this man, and at his wisely unrelenting insistence which I once thought only a stubborn and prosy devotion to set forms. Father Gerard managed to make passable writers of a lively and exuberant group of scribblers. Under his watchful eye and under the constant scourge of his unmerciful blue pencil we contrived to turn out a monthly magazine that had dignity and a measure of grace. Our work "on the staff" was a splendid training in the difficult art of clear, compact expression.

Of course, we nearly all wrote verse sometimes, and I was guilty of a vast quantity of it, and have lapsed into this weakness even in maturer years. I think that the hard work of mastering verse-forms, the rigid adhering to the laws of scansion, the heart-breaking quest of the just and graceful rhyme, are most excellent exercises for the hopeful writer, even for the writer who never expects to see a "poem" of his in print. As I say, I performed such exercises, and I believe they did me good, although I confess I never wrote a real poem. Such training as they gave me was severe; Father Gerard was a relentless enemy of the poetic license. On one occasion only have I known bitter regret for my dallying in the fair fields of poesy. Once, when I had finished an hour's instruction in dialectics in St. Mary's College, Monroe, Michigan (a fine institution which has since moved to acquire metropolitan splendor as Marygrove College in Detroit), the assembled young ladies arose and burst into charming song. A mandolin or some such tinkling instrument appeared from hiding, and to its accompaniment the chorus of young voices chanted—an old "poem" of my own, published years before in the college magazine! Throughout the performance I had to stand, facing the singers, and knowing not what to do but to grin like a suddenly amused Buddha. It was a soul searing experience.

After my ordination, I was assigned to parochial work, and continued in it for more than four years. In 1923 I went to Detroit to teach philosophy in the new diocesan seminary, and in

1927 I transferred, for the same work, to the College of St. Charles
Borromeo in Columbus, where I am still most happily employed.
While I was associated with the Detroit faculty I taught some
classes each week at St. Mary's, Monroe, and lectured in the summer-school at the University of Notre Dame.

My book writing has all been done at Columbus, and during
the last fourteen years I have turned out ten books, covering the
field of philosophy. There is, of course, another in the course
of construction, for this writing is a habit not easily overcome. I
have been told by kind people that the books have done good.
Surely, I hope so. But I know students, and I never allow myself
to think of the mountain of malediction that has been heaped
up for me these fourteen years by tired pupils who have had to
study the books. Ah well, I could show them others that would
really make them squirm. I have tried in all my writing to keep
out needless difficulties and to make needful ones as uncompli-
cated as possible. Indeed, the inspiration and the purpose of
my writing of textbooks has been "all possible simplification
without falsification."

My friends keep telling me write a novel. They have no reason
for this advice, for I have challenged them every one and they
use evasions and subterfuges. But some day I may follow their
advice. And then, if I can fool some publisher, I shall buy a
frock coat, and thrust my hand into its bosom, and have my picture taken, and send it to my friend the editor, to stand boldly
and without apology among the real Catholic Authors!

EDITOR'S NOTE: Dr. Glenn's books, all issued by Herder, include class manuals
in *Apologetics, Cosmology, Criteriology, Dialectics, Ethics, Ontology, Psychology, Sociology,* and *Theodicy,* as well as a *History of Philosophy,* 1929,
and an *Introduction to Philosophy,* 1944.

DOM ERNEST GRAF, O.S.B.

IN A WORLD in which the sparrows in the nearest hedge are the objects of divine care, it would be the height of folly to ascribe to chance any of the happenings in our lives. So I see the guiding hand of God in the fact that, as a boy of twelve, I left Germany, the land of my birth, to enter the small school—Alumnate, it was called—of St. Mary's Abbey, Buckfast, the only pre-Reformation religious house in England which, so far, has risen from its ruins. And at Buckfast I have lived ever since, with the exception of two years spent in Palestine. Now it so happened that most of my studies were made through French—a circumstance hardly likely to be of advantage to a future writer. Yet I look upon this seeming handicap as an immense blessing since it meant the freedom of France's splendid literature. The works of Bossuet, the last uncanonized Father of the Church, as he has been called, have been a constant joy and inspiration to me. Any page, or half-page, of that sublime genius, will always stimulate the mind and open out new vistas.

How did I come to write? Well, the temptation is to say that one just drifted into the thing, but that would be in direct conflict with the opening sentence of this sketch.

Close on forty years ago, that is shortly after my ordination, I was sent one Saturday, to help at one of the Plymouth churches. In the evening I called on a young Irish priest, then an assistant master at a Catholic boys' college. I found my friend seated before a portable typewriter of a now obsolete make—an American machine, I believe, called "Blick." I was interested, for up to that day I had never seen a typewriter. "What are you doing?" I asked. "I am typing an article for an American review," he replied, "Why don't you write too?" Now until that moment such a thought had never entered my head—except that as a school-boy, I once began a Latin epic which never got far beyond the initial invocation to the "heavenly Muse." What could I write about? and, anyway, why should I write at all, and who would want to read what I had to say?

But that young priest, whom I was to meet again, many years later, whilst giving a clergy retreat at Cork, had somehow "started a hare," and thereafter the idea of penmanship began to look less and less fantastic.

Up to that time I had often wondered how the men and women whose names I saw on the backs of bound volumes or on the title pages of magazines, had started on their literary careers—in fact, I still wonder. Is it absurd, or uncomplimentary, to suggest that opportunity, which is said to make the thief, also makes the writer? It may be that there are people who, deliberately and of malice *prepense,* embark on a literary career: are there not philanthropic agencies which promise to teach the would-be writer how to become an expert and even to find a market for his wares?

As for the priest who, in addition to his professional duties, takes up literary work, I think it is true to say that almost always writing is simply part of his priestly task—he writes from the same motive from which he preaches and catechizes, that is, from a desire to procure God's glory and spread His Kingdom. If then, to comply with the wishes of the editor of this book, I must state why or how I ever came to take up writing, I would say quite simply that my only motive was to do some good to as many people as possible—that is, to people one can reach only by means of the printed word. No other motive would have made me put up with the drudgery inseparable from literary work. It is not the poet only who, in Horace's words, *multum sudavit et alsit,* in order to fit himself for his task. A priest, like the Apostles, must needs give himself "continually to prayer and to the ministry of the word" (Acts VI:4). Hence, a priest's writing is usually an extension of his preaching.

My first attempt at literary work consisted for the most part in reviewing for a small monthly called *The Poor Souls' Friend,* a magazine devoted to the interests of the Holy Souls, as the title suggests, and published by the Bridgettine Nuns of Syon Abbey, Devon. In the pages of that magazine I also began a translation of the voluminous Revelations of St. Bridget of Sweden, a task not yet completed, though started some forty years ago. In due course, I sent a manuscript to a London publisher: it was returned with the bitter-sweet mixture of compliments and regrets of which, I believe, even successful writers have had to take an occasional sip. In 1920 I began a monthly series of papers on the Liturgy in the *Homiletic and Pastoral Review.* Through the kindness of the editors and the publisher—Mr. Wagner of New York—some of these papers dealing with the Mass, appeared in book form under the title of *The Priest at the Altar.* Mr. Wagner also published a smaller book entitled *The Cross and the Altar,* and Burns, Oates and Washbourne, by kind permission of Mr. Wagner, brought out a book on the Office: *The Church's Daily Prayer,* this being another series of papers first published in the *Homiletic.*

In the summer of 1930 I went to Palestine where, thanks to a commission as officiating chaplain with the R.A.F., I had exceptional facilities for seeing the Holy Land and some of the adjacent countries. The result was a book entitled *In Christ's Own Country.* During all those years I was also busily engaged in the work of translating other people's books, French and German. In particular, I am responsible for Volumes XXV to XXXIV of the English edition of Ludwig von Pastor's *History of the Popes,* published in the United States by Herder.

It is often said that the printing presses are kept far too busy nowadays—that there is far too much writing, since all that is worth saying has been said long ago and as well, or better, than we can hope to say it. There is much truth in this, but if pressed, the argument could also be urged against our preaching. No sensible person—and most of us hope we belong to that category —cherishes any ambition to say something that no one ever thought of. As the late Abbot Vonier told me more than once, we can do little more than keep the debate going, and present truth in our own way to our contemporaries. If a writer can produce a book or pamphlet capable of holding the interest of were it only a few hundred readers, he may deem himself amply rewarded. And, as a publisher once told me, the "life" of the average book is less than one year.

For all that, writing has its joys and brings great rewards— not necessarily of a material kind. It is also a great responsibility for whilst *verba volant, littera scripta manent.* The pen is a tremendous power for good, as it is for evil: the more Catholics take to the pen, the stronger will be the barrier against the spate of bad or simply neutral literature.

EDITOR'S NOTE: Father Graf's books include *The Cross and the Altar,* 1938, Wagner; *In God's Own Country,* 1937, Burns, Oates; *The Priest at the Altar,* 1926, Wagner; and *The Church's Daily Prayer,* 1938, Burns, Oates.

DOROTHY FREMONT GRANT

WHEN YOU GIVE the thought due reflection, it is rather breathtaking to consider that in the Infinite Plan of creation the Creator allocated a time and a place for *your* soul to begin its earthly probation in preparation for its eternal salvation.

For me the time was October 8, 1900, the place, New York City. Rushing to view his first-born my father, Francis Murray Fremont, a good Episcopalian and a 32° Mason, met with a tragic accident which proved fatal three weeks later. He had anticipated a son. He and my mother, Henrietta Addison Fremont, had chosen a name for a son. They had never considered a name for a daughter. But on his deathbed my father overcame his disappointment by asking my mother to name me Dorothy. He knew then, of course, that I would be his only child and the last of his family line. Unsentimental members of the family have pointed out to me that in 1900 Dorothy was a name popularized by current fiction. But, though I never knew him,

I prefer to believe my father had a deeper reason behind his choice: that he was well aware Dorothy means "A gift of God."

By its very nature a gift is an unexpected surprise, intended usually to be pleasant, but quite often, pleasant or otherwise, it is a great responsibility. A well known modern has written a book to sustain his proposition that "Life Begins at Forty"; but for me it really began at thirty-three. For it was then that I received the Greatest Gift—that of the True Faith. Here was a joyful, tremendous surprise, and yet a grave responsibility. Underlying the enthusiasm of the neophyte was a belief new to me, a serious warning: namely, that there will come another time and another place in the Infinite Plan when to God, my Father and Creator, I shall have to render an account of my probation to earth. Of lesser import, but also a forceful incentive to a fruitful life was my father's choice of my name. I must not disappoint him, either. I do, indeed, pray my mother and father are now in Heaven. Did their "gift of God" give them a surprise by embracing the true Faith? Surely, given equal grace and opportunity they would have done likewise. To my father was it a surprise that one of the first non-Catholics to read *What Other Answer?* was a 32° Mason? He wrote that I had "hit him on the head" and that he was beginning instructions in anticipation of his baptism.

The responsibility attached to the Gift of Faith has been an endless incentive to me to try and use it, and accompanying gifts, well.

From earliest childhood I have wanted to write. Perhaps the inspiration came from the Addison branch of the family tree, or perhaps, more than this, God was reminding me that He had given me an ability which required development by discipline and perseverance. Many people voice an urge to write. Not quite so many are willing to invest the time, the ceaseless effort, study and research, the sometimes overwhelming disappointments.

At long last the latter got my "dander up" as the saying goes.

I determined if all editors were so stone blind to the merits of my works which I began submitting to them in 1922 shortly after my marriage, I would, myself, publish what I wrote. So I started my own newspaper in the Long Island town to which we moved in 1928. This I maintained at a good profit on and off for three years, and when I was not too weary I paused to laugh at all the editors! But when I invested my initial capital of $200, I had not realized that I was buying myself a three year training course which could not harm any writer of popular works and would yield rich experience for the future.

The newspaper editor-reporter-circulation-and-advertising manager cannot pick and choose the topics about which he will write, nor the time he will take to write them, nor even the length of his stories. He is hemmed in by publication dates which do not wait, and space limitations due to the fact that news-stock is not made on a rubber base. Community social and civic events, ninety percent of them uninteresting to "ye editor," must each and every one be presented as though each one was of vital interest to all readers. Further, adjectives are out. The reader will supply his own. Though the paper be four, eight or twelve pages, and the stories column, half, quarter or third column length, each must "tell all" in the first *short* opening sentence. Headline writing, restricted to picas per column, is also excellent discipline for the verbose writer.

After three years of this drudgery, profitable in experience and cash, I sold out my paper and began to take stock of myself. Now I was becoming a ripened Catholic, so to say. As the roots of the faith reached deeper into my heart and soul I began to wonder just how I was discharging the responsibility of the Greatest Gift. Considering the forthcoming accounting I shall have to render to Him Who gave me my ability I decided that all future writing would be "for God." Of course I realized as I reached this decision that I would never make a living as a Catholic author. First because my vocation of marriage consumes a major portion of my time, and second because a major portion of Catholics prefer the secular to the Catholic press (which may be partially the fault of some Catholic authors)!

But, I reasoned, I do not have to make a living: that has been provided by my chosen vocation. Money is not my primary objective. The latter is to be able, when the time comes, to go to God with books written either directly for Him, such as *What Other Answer?* and *War Is My Parish,* or books in no way offensive to Him, such as *Margaret Brent, Adventurer.*

These have been preceded by many articles and short stories in the Catholic Press. My first check from a Catholic editor (or any editor save myself) came from Father Gillis for an item in the *Catholic World* for March, 1939.

How long was the road from 1922 to 1939! And how many and bitter the disappointments!

To aspiring young Catholic writers I humbly suggest a consecration of their talents to the "Apostolate of the Pen." In this apostolate there is plenty to be said; there is a popular, pungent way to say it. Say it *your* way: your family, neighbors and friends understands you, so will others.

There is a Jesuit priest whose works I have admired. In *What Other Answer?* for one brief chapter I tried to approach his style. When he reviewed the book he scorned that one chapter as "weak and poorly constructed!" So, coming Catholic writers, be forewarned and be yourself.

And do not presume the "Apostolate of the Pen" is restricted to apologetics. Why not Catholic fiction? This field, with some admirable exceptions which are increasing, is still a broad expanse of fertile but uncultivated acres. Flies are caught with honey. Why not snare souls for God with strong, morally sound fiction? Your moral training has all the answers for a world run amuck. It is true that financial returns will not likely reach the height of a certain publicized tree which grows in Brooklyn, but God has a way of keeping His apostles decently clothed and sufficiently fed. He will not let you get ahead of Him on the score of generosity: witness the *Song of Bernadette,* written by a Jew as a prayer of thanksgiving to God. Discharge the responsibility your talent places upon you by giving it back to God—you can take *that* with you, but not the money your writing brings you. Leave the cash returns in His hand: concentrate on a good accounting, and above all give ample nourishment to your sense of humor.

EDITOR'S NOTE: Mrs. Grant's books include *What Other Answer?*, 1943, Bruce; *War is My Parish*, 1944, id.; *Margaret Brent, Adventuress*, 1944, Longmans.

WALDEMAR GURIAN

I WAS BORN on February 13, 1902, in St. Petersburg (today Leningrad), Russia. I spent my early childhood in Moscow. I remember my mother's drawing-room, full of pictures dealing with St. Francis of Assisi; my Baltic governess, who later entered a Catholic convent; and my teacher in Russian and Church Slavonic, Bama Efros, who wrote a book on the painter Chagall, a friend of the Maritains. I remember, too, that I almost broke my neck sliding down from the Kremlin, and that I was once rescued from drowning in a lake in the neighborhood of Fuerstenberg (Mecklenburg), where we had gone for a vacation. I have not forgotten my Russian nurse who was called simply Nyanya. She could neither read nor write, but was one of the most intelligent persons I have ever met.

After two years in the Hohenzollern Gymnasium of Berlin, I was sent in 1914 to the Collegium Albertinum of the Dominicans in Venlo, Limburg, Holland. My most pleasant memories of it are card parties, during the periods of recreation, in which the benevolent Fathers participated, the extra fine food and the bottle of wine, which the students received on the feast day of St. Dominic, and the walks to the St. Albert farm, where we got good cake and bad coffee.

I left in 1917 for Dusseldorf to join my mother and to continue my education at the Hohenzollern Gymnasium of this city. I remember well the lessons in mathematics given by an old romantic looking Pole. The students said that he opposed the Imperial German Government; but he told us only about functions and equations. The principal was a very fine man, very kind and human, though in politics he admired Grand Admiral Tirpitz and preached a Pan-Germanism, eager to expand the Reich in all directions as much as possible. At the same time, he knew Horace very well and spoke with tears in his eyes about Goethe's Italian pilgrimage.

There were some Catholic influences. The teacher of religion impressed us by his proofs of God's existence, though some unruly characters among the students claimed that these complicated arguments were unnecessary: a man who believed in God believed in Him without proofs. There was a literary circle directed by a friendly Franciscan where many non-literary topics produced feverish debates. I became interested in the Catholic Youth Movement, which had been completely renewed under the leadership of Romano Guardini. It had started out as a somewhat anti-intellectual, idealistic temperance group, but became under Guardini one of the strongest spiritual influences among the young German Catholics of the early 'twenties.

Guardini stimulated me very much during my years as a student in Cologne and Bonn (1921–1923). It was not too difficult to go to Puetzgen, a village in the neighborhood of Bonn, where the author of the classic, *Spirit of the Liturgy,* was stationed as chaplain of a Sacre Coeur Institute. Here, in a small room with a few chairs, a desk and a couch (on which I slept when the conversation lasted into the night or in the early morning), I became aware of what real knowledge means, knowledge which is based upon participation in realities and which cannot be obtained by an accumulation of facts or by skilful handling of concepts.

But even greater was the influence of Max Scheler who in these years as professor of philosophy in Cologne reached the apex of his Catholic period. He taught me to be always curious about the ramifications of phenomena and he showed what depths can be discovered by a combination of psychological, social and metaphysical analysis. I was fascinated by the strange union in his lectures between an almost childish naivete and an overlucid rationality.

In 1923 I took my Ph.D. under him. After a short period in the editorial offices of the Catholic newspaper, *Koelnische Volkszeitung,* I settled down as a writer and lecturer. I lived in Bad Godesberg, known today the world over as the place where Hitler received the Prime Minister of the Appeasement, Chamberlain.

In 1924 I married Edith Schwarzer, a young teacher and Catholic Youth Movement girl, whom I met in Breslau. A daughter, Joan, was born to us in 1926; she has not inherited my interest in social sciences and history, but is an enthusiastic student of biology and mathematics.

In 1929 I published my first book. It dealt with the political and social ideas of French Catholicism from 1789 to 1914. (I hope sometime to return to my studies on Lamennais from which it originated.) In 1931 an analysis of the Action Francaise and Charles Maurras followed. In the same year I had the honor of speaking in Salzburg (Austria) before the Catholic Academic Association on the mission of the publicist. I also gave lectures at the Hochschule fuer Politik in Berlin. Dr. Keckeis, at that time the leading spirit of the great Catholic publishing house of Herder, gave me an opportunity to write my book, *Bolshevism, Theory and Practice,* and, in addition, an investigation of German nationalism.

I left Germany for Switzerland in 1934, more than a year after Hitler's rise to power. We decided to live in Buchrain, a village in the vicinity of Lucerne on the beautiful Vierwaldstaetter

Lake. Those were happy days in the great forests where I could spend many hours looking for mushrooms. Together with a Bavarian editor and writer, Otto Michael (who is now in Portland, Oregon, dividing his time between Catholic Action and Henry Kaiser's shipyards), I published a news service devoted to the religious and intellectual situation in Nazi Germany. We were accused of being too pessimistic—in reality we were not pessimistic enough. During my Swiss years (1934–1937), I wrote three books: *The Future of Bolshevism, Hitler and the Christians,* and *The Rise and Decline of Marxism;* and I translated Maritain's *Integral Humanism* into German.

In 1937 Father (now Bishop) O'Hara, C.S.C., invited me to the University of Notre Dame where, since the fall of that year, I have taught political science. In 1943 I became an American citizen. I like my work at Notre Dame, a peaceful center of Catholic and American education, where all the conflicts and storms of the world calm down and assume a distant character and a certain perspective; where I have met interesting and kind colleagues; where I enjoy dealing with the fresh minds of students, eager to learn; where the administration, now headed by Father Hugh O'Donnell, C.S.C., has entrusted to me *The Review of Politics,* which was founded in 1938. I hope to continue to contribute to the development of the Graduate School, the direction of which is in the hands of Father Phillip Moore, C.S.C. A walk through the beautiful campus takes me to nearby St. Mary's College, where Sister Madeleva's students have proved to me that young ladies are also interested in politics.

It is too early to discuss my American friends. I have too many and I am winning more and more. But I wish to mention three Europeans who represent important aspects of contemporary civilization and of the Catholic world.

For years I have known Jacques Maritain. I have met him in Paris and Cologne, in Rome and Geneva, and more recently in New York and Chicago. I hope that I will see him and Madame Maritain again in their house at Meudon. Maritain is great not only because he is a philosopher and a man interested in all the aspects of life,—like Max Scheler, but in a less playful way—but he is also a humble man, always eager to understand and to help, for whom there are no unimportant or insignificant persons. Every human soul has to him—and not just in theory—an infinite value. His courage has made him enemies. But, I am sure, the intrigues and often indirect attacks of petty minds and jealous competitors will be forgotten, whereas the works and the personal influence of Maritain will live on.

My Swiss friend, Father Otto Karrer, the author of *Religions of Mankind,* is very different from the French Thomist. He reveals his long training in the excellent schools of the Society of Jesus. He is but slightly interested in philosophy. He is interested in the life and the development of the Christian soul. He could have become, if he had cared to, the German counterpart of Abbé Bremond, the great student of French piety. His own character has been described by his beloved Master Eckehart, who said seven centuries ago: "Even if I were in the highest ecstasy, and a poor man were to ask me for a bowl of soup, I would give it to him at once."

And I remember Carl Schmitt, the brilliant German jurist, who became a typical representative of a nihilism, which made the rise of nazism possible; without an understanding of his mentality, the negative demonic depths of Hitler's movement remain unintelligible. A strong mind, mastering fully the arts of dialectics, he knew everything from Shakespeare to Laski, from the Bestarium to the German Romantics and Bakunin, from the decisions of the Supreme Court to the lyrics of Baudelaire and Daeubler. But he did not take anything seriously except his ambition. The Catholic faith was used by him only as a means, as an occasion for a display of startling paradoxes in order to provoke and to puzzle liberals.

My work has been devoted to the understanding of the modern secularization which reached its peak in the totalitarian regimes and religions of the twentieth century. It is my belief that politics cannot be understood by a specialized technical approach. Theology and history are necessary; the history and development of the Church help to open wide before men's eyes the most distant horizons. It is my aim to show also that even in the struggles of the day the door leading to eternity can be found. But this *sub specie aeternitatis* cannot be obtained by memorizing, by an attitude which despises or pities those who are going in wrong directions, or by a smiling sentimentality which does not sense the power of evil forces and which confuses love with gullibility. We must make distinctions before we can see the true unity.

EDITOR'S NOTE: Mr. Gurian, who incidentally is a convert, is the author of *Bolshevism: Theory and Practice*, 1933, Sheed; *The Future of Bolshevism*, 1936, id.; *The Rise and Decline of Marxism*, 1939, Burns, Oates; *Hitler and the Christians*, 1936, Sheed.

OSKAR HALECKI
Historian

THIRTY YEARS AGO, in 1915, I published as a young man of twenty-five my first three books. Containing almost a thousand pages, they appeared simultaneously, after a dozen contributions to various historical journals. Such "mass production" was possible thanks to the ideal atmosphere which a research worker could enjoy, even during World War I, in our dear old Cracow and its Jagellonian University, where I had graduated with a Ph.D. two years before, and started to lecture in the spring of 1916.

My field was then almost exclusively Polish history. In a Poland awaiting liberation, but being still under foreign rule, the history of our past, especially of our days of greatness, was for me like for so many others, an escape from reality and a guarantee of a better future. For different reasons, partly suggested by my teachers, chiefly Professor W. Sobieski (to whom I owe a special gratitude), I studied with particular enthusiasm Poland's relations with Lithuania and Ruthenia, the "Jagellonian Union," and wrote the history of that great experiment in federalism, from 1385 to 1569, in two large volumes published by the Polish Academy a few years later.

I considered them only an introduction to a comprehensive history of the whole Jagellonian period, a work which I planned in detail, dreaming of a series of eighteen (!) volumes, and which always remained the aim of my scholarly ambition. Unfortunately, I have never again found the conditions which so greatly facilitated my exclusive devotion to pure research in those early days of my academic career.

It was one of the happiest days of my life when, at the very moment of Poland's resurrection, in the fall of 1918, I was invited to occupy the chair of Eastern European History in the reorganized University of Warsaw. Very soon, however, our activities in that rapidly growing school were interrupted by the danger threatening the restored Republic from the east and by the general concern with political problems. I was appointed Secretary General of a Committee of experts which joined the Polish Delegation at the Peace Conference and remained in Paris until the signing of the Versailles Treaty.

That thrilling experience deeply influenced my whole future. I abandoned my ivory tower of scholarship, and although I never became interested in internal party politics, I was attracted by the contemporary problems of international relations. It was especially the League of Nations which became another object of my unlimited enthusiasm, and on my return to Warsaw, after having written a book about the new institution, I organized the Polish League of Nations Union and participated in some of the earliest meetings of both the international federation of such societies and the official Assembly at Geneva.

It was, therefore, with great pleasure that I accepted the appointment in 1921 as a member of the League of Nations Secretariate where I worked for three years, on leave from my University. I was entrusted with the task of organizing the League's Committee on Intellectual Co-operation, a task which meant not only the drafting of numerous reports, but also the rare privilege of meeting some of the greatest minds of our times:

Henri Bergson and Madame Curie, Gilbert Murray and Francesco Ruffini, Lorentz and Einstein. Also my first contacts with American scholars and educators, which had begun at the Peace Conference, were now developed, thanks to meetings with Robert A. Millikan, James T. Shotwell, Waldo G. Leland, Stephen P. Duggan, Henry N. MacCracken, and many others. All these relations were continued when I spent another year in Paris as chief of the University Section in the League's Institute on Intellectual Co-operation and later served on its various Commissions which promoted international co-operation between the universities. I particularly enjoyed presiding over the annual meetings of the delegates of international students' associations for ten years.

Working in the international field, I realized, better than ever before, the universal significance of Catholicism. I had always been a believing and practicing Catholic, deeply convinced that only by applying Christian principles to all human relations, could a better world order be established. But it was a great encouragement to find among the intellectual leaders of all countries so many personalities sharing the same conviction, and ready to co-operate. Besides the "Pax Romana" movement of the younger generation, I found them chiefly in the "Union catholique d'Etudes internationales," a group organized in Fribourg, Switzerland, soon after the war.

The distinguished Swiss writer, Gonzague de Reynold, who a few years later became president of that Union, was also one of the most active members of the Committee on Intellectual Co-operation; and two French priests, Monsignor Eugene Beaupin and Father Yves de la Briere, S.J., particularly impressed me when I met them at the first meetings of the group. I shall never forget the friendly relations I had with them through many years.

Stimulated by these experiences, I also participated more and more in the Catholic Action which between the two wars so successfully developed in my own country. I was, of course, chiefly interested in the youth movement and in the co-operation of Catholic writers whose national association I presided over for several years. A specific problem which attracted me, both as a Catholic and as a scholar, was the program for furthering the cause for the canonization of our great queen Jadwiga, who seemed to me to be the most inspiring symbol of our religious and patriotic tradition. In speaking and in writing, I have discussed no subject more frequently. Among the many members of the Polish clergy with whom I had the privilege of co-operating in this and in other matters, at least Father Jan Rostworowski, S.J., ought to be mentioned.

My growing concern with international and Catholic issues could not but influence the orientation of my historical research. One of the principal results was the publication, in 1930, of my book *Un Empereur de Byzance à Rome,* which described twenty years (1355–1375) of relations between Byzantium and the Papacy, in connection with plans for re-uniting the Western and Eastern Churches and organizing a league against the Turks. Based upon materials collected in the archives of the Vatican and of Venice, the story was continued, seven years later, in my monograph *Rome et Byzance au temps du grand schisme d'Occident.*

In the field of Polish history, the necessity of a synthetic treatment of the chief problems was so strongly felt in the years between the two wars, that, postponing my personal plans, I had to contribute to two encyclopedic outlines, describing the reigns of Casimir the Great and those of Sigismund I and Sigismund Augustus in a political history of Poland, edited by our Academy, and the period of the Jagellonian dynasty, in another collective publication. I also tried to give an interpretation of our whole past, up to 1914. This work, published in French in 1933, was soon afterwards translated into Finnish, and, with an additional section covering the last thirty years, was published in English by Roy in 1943.

Many special questions which engaged my interest during this period of my life, as for instance, the fascinating problems of the philosophy of history, the origin of French-Polish relations, the cultural trends in Poland's eastern borderlands, etc., were approached in well over a hundred articles which, in addition to minor contributions, I scattered in the periodicals of various countries. I have never attempted to collect any of them in book form, and often did not even secure reprints, because most of my time was taken up with extensive teaching obligations. But I certainly do not regret that. It is with pleasure that I remember the years when I had about a hundred students working in my various seminars, and when I had particularly large classes in the School of Political Science, in addition to those at the University. And I was proud to see four of my former students among the members of our teaching staff, while several others awaited their appointments. Only one of them is safe today.

What I had no time to write, I tried at least to summarize in countless lectures, in Poland and abroad. Many of these were delivered at international congresses. The congresses of historical sciences will remain a particularly pleasant recollection, especially as the Polish delegation was always headed by Professor B. Dembinski, the most charming gentleman I have ever met and who, although much older, honored me with his friendship.

Congresses and individual lecture engagements involved a great deal of travelling. Most frequently I went to France, to Switzerland, and to Austria where I like to participate in the International Catholic Summer School of Salzburg. A particularly valuable experience were my visiting lectures at the University of Cambridge, in 1935, followed by the Anglo-Polish historical conference which planned the *Cambridge History of Poland,* and by a lecture in Dublin where I had been before on the occasion of the International Eucharistic Congress. I also was extremely interested by my first visits in Sweden, where I spoke in 1937 at Stockholm, Upsala and Lund, as well as in Greece, in the last spring before the World War II, when my lectures at the University of Athens were combined with excursions to the Byzantine monuments of Mistra and Hosios Lukas, I also remember the beauty of Budapest where we inaugurated in the same spring a Polish Institute, connected with the University.

Nothing, however, could be compared with my first lecture tour in America, admirably organized in the fall of 1938 by the Kosciuszko Foundation. It took me to twenty Universities and Colleges of the United States in ten weeks and proved an extremely helpful experience when less than two years later I came again to this country—as an exile.

Both my private life, omitted in this sketch, and my public activities were cut into two entirely different parts by the fateful date of September 1, 1939. That happened, of course, to all Poles. If I escaped the worst, the ordeal which most of my colleagues had to suffer, it was because the outbreak of the war found me in Switzerland where I had attended a Catholic educational congress at Fribourg. With my wife, I reached Paris and after the invasion of France—thanks again to the Kosciuszko Foundation—the United States. We have lost everything else, and in saying so, I am not referring to material losses, but to all that we loved here on earth.

Fortunately, I was and am very busy during this second World War. During the Paris year, I organized there the Polish University in Exile, taught at the Sorbonne, and edited a review, called *La Voix de Varsovie*. In this country, I was first visiting professor of history at Vassar College, for two years, and then, in May, 1942, became director of the newly created Polish Institute of Arts and Sciences in America. Lecture engagements brought me as far as California. Since 1944, I am also professor of Eastern European History at Fordham University where I teach regularly in the Graduate School, and professor of Slavic History in the University of Montreal, where I go every month for a few lectures. And I write articles, even plan books, as usual. . . .

Everything, however, is so different from what it had been. I certainly love this country and I am grateful to be here, with so many opportunities to do some work which I hope to be useful. But what is happening and going to happen to my own country, undoubtedly the main victim of the war and probably the main victim of peace? Its brief period of freedom, with all its short-

comings, seems to me today a lost paradise. What is threatening
Poland, is so much worse than what I experienced in the years of
my youth, before our liberation. All that remains is the memory
of our past and the Faith which inspired it during a thousand
years.

EDITOR'S NOTE: Dr. Halecki's books include *A History of Poland*, 1943, Roy;
and *The Crusade of Varna*, 1943, Polish Institute.

ROSS J. S. HOFFMAN

MY FIRST PUBLISHED WORDS were fruits of a misspent youth. In 1917, when I was nearly sixteen, the draft decimated the newspaper staffs of my home city, Harrisburg, Pa., and I got a job as a reporter. Within a year I was sports editor, and when I was seventeen I had made the acquaintance of Strangler Lewis, Benny Leonard, Doc Roller, Stanislaus Zbysko, Jack Dempsey, and other great men. I had even interviewed a Democratic candidate for the Presidency, James M. Cox of Ohio. I smoked cigars, drank beer (this began with national prohibition) and thrilled at the sight of my own name over signed articles about the sporting world,—until this last pleasure was taken away by an order that came up from the business office one day with an explanation that it was hurting the paper's circulation. I quit that job to go to college, and although I covered the games for the papers during the next four years my career as a newspaperman had terminated. Its best fruits were the money I earned. Among the bad ones were a habit of writing fast and carelessly, a great love for seeing my own words in print, and a preference for small tasks that can be finished in a day rather than big ones requiring time, pains and the cardinal virtue of patience.

I do not know whether it was good or bad that being a sports writer in early youth emptied me of all that interest. Since the day I wrote my last play-by-play football story I have never witnessed any great sporting event without yawning or cared two pins which side won a championship game. I like sports,—if I can get into the game myself and with a chance to win,—and I believe in their moral value,—especially if they are dangerous to the whole skin; but I do not care much for watching them, and I cannot bear reading about them. It is my belief that sport, not religion, has been the 'opiate of the people' in the last twenty years. Abroad and at home sport has virtually ceased to be sporting; it has been commercialized, politicized, totalitarianized, and even raised to the level of a religion: the cult of physical culture, an abominable and soul-killing heresy. In my opinion carousing in a tavern is far less bad for young men than this sober new puritanism of "keeping fit." Mussolini and Hitler have been its outstanding apostles, and my hope is that whatever happens to "democracy" the war may vindicate the Churchillian cigar, whisky, and roast beef, over pagan teetotalism, vegetarianism and chest-expansion. Otherwise, civilization is doomed.

But to return to my story, I veritably wrote my way through college. I did not write well, but I wrote easily, having a glib and facile articulation that won me much better marks than I deserved. I joined the staff of the college paper and became its editor-in-chief, in which capacity I wrote on every subject under the sun, since campus affairs were too provincial for my spirit. I discovered that it was easier and much more satisfying to the ego to attack things than to praise them, and so I attacked the Treaty of Versailles, the National Administration, the Presbyterian Church (which supposedly ruled the college), Protestantism, Catholicism, capitalism, the Republican Party, and other members of the sinister conspiracy for blocking the advent of a brave new age. So did I gain campus stature as a serious thinker, and

in the general post-war deterioration of college studies I was able
to graduate with highest honors. At that time I may very well
have written more than I had read.

After college I went to Germany, which seemed the fountain-
head of all the most progressive new doctrines. I hoped to stay in
Europe indefinitely and become a famous international journalist. An obscure instinct took me straight to Munich which, if not
the terrestrial residence of His Satanic Majesty Himself, was certainly the contemporary headquarters of some of his ablest lieu-
tenants; for Adolf Hitler, General Haushofer, and Oswald Speng-
ler were all there and each doing his bit for the "revolution of
nihilism." It was 1923 and readers of Lion Feuchtwanger will
remember something of the spiritual abyss which was Munich
after the last war: that awful emptiness preceding diabolic possession. Munich was like Hitler's face in repose. But of course
a twenty-one-year-old fresh from an American campus knew nothing of these mysterious imponderables. I neither met the devil
nor suspected his presence. Instead—and I count it providential
—I saw for the first time in my life that tiny tabernacle which is a
very special dwelling place of God.

One day I went down to Oberammergau and fell in with a
young ex-lieutenant of the Prussian army. He had a knapsack on
his back and was on a holiday *bummel*. Together we tramped
through the valley to Ettal, where the Benedictines have been
since Lewis IV founded the cloister in the fourteenth century.
Faithful to the rule of their sainted legislator, the monks received
us as if we were Our Lord Himself. We spent the day there and
I was nothing short of spell-bound, for I had never before been
in the presence of the Blessed Sacrament. We made our way
back to Oberammergau in the cold Alpine night, and I do not
remember that we talked of Ettal. Rather we discussed the
Treaty of Versailles and how to get back on the road which we
lost for a little while in the darkness. But that day there had
been sewn in me a tiny seed of curiosity about grave and high
matters: a seed that lay apparently sterile for yet some years, but
eventually burgeoned and grew.

During much of 1923 I roamed over Germany, studying "conditions," watching the mark depreciate until you could buy more than four trillion for one of my American dollars. But since even these could not last forever, and since my efforts to earn money by writing articles for the American press were completely unsuccessful (they netted just fifteen dollars which I had to go home to collect) I had to leave the country. I went to Paris—it was the day Hitler tried his *Putsch* at Munich—and then to London and home. As an international journalist I could not have been a more complete failure. But I had profited somewhat by the disagreeable discovery that I was an ignoramus. So I went to graduate school and eventually became a doctor of philosophy in history.

To gain that dubious honor I had to write a book and go back to Europe several times to get material for it. The resulting volume was *Great Britain and the German Trade Rivalry, 1875–1914,* which, by a lucky break, was judged good enough to win a prize from the American Historical Association. To write that book I read five thousand consular reports, handled about ten tons of newspapers and magazines, and during five years choked in the dust that collects on Parliamentary Papers. I could easily have become an economist or a statistician after such great labors, and I know that I disappointed many well-wishing friends by not going on as an "economic" historian. But these studies—and I strongly recommend them for precisely this reason—taught me that economics do not explain man, but man explains economics. If they do not feed the soul richly, they may awaken its hungers. I found that Chesterton was never so refreshing as after a day spent with *Statistische Jahrbucher fur das deutsche Reich,* and that Belloc taken with consular reports from Muscat and Johannesburg gives a balanced diet for the mind. I discovered Newman, Karl Adam, Dawson, Maritain and other expositors of the great truths. I began to go to Mass with my wise Catholic wife. I even began to suspect the existence of God, and presently I found myself a Catholic even before I was a Ph.D. This is not the place for spiritual autobiography, but whoever is interested in mine can read it in *Restoration,* which Frank Sheed published in 1934. It is a piece of historical apologetics written in the convert's flush of enthusiasm. The book was well received, but I have sometimes regretted writing it because it created false impressions of me as a man more interested in religion than in politics, economics and diplomacy. I had merely found a great reality and felt the need to report the fact; after that I went back to history, even sometimes to economic history.

Now the history of the modern state became a more and more commanding interest, and after composing some essays for the *American Review,* I put them together for my third book, *The Will to Freedom,* which appeared in 1935. The next year I went to Rome and there I thought of everything I had ever known, in the light of the great truth that civil and social progress is only achieved when men illuminate practical reason with wisdom drawn from the past. From these speculations came my essays in *Tradition and Progress,* which were published in 1938. The crisis in democratic politics, the fierce controversy over Fascism, and the coming of the war inspired my *Organic State* (1939), a book which offended and, I think, even disgusted many persons who interpreted it as pro-Italian and anti-democratic. I shall always protest the injustice of this view, for I strove to be as objective as Belloc in *The Servile State* or as Machiavelli in *The Prince;* which books, by the way, I strongly recommend as models to all who would study and write of great social and political matters.

As the war became global, my mind, like so many others, has been engrossed by the great problems of how and why the nations have been unable to make and keep the peace. What are nations and what is international community? Why did the League collapse? What prospers, what hurts the well-being of international society? I sought answers to these questions in my *Great Republic* (1942), a book in which I tried to examine the world's state-system in the spirit of Burke regarding political society or Newman contemplating the Church. I tried hard for clarity, but many seem to find the book obscure, and I wish I had taken a longer time to write clearer explanations. But even as the book stands, I think it is my best. Before it was published I engaged with the Oxford University Press to write a history of *The Origins and Background of the Second World War,* in collaboration with my friend, Professor C. G. Haines. We completed that formidable undertaking and our book was offered to the public in the spring of 1943.

And in 1944 appeared my study in American national policy entitled *Durable Peace.*

That brings an uneventful story down to the present date. I was forty-three this year (1945), and I hope to go on being a professor who occasionally writes a book, not for hire but as a by-product of his work and reflections; for only so, I do believe, should books be written,—unless, of course, they are books of fiction or poetry. But such mysteries belong to other crafts than mine.

EDITOR'S NOTE: Dr. Hoffman, who was born in Harrisburg, Pa., on February 2, 1902, lives in Rye, New York, and is a professor of European History at Fordham University. His books include *Great Britain and the German Trade Rivalry, 1875–1914,* 1933, Univ. of Pa. Press; *Restoration,* 1934, Sheed; *The Will to Freedom,* 1935, Sheed; *The Organic State,* 1939, Sheed; *Tradition and Progress,* 1938, Bruce; *The Great Republic,* 1942, Sheed; *The Origins and Backgrounds of the Second World War* (with C. G. Haines), 1943, Oxford Univ. Press; *Durable Peace,* 1944, Oxford Univ. Press.

REVEREND ROBERT EMMET HOLLAND, S.J.

I WAS BORN February 21, 1892, at Olympia, Washington, not of Indian but of American-Irish parents, Joseph Lee and Annie Ellen Kelliher Holland, who had first met at a hand-composition frame in a newspaper and job printing office. I came by my inky fingers quite naturally. Elementary schooling was first in the Public School, but after there was room for more children in St. Aloysius School, Washington, D. C., I finished there, and began high school at Gonzaga High School.

I was admitted to the Society of Jesus, August 14, 1908, at St. Andrew-on-Hudson, Poughkeepsie, N. Y., where after the novitiate I completed my classical studies, and went on to science and philosophy, at Woodstock College, Woodstock, Maryland; there also I had my theological studies; and was ordained priest, June 28, 1923, at Dahlgren Chapel, Georgetown University.

At various times I have been instructor in classics and in English Literature at Boston College High School; Canisius High School, Buffalo—where I also was Principal; at St. Joseph's High

School, Philadelphia. For a short time I was missionary in the Philippine Islands. Presently I am Director of Fordham University Press; a member of the American Institute of Graphic Arts; Chairman of the Publishers and Publishing Committee of the Institute of Social Order. That brings me up to date.

My first discovery of the desire to become a writer was made when one of my teachers in High School praised a weekly composition in English. All I remember of it now was that a boy and a girl stood chatting one summer evening at the gate. I have had the good fortune to *like* to write, and to have been undismayed by the drudgery I soon found that serious and ambitious writing imposes. No number of rejection slips kept me from continuing to try, for whether I was published or not, I enjoyed what I did.

The first book was a brave attempt to be a biographer; it was the *Life of Saint John Francis Regis, S.J.* Father Kavanagh, of Notre Dame University, wrote a syndicated review, which was honest, and to me too painfully so. I was labeled "not a skilful bookmaker," but I went on making them anyhow—another kind.

While teaching at Boston College High School, I found an unusual group of American-boy characters. These went into a series of juveniles: *Reardon Rah!; Dan's Best Enemy;* and *Dan's Worst Friend.* The late Father Francis J. Finn, S.J., did me the honor to read the first of these in manuscript. The electric light failed him, so he lit a candle and finished the story at one sitting. These juveniles were well received; after twenty years they are still in print.

I consider my most valuable work with the pen to be *The Song of Tekakwitha.* Certainly it is my most ambitious undertaking. It is the life of Venerable Kateri Tekakwitha in the verse-form of *The Song of Hiawatha.* It came in its first inspiration as if leaping at me out of an obscure footnote in the copy-pages of that monumental work I was preparing for press, in 1938: *The Positio of the Historical Section of the Sacred Congregation of Rites, on the Introduction of the Cause for Beatification and Canonization, and on the Virtues of the Servant of God, Katharine Tekakwitha.* There I read the fact, so well known to every American school child, that the Iroquois Nation had been celebrated in the poem of Henry Wadsworth Longfellow, *The Song of Hiawatha.*

This was the beginning of my hardihood to do for the real heroine of our American forest, what Longfellow had done for his Indian youth of legendary prowess. The poem is 3860 lines. It has been well received through two printings. Parts of *The Song of Tekakwitha* were set to choral and solo sequence, by Sister M. Edwina, O.S.B., of the College of St. Scholastica, Duluth, Minnesota. This music has been performed in Duluth and Chicago.

My editorial work on *The Positio* and my writing of *The Song of Tekakwitha* were explained to the present-day brethren of Kateri Tekakwitha, who live at Caughnawaga, Province of Quebec. With an imagination characteristic of the American Indian, these modern Mohawks admitted me as an honorary chieftain of the tribe, and named me Ronwasennowanatha—"One who causes her name to be considered great."

EDITOR'S NOTE: Father Holland's editorial acumen and his knowledge of and taste in the graphic arts are largely responsible for the prestige of Fordham University Press among the university presses of the country. His own writings include the juveniles *Reardon Rah!*, 1923, *Dan's Best Enemy*, 1924, and *Dan's Worst Friend*, 1928, all published by Benziger; *Life of St. John Francis Regis of the Society of Jesus*, 1922, Loyola Univ. Press; *The Song of Tekakwitha*, 1942, Fordham Univ. Press. The Music for *The Song* is published by the Paul A. Schmitt Music Company.

ERIK M. RITTER VON KUEHNELT-LEDDIHN

I WAS BORN on July 31 in a small Styrian resort. The fact that I saw the light of day on the feast of St. Ignatius seemed to have had a certain effect on all my future life because, although remaining a layman, the Society of Jesus had always a major influence on my destiny. Physically and spiritually.

The years of my elementary school I spent in a medium sized town not far from Vienna. Baden—this the name of the city—was the G.H.Q. of the Austro-Hungarian Army during the First World War and I still remember the many illustrious persons, generals and diplomats, who came as "guests" to the house of my parents. The word "guests" has to be put in quotation marks because our hospitality was limited by the food situation. Better than our social life I remember the hunger of 1918 and 1919. The fainting of children in our school was almost a daily occurrence. Many of them had swollen bellies from malnutrition. Three or four times a month we feasted on horse meat. These meats were high-lights in our desolation.

Yet there was in our family and in our country a remarkable lack of hatred for the enemy. Our education was French and we had a French governess; my "Sunday's best" was a British sailor uniform with a cap bearing the inscription "H. M. S. Renown."

The years after the war were darkened by the complete dismemberment of our country which presaged a gloomy future for the whole coming generation. My father who had risked his life in pioneering work in the field of X-ray research lost his leg. He succumbed finally on Christmas day 1932 to his ever aggravating ailment. He was a very devout Catholic with an almost complete contempt for science, including medical science. He was acutely conscious of the fact that his work was only conducive to the salvation of bodies but not of souls. Yet in spite of his illness he was one of the most humorous men I have ever seen. Rarely he spoke a serious word.

In 1919 I passed the entrance examination for a "Gymnasium," a combination high school and college which puts the main stress on Classic languages, history and literature, not on gymnastics as the reader may be tempted to believe. The survival rate in this type of school is extremely low. After four years of calamitous studies in Baden with more conditional examinations than hair on my head I was put as a punitive measure in a boarding school in Vienna—the Theresianic Academy. There I learned a great deal, but I loathed the place, from which also the late General of the Jesuits, Wlodzimierz Ledochowski, had graduated. The spirit of this school, although religious instruction was given, as in all other state-schools, was pagan, collectivistic and authoritarian. My spirit of opposition drove me straight into the arms of the Church.

At the age of ten I visited Denmark, at the age of twelve I spent my first summer in England. At the age of sixteen I wrote and published my first article; more than that—I became Vienna Correspondent of the *London Spectator,* a highly respectable British weekly which I kept successfully in the dark about my age. Soon I had visiting cards printed with my name and my "official position." I used these to accompany my various articles which I turned out in great numbers. Many of these were accepted and I felt immensely proud.

At the age of fourteen I had joined a political group of Catholic tendencies. Politics colored all my adolescence. I graduated with a B.A. at the normal age of seventeen. At that time I studied Hungarian assiduously and added Japanese and Russian to my schedule. (I practised Japanese with the Nipponese Military Attaché in Vienna—Tomoyuki Yamashita, the conqueror of Singapore and Bataan). I already then planned to study in Budapest, the Hungarian capital, because Vienna, the dying Queen of the Danube, bored me not a little.

I started my graduate studies at the University of Vienna but continued them in Hungary. My university years were crammed with travels since physical attendance is not required in our graduate schools. As my parents disagreed with my desire to live in Hungary I had to live there on my own. It almost ended in a catastrophe; for weeks I starved on bread and water. At last I managed to get a contract from a newspaper and at the age of twenty I went as the first Hungarian reporter to Russia; I was just beginning to write in Magyar with greater fluency. At that time I had also finished my first novel (about the Balkans and Eastern Europe) which I published under a pseudonym in Vienna.

From now on I led a truly adventurous life. I took abode in one European country after the other, worked on a novel or an article, dashed back to Budapest for my examinations, climbed mountains, conversed with political conspirators, statesmen, hoboes, peasants and scholars. I spent almost a year in Lapland, but Helsingfors, London, Sofia and Corfu must also be mentioned as my "headquarters." I neglected naturally my studies and when I received my M.A. in 1934 I was almost three years behind schedule, but even before taking the doctor's degree in Budapest I started to study theology at the University of Vienna. (There is to my great sorrow only one place in the United States where I could complete this study as a layman). I wrote then also successively *Gates of Hell* and *Night Over the East*.* Of a trilogy on

* The American edition does not bear my name; it was totally cut and emasculated.

the devil (*In the shadow of Satan*) only the third volume (*Moscow 1979*) was published in English.

National-Socialism in Germany made my "literary" work increasingly impossible.   Since Austrian publishers depend almost wholly on the German market this attitude of the *Reichsschrifttumkammer* was a severe blow for me.   The *Gates of Hell* was confiscated, released and again confiscated.   *Night Over the East* on the other hand was available for three years until the final blow fell.   These journalistic novels have a certain documentary value, but little else.   They found their way to this country as well as to England in translations.

I had to look for other financial resources and took up teaching for one year in an English college.   Before going to the United States I took my Ph.D. and thus became a Hungarian "academic citizen."   From 1937 till 1938 I taught Geopolitics in Georgetown University.   I led then the existence of a commuter between this country and Europe.   On the first of these trips I married an Austrian to whom I had been previously engaged.   My wife has been to me a faithful and patient collaborator and a painstaking translator.   Her English is infinitely superior to mine and the transformation of *Moscow 1979* into its published form is almost entirely her work.

The war put an end to our commuting and separated us from our small boy, born on a trip to Europe.   I had, in the meantime, changed from Georgetown to St. Peter's College, Jersey City, where I still act as a Chairman in the Department of History and Sociology.   We then started to explore the United States.   Every summer we toured at least 14,000 miles with the result that we know God's Own Country better than most Americans.   My collection of colored slides has grown to an impressive size and the groundwork for a *magnum opus* on the American West has been laid.   Once the war is over and we have returned to our native land we will make an honest effort to acquaint Europeans with the real America which, after all, is quite different from the picture which has been presented to us by the movies.

My literary activities have now been suspended entirely.   Catholic literature has undoubtedly a great future in the English speaking world but the present outlook is still rather grim. Most Catholic publishers and a considerable section of the Catholic public suffer from puritanical and Jansenistic inhibitions, and oppose bitterly any attempt of a fuller representation of life. Non-Catholic publishers, on the other hand, are very reluctant towards the publication of Catholic literature, except in the case of authors who have earned an initial success prior to their conversions. (The Catholic masses, one must admit, view these authors with unreasonable suspicion, so that we can speak about Catholic authors read by an agnostic public and a Catholic public reading Puritan authors). The reluctance of secular newspapers to review books of Catholic publishers who are not among the big advertisers as well as the tendency of Catholic newspapers to praise Catholic literary productions almost indiscriminately have aggravated the situation.

Another major difficulty lies in the field of language and thought. My immature works written at the very beginning of the third decade of my life could easily find a reading public in this country. Now I become more and more "untranslatable." Few Central and East-European writers have adapted themselves to the Anglo-Saxon mind; their very trend of thought is extremely alien. Even the common ground of our Faith can hardly over-bridge the considerable abyss between two very different cultures.

Of my own, even more mature work, I have a rather low opinion. But I regret that very much material from the European Continent does not find its way to this country. Some of these works could be translated and marketed without a financial loss. I myself cannot do much else in the meantime but wait. *Ego dormio sed cor meum vigilat.*

EDITOR'S NOTE: Mr. Kuehnelt-Leddihn's books include *Gates of Hell*, 1935, Sheed; *Night Over the East*, 1936, id.; and *Moscow 1979*, 1940, id.

MICHAEL DE LA BEDOYERE

I PASS OVER details of birth, parentage and early life, as being of no interest except to myself, mentioning only that my French name does not make me French, for by blood I am three-quarters English and only know France through short holiday visits.

My education was very thoroughly Jesuit, including two Jesuit schools and a period in the Society itself. That was brought to an end for diverse reasons, but one at least included the contact with a great University, namely Oxford, where I studied and succeeded under the Jesuit mantle in the form of Campion Hall, a residence of the Society for its own students.

Nothing could have been pleasanter than the Jesuit life, and to it I owe any good habits I may possess—chiefly the habit of never being happy unless I am thinking fairly hard. Equally I have never regretted leaving the Society for its mental discipline would have suffocated me. (In any case, it became quite obvious to my superiors and myself that I might, with luck, make a moderate Catholic layman, but must certainly make a very highly-strung and impossible priest. The more elbow-room I am given, the straighter my course! Reading over that last sentence, it strikes me that it might be taken as a criticism of the Society. It is not. It is a criticism of myself. My admiration and love for the Society are unbounded, and I am never so happy as when paying a visit to a Jesuit house or college).

One of the troubles of beginning an ecclesiastical career and giving it up in mid-course is that you are thrown on the world at an awkward age when most of the buses that lead to a career have been irretrievably missed. Many such find a refuge in school-mastering. I was luckier at first because my academic qualifications enabled me to obtain a post in the University of Minnesota where I taught logic and moral philosophy to large numbers of men and women who were convinced that a course of logic would somehow enable them to make money more easily, while philosophy had all the attraction of divination and astrology! I got a little tired of disabusing them, but domestic reasons, rather than philosophic ones, made it necessary for me to return to England.

At this point I was grateful to the capitalistic system (which I have since ungratefully criticised) for enabling me to have a private income of modest dimensions. However, with an increasing family it had to be augmented. The simplest way—and the most comfortable—was to sit at home and write. I had already made my debut in this art with a small volume called *The Drift of Democracy*. It earned me about a hundred dollars and ·sold about a thousand copies. I realised perfectly well that to earn your living by writing you had to choose a fashionable subject and have a stroke of luck. At the time one of the fashionable crazes was for slick, debunking biography. I looked for a possible subject in a biographical dictionary and settled on Lafayette. His life was not well known in England. He lived through four revolutions in the most fascinating of periods of history. He was a father of liberalism. He was brought up a Catholic. His American adventure appealed to me on my return from America. In nine months I had completed a full-length biography, of which I had, however, little hope, if only because it was too seriously treated. However, to my great surprise, it was taken by the first publisher to whom I sent it and very widely praised in the press— being compared, as a companion volume, with Duff Cooper's best-selling *Talleyrand*. But someone made a mistake, because it never caught on. However, it earned me a commission from another publisher to rewrite the life of George Washington from a British point of view. This went better and was even more widely praised (being published in the silly season when reviewers were glad of an opportunity of airing their views on history— some of the more popular papers even made a headline of my debunking the lie-and-little-hatchet story!). Still, at that rate, I should have to write about four biographies a year to earn a schoolmaster's salary! I was asked to follow up with a life of George III. Someone must have overheard my publisher's original suggestion, for, before I had finished, lives of George III were popping up like sparrows at feeding-time. My labours resulted only in my being able to write a crushing review of the efforts of one of my competitors.

However, my writing efforts turned out not to be in vain, for the late Charles Diamond came across my *Drift of Democracy* and liked it well enough to ask me to contribute regularly for his newspaper, *The Catholic Herald*. From this piece of luck my career, such as it is, really began. (Two other jobs were then occupying me. I was asked to contribute 60,000 words to a big six-volume *History of European Civilization* for which I was paid more heavily than for all the rest of my writings put together. It turned out to be quite the worst effort of my writing life. Some parts I can't even understand now! The other was assisting my uncle, the late Algar Thorold, in his editing of the *Dublin Review*. I should mention here how much I owe to his guidance, his breadth of view, his immense culture, and the deep Catholic devotion which marked the last years of his life when I knew him best. Through him I made many contacts, for example, with T. S. Eliot; through him I was introduced to the work of von Hugel, the deepest Catholic thinker of our times, as I believe, and I have in fact been commissioned to write his life, though when it

will be completed is another question!   And while I am mentioning influences, I must also name Father Martin D'Arcy, S.J.,
who taught me as a boy and with whom I have remained in close
contact all my life).

To return to my story.   The old *Catholic Herald* was a once
powerful organ of Irish nationalism in this country, but at the
period when I met Diamond the question was dead and his newspaper was dying—so, alas! was he.   However, C. D. never gave up,
and his last years were devoted to trying to re-establish the paper
as the organ of the younger generation of Catholic intellectuals.
He never really got going, and he died at a moment when his
fortunes were at a low ebb.   Because I happened to be on the
spot, I helped to keep the paper going with Miss Bottrill, Diamond's secretary.   By a series of extraordinary coincidences—the
full story of which must be told one day—a number of interests
came together and the old paper was bought by a new company
which cherished precisely the ideals which were moving Diamond
just before his death.   Matters did not go too easily and there
were about two years of experiment and tension between conflicting personalities.   However they emerged in the end in a
situation satisfactory to myself, for the revived paper was firmly
in the hands of E. Vernor Miles, a convert lawyer, who neatly
married Miss Bottrill, Charles Diamond's secretary and later my
own, and I was equally firmly placed in the editorial chair where
I remain.

Such serious contribution to the welfare (or otherwise) of my
fellow-countrymen and especially, of course, fellow-Catholics
must, I suppose, be found in these seven years of editing a Catholic journal that has broken away in many respects from the tradition of such journalism, that started slowly because of this break
with tradition, but which today is established as a leading feature
of British Catholic life, which has affected all Catholic journalism
in the country and which enjoys a circulation more than five times
as great as when it was taken over from its founder.

What was the principle which guided us?   It was simply the
truth that *all* news (from ecclesiastical to football, from politics

to art, from economics to literature) was Catholic news, because all news is news of what is right or news of what is wrong, of what is in harmony with God's design and what is not. This meant that we broke away from the tradition that a Catholic paper is only properly concerned with news of the sacristy, the doings of the clergy, the devotional affairs of the Catholic people. In practice we have had to compromise, and I myself was never a defender of the view that this correct principle can in fact be rigorously applied. A Catholic paper must, I think, cater for the domestic news of Church life which would otherwise be unobtainable by the public, but that news must be given against the far more important background of the news of the world in all departments of human activity, studied in terms of the Christian outlook. And the views of a Catholic paper must be given, not in the narrow categories of sectarianism but in the wide and deep sweep which is the essence of the claim of the Catholic Church to be one, true, all-embracing, apostolic.

The attempt to carry these ideals into effect in the course of week-to-week journalism, writing up to 5000 words for each issue and each word (one hopes) consonant with such principles, has naturally left its mark on my own mind and outlook. I have come to see more and more clearly the way in which Catholics today are the victims of sectarianism, how they lamentably fall short in the minds and lives of the nobility and grandeur of God's Church. This leads to two errors that seem at first sight contrary. On the one hand they reduce the Church to the status of a sect among sects; on the other they raise the Church to a position of almost totalitarism and narrowly-conceived authority, totally out of keeping with its real tradition and spirit. I seek to remind them of the truths that God is greater than His Church and that God's Church is greater than anything "cut-off" from any of God's creatures. I seek to remind them that they and the Church are part of God's grand design for the world, just as is the State, the family and other natural or necessary societies and institutions.

Christianity, Catholicity, covers all this because it gives the order according to which every part of God's creation finds its allotted place. There can be no division in the Christian life. You are not more Christian when carrying out God's will for ecclesiastical life than His will for secular and family life—more Christian on Sundays, so to speak, than on weekdays. The Church was founded by Christ for a special purpose, to provide the machinery, as it were, for the life of grace which raises man to the status which God intended for him and to teach and preserve the truth which God has revealed to mankind. That purpose gives to the Church direct authority in faith and morals and indirect authority on all human behavior, because all human behaviour has a moral import.

But for all that nine-tenths of our lives do not come under the direct authority of the Church; nevertheless the ten-tenths must be Christian, that is, in harmony with God's design. The Church is the greatest thing on earth because it is God's specially commissioned institution for the most important of all God's purposes, but the things that happen on the earth, the living of its people, their cultural and technical activities, the societies they form—these things fall outside the Church's direct authority, but not outside God's design.

The Catholic, therefore, and all human beings in so far as their knowledge and conscience take them, are bound to a hundred-per-cent service of God, daily and Sunday, in the market-place as well as in the church, but they are not bound to a totalitarian subjection to an institution that has its special place and its special authority in God's design. The complete Catholic life, I have suggested, is to be found in the human person who unites within him religious and secular, each with its appropriate loyalties and the second in certain very important respects subject to the first, in a Christian harmony reflecting the harmony of God's own Will.

The Church of God is too grand to be a sect, narrowing men's lives to any merely ecclesiastical outlook, and the Church, as the bride of Christ, shares the compassion and charity of Christ towards all men, while vigourously witnessing to Christ's unchanging truth by which it is the duty of all men to live and apply for themselves to secular as much as religious life.

Such considerations as these (here expressed very briefly and, I hope not erroneously) I have tried to apply to contemporary conditions in a fuller way than is possible in weekly journalism in two books, the first called *Christian Crisis* and the second, *Christianity in the Market Place,* as well as in speeches, pamphlets and articles. But the more one dwells on such matters, the more important it seems to study them in their detail, in their day to day application to concrete cases, and because of this I have lately been moved to experiment in fiction in the hopes of writing a truly Catholic novel. My first novel, called *The Shrine,* but published under a pseudonym because I wish to keep this experiment separate from journalistic and other writings, was published in 1943 in Britain. I am engaged in writing a second novel whose purpose is not so much the illustration of my views but the better mastering of the technique of fiction. My hope is that if I am able to do this sufficiently well I can embark upon a series of novels in which, I think, my ideas can be put over more effectively than either in weekly journalism or in heavy essays.

(In case it may interest anyone I have five children and I paint as a hobby.)

EDITOR'S NOTE: Mr. de la Bedoyere's books include *Christian Crisis,* 1942, Macmillan; and *Christianity in the Market-Place,* 1944, Bruce.

ROSALIE MARIE LEVY

THIS IS CERTAIN that God's ways are not men's ways. How could they be?

"All the ways of the Lord are mercy, and truth, and justice" the Book of Tobias assures. And our Blessed Lord Himself testifies: "Behold, I stand at the gate and knock. If any man shall hear My voice, and open to Me the door, I will come in to him, and will sup with him, and he with Me" (*Apoc.* 3:20).

In spite of the fact that God desires that "all men shall come to the knowledge of truth and be saved," He does not force anyone. He died for all—Jew and Gentile, pagan and unbeliever, and His only wish is that all become partakers of the merits of His toil, His suffering, His death. These are the thoughts which are mine as I view my life.

From all eternity our Heavenly Father knew that He would create me, and that, although born of Jewish parents, I would be brought to the knowledge of His Divine Son and be given the opportunity to cooperate with Him in the salvation of souls. It remained for me, however, to consent to that invitation, somewhat in the manner in which it was required of the Blessed Virgin Mary, to assent, when the Angel Gabriel appeared and asked if she would become the Mother of the Messias. God sent no angelic messenger to visit me. Instead He planned my life, as He does that of every human being, in such a way that eventually these circumstances led me to the portals of the Church which the Saviour of the world established upon Peter. Thus I face the duty and the privilege of the decision: whether I would or would not accept the grace offered and ask for Baptism. An humble, yet confident, choice was made after taking a course of instruction and praying for the light to know God's holy Will. Since that hour, from the depths of my heart, I have thanked the Bestower of All Gifts for the "pearl of great price"—the Faith of the Catholic Church.

The story of my conversion is told in the Introduction to *The Heavenly Road,* the first book which I published in 1919. Many may wonder why I prepared this book and why I published it personally. Some people are born with the gift to write; others acquire the ability through reading, travel, study and practice. I cannot claim to belong to either group, for there was but one reason motivating the desire of "getting into print," and that was the urge to share with others the great grace God had bestowed upon me by helping them, especially the Jews, to recognize that Jesus is their Saviour.

The persistent urging of the late Sister M. Pauline Finn, B.V.M., of the Visitation Convent, Georgetown, D. C., whom I met on the day of my First Holy Communion and Confirmation, and of the late Rev. Lewis J. O'Hern, C.S.P., caused me to write a short sketch of my conversion, which was published in *The Missionary* magazine. The same Sister, ever awake to the wish of Our Lord that the true Faith be brought to the "Children of Israel," greatly encouraged my thought of writing something that might be helpful. Consequently, in 1918, I prepared the manuscript of *The Heavenly Road,* a copy of which was submitted to several Catholic publishers. All returned it with the comment, "There is no need for such a work." Feeling that there was a need, and if there were not there should be, I proceeded to publish the work myself, and I gave the manuscript, bearing the *Imprimatur* of the late Cardinal Gibbons of Baltimore, to a printer in November, 1918. The book appeared early the following year. Five years later (in 1924) when the manuscript for a second book, *Why Jews Become Catholics*, was ready, once again I submitted it to Catholic publishers. It met with the same fate as that of *The Heavenly Road*, and so I proceeded to publish it myself. In 1926 I published *Judaism and Catholicism*. I had actually gotten into the publishing business!

Aware of the fact that there are innumerable souls who "know not Christ," and who have not the slightest inkling that Jesus dwells in their very midst, in the tabernacle on the altar in all Catholic churches, which many pass daily without a thought of man's Eucharistic King, I could not restrain the wish to tell all men about their Hidden Savior and to invite them to visit Him. In recent years, frequently I urged some such passerby to enter our churches, particularly at the hour of Benediction, but each one declined for one reason or another. After talking to Our Lord about the matter, the idea came to me to prepare some little books, to be sold at a nominal price, that would aid the friends of Christ to love Him more and to enable them to pray better during their visits to Him. The outgrowth of this was that I compiled and published in 1926 a First Series of *Heart Talks With Jesus*. Since then, after my regular business hours, I have published four additional Series of the *Heart Talks With Jesus* and two Series of *Heart Talks With Mary*. I also prepared the manuscripts for two published by the International Catholic Truth Society of Brooklyn, N. Y.

Naturally I was much encouraged by the hundreds of kind, unsolicited letters received, telling of the wonderful consolation derived from the use of these devotional books. They have also, with God's grace, been instrumental in converting a number of Jews and others to the Catholic Faith. Recently one person when informed that she had an incurable disease became so despondent that she attempted to take her life. In this she failed;

but she refused, persistently, to make her peace with God. A friend of hers, who had received a copy of *Heart Talks With Mary* as a gift, offered to read some of its prayers to her. When the reading was finished she asked to see a priest. She went to confession, received the Last Sacraments, and died a week later. Deo gratias!

In 1928 I published a Holy Hour booklet for the Conversion of Israel. In 1940, as a tribute to the late Rev. Paul R. Conniff, S.J., my spiritual director for twenty years, I published *Stepping Stones to Sanctity,* which contains gleanings from his holy wisdom and sincere piety. This book has also been appreciated by many.

During the twenty-five year period of my publishing books close to 150,000 copies have been sold. In addition to these English copies, there were 25,000 copies of *The Heavenly Road* in German, and 2,000 of *Why Jews Become Catholics* in Polish. Four special editions of *The Heavenly Road* were printed for free distribution in my effort to spread the Faith.

Not content with the "written word," I longed to make use of the "spoken word" in order to bring the knowledge of the true Faith to the man on the street. This opportunity was vouchsafed to me through my founding the Catholic Lay Apostle Guild and its approval by His Eminence, the late Patrick Cardinal Hayes of New York. It was on May 5, 1936, that the Guild held its first meeting at Franklin Triangle, facing City Hall Park, in New York City, and its second meeting on May 8 at Union Square. Since then between 25,000 and 35,000 leaflets have been distributed by the Guild each year.

Sister Editha, of the Sisters of Notre Dame de Namur, who instructed me in the Catholic Faith in Washington, D. C., in 1912, urged me, when I visited her in Cincinnati, Ohio, in 1942, to write an autobiography. At first I was reluctant to do so, but upon further consideration it seemed to me that God might deign to use this volume as a means of converting others. Hence, upon the advice of my Spiritual Director I undertook the task, which was a labor of love, to make known the great mercy of Jesus to one who was most unworthy of His Affection and benediction, and to thank Him publicly for the many blessings and favors He had so bountifully bestowed.

Details of my conversion, of the work of the Catholic Lay Apostle Guild, of the Guild of Our Lady of Sion, of my two visits to Europe and the Holy Land, and of various other activities since my conversion are contained in this, my fifteenth publication, *Thirty Years With Christ*.

EDITOR'S NOTE: Miss Levy was born in Delhi, Louisiana, in 1889, and, after a business college education, engaged in secretarial work for nearly twenty years. Since 1929 she has confined her activities to writing and lecturing. Communications concerning the availability of her publications may be addressed to her via P. O. Box 158, Station O, New York 11, N. Y.

REVEREND VALENTINE
LONG, O.F.M.

IN APPROACHING THIS EGOTISTIC SKETCH I am reminded of John Jay Chapman's opinion of such attempts and feel like one who has had a wet blanket dropped over himself and typewriter. "Autobiographies," says J. J., "are fairy tales . . . the more interested a man is in himself, the greater liar he becomes." Upon invitation, however, I shall go on to analyze my motives for writing, as if Chapman had not spoken out, like that other of the name, loud and bold. It may prove as silly as taking one's nose apart to see what makes it run. But I have promised; and I must see the thing through, if only not to be a liar.

To begin: whatever induced me, an otherwise fairly good-natured Franciscan, to do it—thrust myself in the face of readers? (A brief pause for examination of conscience.) Because I wanted to, I believe the answer is. Not that a variety of motives were not mixed in with the desire; they were. But the answer nevertheless stands pat, Mr. Chapman. I shall not be inveigled into amplifying the statement. I follow Mark Twain's advice, for the present, to "always dress a fact in tights." (Never mind the contradiction, and kindly charge that split infinitive to me.) And then remember what I repeat: I began writing for pretty much (ah! he qualifies) for *just* the reason then that people eat cream puffs and attend baseball games. There was no force of circumstances to be blamed, nothing of necessity to urge.

Teaching English at St. Bonaventure College and being a priest in the world-wide Church of God was more than sufficient vocation. I took up writing not from want of a livelihood, nor of something better to do. Tossing off articles for magazines and imposing an occasional book upon the market may or may not rank superior to that other avocation of instructing students, but heaven knows neither one nor the other will ever see the day when it takes precedence in any possible way over saying Mass and administering the sacraments. "Then why," as must have wondered those students of mine who suffered low marks, and those readers who have shut me up with a yawn, "why didn't he stick to the divine business of Christ exclusively?"

Well, it will soothe the memories of the former to be told, that at last, although too late, their professor of literature has meekly and ignominiously given up *cum permissu superiorum,* and upon his own request—after Uncle Sam had seriously threatened to empty his class-rooms. And rightly so; since by no stretch of the imagination could such stuff as "Ode on a Grecian Urn" be considered of assistance in training potential soldiers. But while my professorship, to shift gears back to the more provocative first person, has ended in a great global war, I must report to the dismay of those others that I still write down my choicest thought, and with it go pestering editors.

I was packed off, then, from a beautiful campus, having left behind a shaft of textbooks I had loved, and with a Portable Royal and a hundred quiet memories came to the bustling scene of New York parish life—on the East side at that. Those closed books may be looked upon as a casualty of war; my priesthood and typewriter survive. The faithful old companion remains open, here on my desk, to the punches of two sturdy index fingers.

It can still be heard clicking off words at intervals, sending academic sounds from a fourth-story window into a neighborhood of more elemental noises, indeed of every kind known to the human throat in various stages of development.

It is a good place in which to write, if done leisurely and under no obligation to continue when the pressure of distraction from that outside world becomes too acute. To maintain a writing schedule against these high moments of teeming life amid tenements would be to invite a nervous breakdown. If ever I thought of trying it—which of course my vocation would prevent anyhow —I should first pick myself out a cozy psychopathic ward, in advance. It would be only a matter of time.

On the other hand, that former environment among trees and lawns, blackboards and students, could not match the human interest of this present outlook—my window faces the rear—where a network of clothes lines, five stories deep, displays every domestic secret from grandpa's long-legged underwear swinging in the breeze to mamma's more delicate fabrics and some little newcomer's tremulous brevities. No rainbow of the sky can rival the poetic contrast of a New York wash, in the midst of which the flimsiest pink handkerchief might hang, like a dream all a-flutter, beside a stolid polka-dot brother. This territory behind the houses was a revelation to me. The fiction I have read of New York family life invariably approaches the subject by the front door. But back in the spaces where fire escapes constitute a world of back porches, changeable after nightfall to love's starlit verandas, dialogue has been found stranger than fiction. One's window must be kept open in hot weather, you know.

From this, I hope I have not implied that I am at present deeply engaged in some monumental work that will offer the public a view of my neighbors denied the street, a view from my back window. I am doing nothing of the sort. I merely eavesdrop and let it go at that. I have learnt my lesson, having once written an intimate novel of Catholic college life, and then, though finding a willing enough publisher, failing to obtain the necessary ecclesiastical approval. I had thrown in too many coeds, it seems. Nothing against faith and morals, understand; but, I was told,

and correctly so, that people are very tender to shocks from a
priest who describes girls as having bodies as well as souls. I am
airing no grievance: the censors in question were real friends who
have spared me, I am sure, the embarassment of *scandalum pusil-
lorum* by advising against publication.

And to show how true their judgment was, how much Puritanism lingers, let me mention a letter from some good soul who read
my *Not on Bread Alone,* my ugly duckling of a firstborn. She
liked it, was even edified. But why did I betray such disrespect to
St. Francis? she wanted to know. Nor did she leave me in doubt
where I had gone wrong. She cited the page. And here, believe it or not, is the shocking passage:

"St. Francis could have defeated the worldling at happiness
even in the favorite haunt of the latter, in the glamour and
sensuous atmosphere of a night club. The Assisian would have
stayed sober at table, fresh, eager, with a pair of dark eyes a-glitter
and dancing from curiosity and wonderment. It would have been
a strange, poetically uproarious place for him who dreamed not
of sin, a place which presented such odd spectacles, as a row of
chorus girls hopping into view all on the left leg, with their right
extended and swinging gayly from the knee. Surely this was organized beauty gone funny, and worthy of trial in a circus. It
was a comedy of motion, a breaking away from the prosaic custom
of just walking one's legs; and to a servant of God with the easy
sense of humor which St. Francis possessed, it meant nothing more
harmful than an enticement to laughter."

The well meaning tertiary who wrote the letter, however, considered it far from a laughing matter. I stunned her, she said—
terrible thing to do! Her conscience forced her to protest, she
said. And, of course, if she were the mother of a chorus girl I
could have better appreciated her tone. As it was, I felt a little
stunned myself.

But I really felt good over the generosity of reviewers towards
that first book, and the companionable warmth of its "fan mail."
It made me want to write more, which I did—a fool doesn't need
much encouragement. And a note, I well remember, from one of
my favorite authors, G. K. Chesterton, went straight to my heart.

I afterwards wrote an article out of admiration for the gallant apologist, which was published in *Columbia* magazine the very month he died. My confreres have ever since hinted, darkly, that G. K. took one look and could stand this earth no longer. May his great soul be with the saints!

Recognition is always sweet. But whether it comes slowly or soon, or never, writing will remain its own reward. And if Mr. Chapman cares to turn over in his grave at that statement, well, that is his privilege. To me, writing is essentially a recreation. To return from a sick call full of deep impressions of the dignity of Catholic death, or from the parlor where love has been canonically readied for the romantic sacrament, or from the pulpit where one sees the glory of the Faith upon such a varied assortment of faces, or from the occasion of a First Holy Communion where the especial Friend of children has been distributed to the most eager little mouths in the world: to return from a hundred such scenes to a favorite chair, with pencil and pad and a good cigar, and to jot down sentences while the mood lasts, correcting and revising, and then tapping the finished draft on a typewriter —what happier way to waste away leisure and prepare for a return to the more serious business of administering sacraments and comfort to the flock of the Good Shepherd!

In case anyone is interested in additional and more fundamental data, as the good editor of this book seems to be, I hasten to reveal that I was born at home, October 28, 1902. The event caused no stir in the town of Cumberland, Md.; yet somehow was hailed as a blessed event within the family circle. Mother liked to think that she held in her arms a future missionary—there was a mission in progress in our parish at the time. Moreover, her friends who came in to look me over, between sermons, encouraged her in that hope. She has told me they were practically unanimous in considering my voice strong enough already to carry God's word to the farthest pew. So, no doubt, were the neighbors who tried to sleep of nights. Dear old dad, for his part, handed out plenty of cigars that week—even to Republicans, who joined in to smoke to the good news that another potential Democrat had arrived on earth. I suppose a birth transcended politics even in those days when both parties still knew their own minds.

Having been duly baptized William George and, according to my godmother, quietly, "like a little gentleman," I six years later took up studies at Saints Peter and Paul's parochial school, Cumberland, Md. There the Ursuline nuns proved models of patience toward a pupil who more and more preferred baseball to textbooks. It was the heyday of Christy Matthewson and Honus Wagner, and it was a deeper humiliation not to know what the heroes of the diamond had done yesterday. Nevertheless, I was graduated—what easier way to be rid of me?—and was promptly wished upon the Capuchin Fathers at St. Fidelis College, Herman, Pa.

It was a preparatory seminary where young candidates to the priesthood were trained either for the Capuchin Order or for the Pittsburgh diocese. I landed in neither. With great admiration for everything Capuchin, except the wearing of a beard, I betook myself—with diploma and razor—to the Franciscans and, in their monastery church at Paterson, N. J., was canonically received. I had just finished making a novena to Our Lady, and coincidentally or otherwise, the ceremony took place on the feast of her Assumption, 1921. I was proud to be a member of the Order that has loved her so gloriously through its history.

In exchange for having given myself to the Friars Minor, I found them giving me the name Valentine, which of course supplanted the less romantic William George, with the blessings of the Church. A fine sense of humor has prevailed in our Order from the start. Be that as it may, I have ever since known and felt that joining the Franciscans was a wise move on my part, whether it was on theirs or not.

How I came to indulge in spasms of writing while teaching as a priest at St. Bonaventure College in upstate New York, and why I still do so indulge in my present environment, I have already stated. Why does a person scratch and itch?

EDITOR'S NOTE: Father Long's works include *Not on Bread Alone*, 1934, St. Anthony Guild; and *They Have Seen His Star*, 1938, id.; as well as many pamphlets.

**REVEREND FREDERICK M.
LYNK, S.V.D.**

LIKE MOST OLDSTERS I like to reminisce. Looking back over the road you have traveled and reading its story in the eyes of Memory sitting by your side on a quiet spot in the fading glow of life's sunset is apt to bring smiles and tears and above all gratitude to the reminiscing mind. No matter what the course has been, you cannot help discovering a guiding hand reaching out from behind the clouds and deftly pointing the direction to take and giving the grace to follow it. I often wonder whether we shall reminisce in eternity on our childhood days in heaven, say after a million years of bliss, just as we do about our earthly childhood after a few decades of life.

I believe every human life, no matter where lived, in the jungles or in the cities, in the slums or in a palace, is intensely interesting, if only a skilled teller could be found. However, I have more than a sneaking suspicion that autobiographers are not best suited for that task. They know too much about themselves and may lack a sense of proportion, both regarding their entire

place in the scheme of things and the relative importance of the
happenings and influences that moulded their lives and careers.
Only after we have entered the light of eternity we shall be able
to see all the hidden threads and skeins that were woven into our
life's pattern.   But now that I have expressed my doubts about
the wisdom of trying to write a chapter about myself for the
Book of Catholic Authors I will start without any further ado.

My cradle—in those days they had big cradles and they were
seldom without an occupant—stood in a picturesque and entirely
Catholic village of the Rhineland.   There were twelve children
though only seven reached adult age.   My mother's name was
Mary Anne and it seemed to fit her well, for she often reminded
me of Mary of Nazareth when she was younger and of St. Anne
when she was older.   She was a working, praying and—singing
mother, a poetess, although she never wrote a line of verse, a lover
of Nature, who often showed me birds' nests as a reward for
"being good."   I mention this only because, I believe, I inherited
what little poetic vein I have from her.

The pastor who had a Polish name, Gadomsky, was a scholar
and a most zealous priest.   He picked four or five boys, me among
them, to prepare for college.   Within two years we finished four
classes and at sixteen I left home to make all my later studies in
other countries.   The priest was an amateur poet and encouraged
his students to similar poetic efforts.   I remember my first one
written for a friend's album when I was less than fifteen.   It was
inspired by a Latin saying we had just learned, "quidquid agis,
prudenter agas, et respice finem."

During college days I perpetrated a great many more "pomes"
but only a very intimate circle of friends knew about it.   During
Philosophy we had a mimeographed class paper, Palaestra, and
I contributed a verse or short article now and then under a pen
name.   I wanted to be a missionary among the heathens and I
dreaded the idea of being appointed to a professorship after
ordination, as Father Prefect had hinted.   The thought of becoming a "missionary of the pen" which I later became, did not
come from me but from the saintly founder of the missionary

Society of the Divine Words, Father Arnold Janssen. He appointed me for Japan and in his last chat with me in the garden of the generalate he told me I should go to Japan and write "religious tracts" for the heathen Japanese. He was always a great believer in the apostolate of the press. I was a bit dumbfounded but I knelt down in the green grass, he placed his fatherly hands on my head, pressing them down hard I thought, and gave me his blessing. I never got to the land of the Rising Sun but I still feel that his advice and order had a great deal to do with my journalistic career. It set me thinking and working. I had hardly reached Techny—and this is almost forty years ago—when I wrote a description of my trip across the ocean which was printed in one of our monthlies.

I was supposed to remain in the States for a year or two to perfect myself in English and French and then go on to Japan. I was fully willing and determined to go, even took a course in Japanese at the University of Chicago, but because of the scarcity of teachers I was recalled to Techny and assigned such subjects as United States History, Religion, Arithmetic, German, etc. I groaned, and accepted (there was nothing else to do) but all the while wrote articles, poems and even a few stories for our magazines, nearly all under a nom-de-plume. You see, I was ashamed of claiming my first brain children. Nevertheless, when the general wrote two years later that I should get ready to go to Japan I respectfully submitted to him half a dozen reasons why I should wish to stay on a little while longer in the Land of the Stars and Stripes. I never received an answer for the good man died six months later and the trip to Japan was never mentioned again. In fact, the same year, 1909, I took over the editorship of the *Christian Family,* and I've kept it ever since, in days when it had 10,000, 50,000, 100,000 or 70,000 subscribers. We print about 70,000 copies now. I like to see the hand of Providence in all this.

I suppose every editor could tell a long story about his experiences with engravers, compositors, printers, contributors and readers and above all, with that ubiquitous individual known the world over as the "printer's devil." It is a very annoying "devil," who sometimes prints the very opposite of what you wish to say. To save money and practice writing I contributed, besides editorials, a large number of articles and poems, under as many as five or six pen names. I still use some of them, but "A Monsignor," as some of our good brothers suspect, is not one of them. That dignitary of the facile pen and deep philosophical and theological knowledge, can write better than I.

Only two or three times I have submitted verse to other magazines. The old *Century,* long out of existence, returned my twenty lines with a beautiful rejection slip. Being the first I had ever received I kept it as a souvenir. I made a bet with a friend my poem would be back within ten days, and I won the bet. *Extension* paid me five dollars for a verse entitled, "My Wealth," and even five dollars seemed a good deal of wealth in those days. I sent three or four of my poems to *America,* in New York, but those "terrible Jesuits" did not even acknowledge the receipt of them. The *Servite* has published quite a number from "Mary's Little Troubadour."

After these experiences I quit sending poetic attempts to any paper. I was cured. Nevertheless, I published a hundred pieces of verse under the title *My Woodland Forge,* at the price of a dollar, and, believe it or not, in less than seven years we sold the whole edition of one thousand. (A lady who bought a copy assured me that she enjoyed my "Valley Forge poems" so much!) I have published three small poetry booklets since, three thousand copies each, and I expect all of them to be sold in less time. All appeared with ecclesiastical approbation, though I was informed before the last one came out that the censor opined, the little volume "had no literary value." He had counted the "feet" of some lines and found them "wanting." Of course counting absent "feet" is not the censor's business. He did not question orthodoxy. Censors seldom write books themselves. I would always rather write plain language for plain people than for the "blue stockings."

I feel deep down in my heart, I am still a country boy. I am not aspiring to a niche in the hall of fame, (sour grapes you may think), but it does give me a little joy when I see some of my verse reprinted in Canadian, English and American Catholic papers (usually without acknowledge to the *Christian Family*).

You can see, it is nice to be your own editor who out of sheer self love will accept most anything you write, unless a last remnant of humility or common sense causes him to bar your contribution. I am planning to publish half a dozen more poetry booklets. Costing only ten cents they are likely to reach a much wider circulation than if I published my "collected works" in one volume. Frankly, their purpose is not literary, but religious, as their titles indicate: *Mary's Little Troubadour,* dedicated to the Mother of God, *The Little Minstrel of the King,* dedicated to Jesus Christ, and *Consecration,* dedicated to the priests of God. The title of the next booklet will probably be, *Toward the Dawn,* a title sufficiently broad to cover a great variety of verse. Incidentally, I wrote "words" for some forty songs and hymns. The composers being well known, I cherish the hope that these words and melodies will still be sung by some good people long after all my books and booklets are completely forgotten.

Since Techny is in the "pamphlet business" and since I had been "officially" appointed a pamphleteer by our saintly founder I also wrote a number of booklets in prose: *The World's Best Prayer* (on the Our Father), *Mary, Our Mother* (on the Hail Mary), *Therese Neumann, the Passion Flower of Konnersreuth* (of which more than 100,000 copies were sold), *The Music of Life, The Art of Right Reading, Sacred Voices,* and translated *Chinese Martyrs, Why We Should Pray for Our Priests* and the plays *Garcia Moreno, The Angel of Peace,* Calderon's *Mysteries of the Mass* which was performed many times at Techny and other places, and *Viva Cristo Rey.*

In the course of years I translated six or seven serial stories for the *Christian Family* and several books: *Seeking the Sun* by Augustine Wibbelt, *The Holy Eucharist and Christian Life, Sister Therese of the Holy Trinity, Our Belief in Providence, When Jesus Walked the Earth, Mary of Magadala, The King of the*

Ages, Jehuda Ibn Esra's Way to God, What the Seer Saw, an interpretation of the Apocalypse, and three or four smaller books. *Watchfires* is a collection of meditations and readings for the year which first appeared in the *Christian Family.*

The most important of the translations and adaptations was that of the *Life of Arnold Janssen* by Father Fischer, S.V.D., published in the United States in 1925 and in a smaller edition in England a few years later.

For almost seven months I worked on this large volume, five or six hours every day, and handed the finished manuscript to the Provincial during Holy Week. I was exhausted and nervous from overwork. When the double jubilee, silver for Techny and golden for the Society, finally arrived there was not a single copy available for the 15,000 people who had come to Techny to help us celebrate. On account of Labor Day the Chicago factory which had bound the books was closed. That little disappointment added to my feeling of exhaustion and in my desperation I went to Father Provincial and told him I needed a Sabbatical year, and would like to go to Europe. To my surprise he said he would endorse my petition and send it to Father General. I wrote to Rome and in four or five weeks I had permission to travel. I rejoiced but told only a few intimates about my luck. I worked feverishly to collect the necessary funds—for the permission included the proviso that I must secure the funds myself —and in about seven months I had $1,700 and was ready to start upon my 50–60,000 mile trip through Europe and the Near East.

Globe trotting is fun when you have enough money and know a little about the languages spoken in the countries you visit. I had supplied myself with several neatly bound diaries and faithfully entered the day's experiences every night. My first travel article was mailed an hour after I left the boat and appeared a month or two later in the *Christian Family.* It was a novel experience, this long distance editing. With sufficient material set aside for each month, articles and poems chosen in advance, and writing chats and editorials en route, it was done. Later I sent articles from Tyrol, Italy and Palestine. In all I wrote more than

a hundred articles about my experiences in some twenty countries and then collected them into three volumes. The first was:
In the Homeland of the Saviour. We had seven hundred advance
orders for that book and two months later ran off a second edition which was sold in a few years. The book is now out of print.
My next volume was *At the Shrines of God's Friends,* describing
some twenty-nine pilgrimages, and the last, *Strolling Through
Europe.* I am told this volume is about sold out too.

Readers and reviewers have said some kind things about these
travel books, and some Catholic high schools have put them on
the list of prescribed reading.

"Habent sua fata libelli" is an old saying. I could tell a great
deal more but the story might not be edifying in every detail.
So I refrain. Journalism is a fascinating career, even when combined with the duties of residing Chaplain of a large city hospital, as I did for nineteen years. I attended the constitutional
meeting of the Catholic Press Association, and also the silver
anniversary meeting at Columbus, Ohio. Catholic America now
has a large number of fine Catholic magazines.

Good Sister M. Joseph has long urged me to become a member
of the "Gallery of Living Catholic Authors," and at last I have
complied. I expect to continue writing and translating books.

I find translating from half a dozen languages is a joy (and
sometimes a headache). The surest way to find out if an author
is really worthwhile is to translate him. Incidentally, you learn
a lot about the soul and temper of both his language and yours.
Nothing better can be recommended to the aspiring young writer
than to learn a classical language, Latin, for example, and one
or two modern languages. There is a wealth of Catholic literature in French, German, Spanish, Dutch, Flemish, and Polish.
Many of our best books are translations and more should be
welcome to enrich us and bring about a better understanding
and cooperation among Catholic peoples.

Just a few months ago I began to study Danish and Norwegian
and before long I hope to read Johannes Jorgensen and Sigrid
Undset in the original.

I have had half a dozen operations, developed diabetes and lived in a hospital as quietly as possible, but I still write editorials, chats, poems and articles and answer questions of inquisitive Catholics, translate a book or two every year and keep wondering when the Good Lord will call me away from my desk and ask me to lay down my trusty pen or give up my Remington noiseless.

Several years ago a student friend of mine asked me how many words I had written up to that time. Of course I did not know. We began to figure averages, and he came to the conclusion that it was more than a million words. That rather frightened me. It may be two or three million before I stop. If God demands an accounting of every word spoken, He must be even more strict in regard to words written. Of course being a "missionary of the pen" I have tried to write only helpful things, but I do feel a good deal like the missionary who lay dying in China after thirty or forty years of hard work. One of his confreres tried to comfort him, saying the divine Judge would bountifully reward him for his labor. The dying man smiled and said: "If the Lord doesn't start talking about it, I won't mention it."

EDITOR'S NOTE: The Mission Press, Techny, publishes Father Lynk's works, including *Fireside Melodies*, 1914, *Strolling Through Europe*, 1936, *Watch Fires*, 1931, and *Mary's Little Troubadour*, 1941.

VERY REVEREND JOHN A. McHUGH, O.P.

I AM NOT VERY ENTHUSIASTIC about writing this sketch of my literary career. The editor of this work has asked me to prepare it, but I wish someone else could do it for me. I feel that what I have written is hardly worth much attention. With this open confession, however, I will set down a few data which may explain my literary efforts and why I have been asked to write this brief outline.

While I lived at my home in my native city of Louisville, Kentucky, I sometimes used to picture my name with a "Reverend" before it and an "O.P." after it. If I ever visioned my name printed as author on the back of books or signed to articles, I am not aware of the fact. I knew, of course, that the clergy are considered well educated men, but I did not think that every well educated person had to be a writer.

Nevertheless, I often heard the praises of writers sounded, and so at an early period I conceived a great respect for them. There were three authors especially whose names had local associations connected with them. My father often spoke of Father Abram Ryan, "the poet-priest of the South," and often read his poems. When I was six years of age, Father Ryan came to Louisville to make a retreat with the Franciscan Fathers there as a preparation for a life of Christ which he intended to write. Unfortunately the poet-priest died during that retreat. Naturally this incident aroused a fresh interest in Father Ryan and his works.

Then there was the famous John Lancaster Spalding, Bishop of Peoria, Illinois, who had been a pastor in Louisville. He was widely regarded as an outstanding theologian and scholar. My mother was devoted to him as a zealous and learned priest, and I often heard her speak in his praise. I still have his *Glimpses of Truth* (The Grafton Press, N. Y., 1901) which she autographed to me over forty years ago.

My mother was also a great admirer of Mary Anderson, a Louisville girl, noted both as a devout Catholic and as a Shakespearean actress. She was known as the "our Mary" of the American stage. It was through her fame as an actress, probably, that the great and immortal name of Shakespeare was first impressed upon me. About this time also I listened with great interest, though not with much understanding, to remarkable readings and recitations from Shakespeare's plays by the noted orator, Father Stafford, of Washington, D. C.

In later life the attraction for these authors—Father Ryan, Bishop Spalding and Shakespeare, grew upon me as I read and studied them. I have gone over them many times and I have read studiously all of Shakespeare.

My reading at home, apart from necessary school matter, was mostly historical—ancient and modern, Church and American; biographical, especially Alban Butler's *Lives of the Saints;* and fiction, such as *Fabiola,* Cooper's Indian stories, Uncle Remus, Father Finn's boy heroes. I used to like to read also the many beautiful passages found in the school readers and elocution books of that day.

My introduction to writing came through the preparation of compositions and debate-matter as a part of class work. I recall the difficulty I had in searching for data for a sketch on Christopher Columbus, until a priest I knew gave it all to me in a few minutes. Also I remember the tribulations I had in putting into order arguments for a debate, and in trying to write with originality and good expression. But I liked writing enough to work at it on my own initiative, struggling once to produce in playform the life of a martyr, and another time an historical address. As there were eleven in my family, I could always find there both enough players and a sufficient audience. The play, I think, never got beyond rehearsal, while the address put the audience to sleep.

But my interest in things literary did not fail, and I think it was the literary fame of two Dominican priests that contributed in a measure to my entering the Dominican order. The name of Father "Tom" Burke was a household word in Louisville in my boyhood. I used to hear my elders speak of his eloquence and extraordinary influence over non-Catholics as well as Catholics. People were simply enraptured by his discourses. He himself said that he made no special pretence at style, but his published sermons and lectures, even as they read now, explain why he was called "the prince of preachers." Father Louis O'Neil, O.P., founder of the *Rosary Magazine,* was a member of St. Louis Bertrand's community in Louisville, during the Columbian celebrations of 1892, and played a conspicuous part in them. He was a fluent and eloquent speaker and attracted much attention. I recall his fame as an historian, a literary man, an orator; and also the scholarly and religious work he wrote on the art of reading (*Why, When, How and What We Ought To Read,* Boston, 1893).

During my life as a Dominican I have read much, and written not a little. While my reading has been chiefly ecclesiastical, literary works so called, both English and Latin, have not been neglected. I have received considerable encouragement and assistance in the use of the pen, and have worked at it with enthusiasm. As a student I wrote Latin dissertations on a variety of subjects, English essays of a literary kind, and sermons. My first published matter was in the form of book reviews for *The Rosary Magazine,* and a column each month in that Review for the Rosary Confraternity. Since ordination I have been chiefly engaged in teaching theology and other ecclesiastical subjects, at the Dominican House of Studies, Washington, D. C., from 1908 to 1915, and at Maryknoll Seminary on the Hudson from the autumn of 1915 to the present time; and, since the summer of 1916, in editing *The Homiletic and Pastoral Review,* New York. My earliest writing as a priest was the preparation of sermons and class lectures on dogmatic theology. In the course of years these manuscripts naturally increased in bulk, and have proved useful as helps to other writing. I also contributed a number of articles on Dominican hagiography and on doctrine to the *Dominican Year Book* and the *Catholic Encyclopaedia.* For *The Homiletic and Pastoral Review* I have for many years written a great number of articles, sermons, moral cases and book reviews, while contributing also to *The Clergy Review, The Sentinel of the Blessed Sacrament, The Torch* and *The Catholic Biblical Quarterly.* My first books were *The Casuist,* a collection of cases in moral and pastoral theology (1917) and *Preparation for Marriage,* canonical questions and explanations (1919).

Most of my writing has been in collaboration with Very Rev. C. J. Callan, O.P. In spite of infirm health, Father Callan is well known as an unusually forceful speaker and a leading influence in the cause of the apostolate of the press. The two flourishing Dominican magazines, *Dominicana* and *The Thomist,* are due in large measure to his initiative and activity, and we two sponsored the idea of *The Catholic Readers' Digest* years before it was heard of in public. I feel that association with Father Callan and his zeal for letters has had much to do with the most of my own writing. Between 1912 and 1942 he and I have produced together some twenty-five different works on homiletic, theological, devotional, liturgical, Scriptural, and literary subjects.

For the help and encouragement of young writers and of those who aspire to write, I have been asked to offer some suggestions. Let me say that my own ideal writers are St. Thomas Aquinas and Cardinal Newman. From their examples and words one may gather, I think, all that is most necessary for the writer's art. Perhaps the most important points from them may be summed up under four directions regarding: purpose, writer, matter, expression.

1. Aim at the highest objectives. Discourse is given man in order that he may express the true, the good, the beautiful; and written discourse, since it endures, has a special responsibility. Writing is not for its own sake; neither is the writer its end, though there is a special crown, as St. Thomas says, for those who instruct others. St. Thomas himself aimed high; and we see in the Prologue to his immortal *Summa Theologica* how he opens with the declaration that his purpose is truth and instruction. Newman agrees with all this, and his statement on preaching can be well used here, namely, that aim, intention, earnestness is "the one thing necessary" above all.

2. Work hard at writing. One may find it a labor of love, but even so, labor it is, even for the most gifted. Aquinas knew this from experience, and, in the Prologue before mentioned, he calls to mind the difficulties of his task, and the need of divine help and his own effort. For the execution of his plan he spent day after day, and year after year, at his desk, reading, studying and thinking, comparing and consulting, writing and rewriting, correcting and deleting, until the end. Newman likewise had to revise, correct and polish as much in his old age as in his earlier years. He tells us that he was always obliged to take great pains with everything he wrote.

3. One should be definite. Though there is a vast number of subjects to write about, an author has to spare both his own and his reader's strength by limiting his composition to something particular. What Newman says for the preacher holds good for the writer also; there must be a definite group addressed, a definite matter discussed, a definite personality who speaks. St. Thomas is again an illustration. In the Prologue to the *Summa* he proposes to discuss the Christian religion—a very large theme. But he limits himself to students of theology and to what is useful

for them; also to matter strictly theological, as distinct from arts and sciences, poetry and philosophy, and the like. Though St. Thomas seldom speaks directly of himself—as was proper in a concise and technical study, his Prologue serves to introduce him sufficiently to the reader. He appears there as one who has had long experience with books and men and schools, as one who speaks out of the abundance of his special reading, thinking, teaching and writing.

4. Write with style. One who writes without sufficient art does justice neither to his subject, not to his readers, nor to himself. A worthwhile subject deserves worthwhile presentation. The reader deserves to be addressed in a manner that will appeal to his intelligence, will, and feelings. As for the author, he owes it to his own reputation and influence to write well, since defective language is a sign of defective thought. St. Thomas certainly did not spare himself in the matter of style. He was most considerate of his readers, proposing to himself to spare them every confusion and weariness. He resolves, therefore, to write, with all possible lucidity and brevity. He succeeded so well that no better model of accuracy and conciseness can be found. Adornment and amplification would have been out of place in a technical work like the *Summa*. But St. Thomas recognized their value. Often he quotes the rhetorical St. Augustine, and sometimes others who excelled in oratory, poesy, wit or fancy. He justifies a figurative speech as pleasant and agreeable to the nature of man. Newman on the other hand, was a great rhetorician, but he did not separate language from thought. The one quality of style he aimed at always was the difficult one of clearness, whereby the writer expresses his meaning exactly. Like St. Thomas he seeks always to be thoughtful of his reader. Vivid exactness, he says, is the very soul of expression in all great writers.

REVEREND VINCENT McNABB, O.P.

(1868–1943)

FATHER VINCENT MCNABB was born on July 8, 1868 at Portaferry, on Strangford Lough, County Down, Ireland. He was the tenth of eleven children, and the seventh son of James McNabb by Ann Shields, his wife. His father was a sea-captain, and the family moved to Belfast during Father Vincent's early childhood, and later to Newcastle-on-Tyne. When he was four days old he was baptized and placed under the protection of St. Joseph, whose name he bore; it happened to be July 12, the anniversary of the Battle of the Boyne, a fact which Father Vincent used to declare accounted for his "Protestant stomach"—his life-long internal weakness. He used to refer to his life in a large family as the best training for the future religious in the virtues of poverty, chastity and obedience. In childhood he had a very serious illness, and was given up by the doctor, but after many months of tender care and open-air treatment of a primitive kind, he recovered. He was sent to the diocesan seminary of St. Malachy, in Belfast, and for a short time he was at a school in England. In November,

1885, he entered the Dominican novitiate at Woodchester when just seventeen years old. His own account of his vocation is simple. "I did not want to go to Hell, so I went to Woodchester." Here he was clothed in the habit on November 28 of that same year by the Provincial, Father Antoninus Williams, the uncle of the present Archbishop of Birmingham. His profession followed in due course and he was raised to the priesthood by Bishop Clifford of Clifton on September 19, 1891. Three weeks later he went to Louvain, where he took the degree of Lector of Theology, July 14, 1894, and then returned to Woodchester as Professor of Philosophy. In 1897 he was appointed Professor of Dogmatic Theology at Hawkesyard, and he remained there until he was elected Prior of Woodchester in 1900. From 1906 till 1908 he was at St. Dominic's, London, and then he went to Holy Cross, Leicester, as Prior. In 1913 he sailed to New York and preached throughout the United States, collecting funds for the building of the new church at Leicester. He became Prior of Hawkesyard just at the time of the outbreak of the first World War, and when he had completed his term of office he came to St. Dominic's, London, where he remained, and seemed to be perpetual Sub-Prior, till the time of his death on June 17, 1943.

His was a truly amazing life. If Father Bede Jarrett, who died in 1934, was described as "extraordinarily ordinary," then Father Vincent (an utterly different type of man) could only be described as "extraordinarily extraordinary." He was a familiar figure trudging the streets in his very ancient habit, big boots and battered hat, appearing like a friar who had strayed into this century from the thirteenth, looking, as someone said, "like John the Baptist risen from the dead." This astonishing man, eccentric (judged by our normal modern standards), egotist (exactly as St. Paul was an egotist), individualist, demonstrative in all he did and said, speaking in superlatives, emphatic and explosive, unique and original (to use two of his favourite words), combined all these characteristics with an unblemished life and an undoubted holiness. Poor with an almost starkness of poverty, ascetic to extremes—for years he never slept in his bed, but on

the floor—he had a sense of humour and simple fun which, together with his love of community life, kept him sane and preserved him from the dangers of fanaticism. His outstanding virtue was charity. He would denounce abuses and evils with all
the fierce vigor of a major prophet, yet never was he known in
public or in private to give voice to an uncharitable or unkind
judgment of any person. He could be terrible in argument, but
if he thought he had given offense, a dramatic apology would
follow, a prostration at full length on the ground, more disturbing than the offense, which may not even have been noticed. But
these "liturgical" gestures (he always explained they were prescribed in the Dominican Ceremonial) were quite sincere. Credible witnesses tell how he once silenced a very objectionable
heckler at Marble Arch by stepping off the rostrum and kissing
the nasty fellow's feet. The present writer once witnessed something of the same kind when, at an open-air meeting on Parlia-
ment Hill, he solemnly announced that, as a public act of repara-
tion for the sins of Catholics (his own included), he would kneel
down and kiss the feet of the Anglican Bishop who was taking
the chair: a solemn rite which he then proceeded to perform.
The cynical onlooker might be tempted to judge it play-acting,
but it was not. Father Vincent saw each thing separately and
intensely and in itself and apart from its surroundings, and it
did not matter to him what people thought. His was holiness
after a medieval model.

The explanation of this strange, lovable friar is to be found
in the conviction that grew upon him with the years, that he
must put all his energy into his vocation as priest and preacher.
"Woe is me if I preach not the gospel!" All he did, his crusade
for social justice in the spirit and letter of the papal Encyclicals;
his inauguration Lectures in Scripture and Theology for layfolk;
his work for the Catholic Evidence Guild—all were the outcome
of his complete absorption in the cause of God. Things were
desirable in so far as they provided opportunities for preaching.
What seemed to be a vulgar cult of publicity was actually the
method of his apostolate. The way he died proves the complete

sincerity and success of that method.   He became a living sermon.

The evening of his life must have brought many consolations. For years he had been writing his books and articles on old scraps of paper and re-using his envelopes out of holy poverty, and he was pleased to find many who had laughed at this practice now doing it themselves in the interests of national economy.   He once proposed a scheme for evacuating the big cities and putting people on the land at the rate of 10,000 each year.   He was called an impracticable dreamer at the time, yet he lived to witness and smile at the wholesale evacuations from our cities during the blitz at the rate of more than 10,000 a day.   The posters exhorting us to "grow more food," "dig for victory," "use shank's mare," gave him pure joy.   The eccentric finds his genial critics adjusting their circles to his.

Father Vincent belonged to the class of whom St. Paul spoke, of those "having nothing, yet possessing all things."   Alike the greatest and the least of men were debtors to him.   One knows the deep obligation that G. K. Chesterton acknowledged; and the abiding friendship and respect of Hilaire Belloc, who made the long journey from Sussex to attend his Requiem.   Among his audiences at Hampstead and Hyde Park and elsewhere in the open spaces were multitudes of simple folk who were not slow to speak of the way in which he had altered their thought and enriched their lives.   He passionately loved the poor, and came, in conjunction with Belloc, to see how a Socialist society would stereotype proletarian status and fix the poor forever in a condition of dependence on State officials.

Among the laity, not the least of his titles to remembrance and to gratitude was his pioneer work in making the philosophy and the theology of St. Thomas Aquinas available to lay men and women.   In course of time his students formed the Aquinas Society, which, in the decade before the war, introduced to English audiences such philosophers and theologians as Reverend Fathers Garrigou-Lagrange and Sertillanges, Monsignor Leon Noel, and Messrs. Jacques Maritain, Stanislas Fumet, and Jacques Chevalier.

One may also refer to his interest in the restoration of Christian conceptions in the English law; and in the foundation of the Thomas More Society. He had a real devotion to St. Thomas More; and liked to trace the links which bound him (through their common friendship with Erasmus) to Franciscus de Vittoria.

Father Vincent's death was in keeping with his life. Warned of it for some months beforehand, he used even that as a sustained sermon to attract people not to himself, but to the God Whom he loved and for Whom he lived. Up to the very end, with the help of another friar, he said all his Office and prayers of obligation, and he seemed to be entwined in his big fifteen-decade rosary. At the very end, he sang the *Nunc Dimittis* in his loud, clear voice, gave instructions about his coffin, and requested that the words of St. Peter, "Lord, Thou knowest all things, Thou knowest that I love Thee," be inscribed in Greek upon it; made his Confession, renewed his vows, and declared himself ready for death, saying, "I have no fears, thank God." And so he died; his mental vigour and prodigious strength of will holding out to the very last.

Father Vincent was the authentic friar preacher.

EDITOR'S NOTE: This chapter was written from material from *Blackfriars*, Oxford, and *The Tablet*, London. Father McNabb's books include *Eleven, Thank God*, 1940, Sheed; *Mary of Nazareth*, 1940, Kenedy; *Old Principles and the New Order*, 1942, Sheed; *St. Mary Magdalen*, 1940, Burns; and *Some Mysteries of Jesus Christ*, 1941, id.

SISTER MARY ALOYSI, S.N.D.

(Mary Agnes Kiener)

THE YOUNGEST of a family of ten children, my childhood memories revert to loved home associations: a mother's quiet, gentle ways, alert to our problems and easily composing differences; a father's beautiful tenor, leading in his favorite "Salve Regina" of an evening when work was done; brothers and sisters sharing the rich countryside, the joyous enthusiasm of children in the beauty of flowers and fields, and endless woods, roamed in carefree abandon.

There were several years of public school in the grades in a little red brick schoolhouse; a dynamic teacher who gave unwittingly—for she was of a different faith—the first external impulse to a religious vocation. "Mary," said Miss Emma Farr to the wistful girl just turned ten, "I think you ought to be a teacher."

As new horizons spread out before the young girl, the freedom of the countryside was still to her the very breath of life. First Holy Communion at ten in old St. Patrick's, in what was then

Rockport, opened new vistas, and then came life in the city. After two years at St. Patrick's school (Cleveland), under the tutelage of Mother Felicitas of the Ursulines, a true friend, the grades were completed and there came a turn in the road. Our Lady beckoned with unmistakable gesture.

Convent school at thirteen with the Sisters of Notre Dame, among the happy aspirants to the sisterhood; the religious habit at sixteen, and mother's early death within four weeks; first vows at nineteen, January 2, 1901,—these are the "log" of a beautiful apprenticeship, shaping for Christlife. It was a glorious time. The most delightful period of an essentially happy life!

Among the scholarly religious to whom it is a privilege to be indebted, two exerted the strongest formative influence, not only during high school but beyond through decades of labor in the educational field. Resourceful and brilliant in conversation, Sister Mary Aloysius, sister of the late Right Rev. Monsignor George Murphy, D.D., won our affection and esteem by her innate tact and courtesy. Sister Mary Girolama, whose genius Bishop Horstmann admired, seems to have shared the insight into human nature and wealth of learning of her brother, the moral theologian, Rev. August Lehmkuhl, S.J. Her personality left its impress on a whole generation of teachers, both religious and secular.

Preparatory years and teacher training over, and our spiritual fortifications strengthened, we were sent out to try our mettle in the classroom. This business of learning how to teach after the rudiments of the art had been acquired was so absorbing as to leave little leisure for writing.

Teaching experiences in Notre Dame Academy, both in Cleveland and in Covington, Kentucky, the grades and commerce high school until 1917, with added duties of principalship at St. Peter's, Canton, Ohio, for nine years, gave zest for the advanced work that lay ahead.

As a member of the pioneer staff of the Girls' Catholic High School, Cleveland, organized in 1917 by the late Monsignor William Kane, D.D., I taught mathematics for three years until a leave of absence from 1920 to 1923 turned the page to a new chapter in my life-story. Mother Mary Cecilia, Superior General, had acceded to the appeal for sisters to take over the domestic work at Holy Cross Seminary, at Notre Dame. When Mother Mary Evarista selected the sisters for the charge, I was designated as one of the group to study at the University of Notre Dame, that "beauteous place where nature teems . . . and learning calmly grows apace, while fancy dreams." But fancy found scant leisure for dreaming. Our Lady's school made large demands on time and effort, and the sequel shows that scholarship has its own compensations.

The combination of a great scholar and a great teacher is rare. What if it be found, not once, but six times in as many years—in the field of English. Witness of this is Father Charles O'Donnell, in touching whose poetry we touch immortality; Father Carrico's passion for perfection; Father Cavanaugh's scholarly wisdom and elegant grace; the contagious enthusiasm and superb craftsmanship of Charles Phillips; George N. Shuster's versatility and critical acumen; the vision and wit of Fred I. Myers. Inasmuch as philosophy was pursued as a minor in graduate work through to the doctorate, loyalty permits me to express indebtedness to two scholars who carried on the Thomistic tradition at Notre Dame, Fathers Charles C. Miltner and Matthew Schumacher.

Summer Schools only enriched the opportunities afforded by the regular academic year, and the harvesting has been perennial. The Bachelor of Arts degree in 1922, the Master's degree in 1923, and the doctorate in English in 1930, sum up these seven years of plenty. In these scholarly contacts with great minds lay a justification for the sacrifices religious superiors made to bring higher education under Catholic auspices within the reach of the sisters, thus to lay the foundation for subsequent service at the college level in their own schools.

Notre Dame College for women, in South Euclid, Ohio, was founded in 1922. Returning to Cleveland in 1923, after receiving the Master's degree, I was appointed to teach English in the college, and for a year to serve as acting dean. A sabbatical year, 1927–1928, gave the opportunity for completing the work towards the doctorate; another, 1929–1930, was spent in research at the Library of Congress and the final work on the doctor's thesis. Entitled *John Henry Newman, the Romantic, the Friend, the Leader,* it was written under the direction of Charles Phillips, who suggested the theme at the outset, and thus was largely responsible for the greater piece of work that grew out of the dissertation. When the degree was conferred in 1920, I was the first sister to receive the doctorate in residence at the University.

Several manuscripts in process of translation with a view to publication were accepted by the University toward satisfying the language requirements for both the M.A. and the Ph.D. *Jesus, the Model of Religious,* a two volume work of meditations, published in 1924, was the first of a series of eight or nine books that followed within a decade or two. Of these the last two are original works: *Draw Near to Him,* and *Praying with the Poverello,* a paraphrase of St. Francis' prayer for peace. Articles also appeared then or later in *Ave Maria, Columbia, Catholic Educational Review, Sponsa Regis,* and other reviews.

Enrichment of background and fresh enthusiasm came with a year of European travel in 1936–1937, at the kindly instance of Rev. Mother Mary Antonie, Superior General. Oxford and Oriel College, fragrant with memories of Newman; Miss Grace Guiney and her sister Ruth, cousins of our beloved poet, Louise Imogen Guiney,—Grace the editor of Louise's unfinished *Recusant Poets,* in collaboration with Edward O'Brien, who had known the poet. On the Continent there was the sweet simplicity of Ruth Schaumann, Catholic mother, poet, artist, and sculptor, in the suburbs of Munich. In the Netherlands, the Catholic University of Nijmegen with its scholarly tomes of the *Acta Sanctorum,* triumph of the Bollandists; Dr. Maria Montessori lecturing under the auspices of the University of Utrecht. Along the Rhine, was historic Maria Laach and its glorious Benedictine tradition; the monastery and spirit of the medieval saint and scholar, Hildegard of Bingen-on-the-Rhine; the magnificent Church of St. Ursula at Cologne; and many another cultured and historic spot.

The written word is intimately bound up with the personality and life work of an author. It should be evident from the subjects chosen for the bachelor's thesis, *Quintilian, Teacher of Rhetoric,* and for the master's, *Womanhood in Modern Poetry,* that there was design in the pursuit of higher education, envisioning the teaching field, in which a religious should find her greatest usefulness and richest influence.

There is a difference, however, in the nature of the books turned out. It so happens that my volumes are for the most part spiritual, though the Newman book is wholly cast in an academic mold. A number of them are translations undertaken at the instance of priests who felt that the specific books should be made available to a wider reading public. Close upon the heels of the suggestion came the determination to do the job. And here, I believe, it is *fabricando fit faber.* Never has there been regret for work thus assumed, with the sanction of religious obedience lighting the way. From this point of view, work of this kind must be accounted a singular blessing. The writing of spiritual books gives breadth of vision and deep soul-peace.

Occasional lectures on my favorite subject, Cardinal Newman, and other literary topics, seem to uncover new reserves to enrich both the writing and the teaching that are my happy lot.

In glancing backward, one naturally pauses to give thanks. A home where the sanctities of family life and culture were held in high esteem; my own religious Congregation, cherishing high ideals of Marian virtue and learning; the University of Notre Dame and the Lady of the Golden Dome. I pay tribute in Patmore's words:

> Mother, who lead'st me still by unknown ways,
> Giving the gifts I know not how to ask,
> Bless thou the work!

EDITOR'S NOTE: Sister Mary Aloysi's books include: *John Henry Newman, the Romantic, the Friend, the Leader,* 1933, Collegiate Press; *Jesus, the Model of Religious,* 1924, Pustet; *Meditations on the Seven Dolars of Our Lady,* 1931, id.; *Splendor and Strength of the Inner Life,* 1940, id.; *The Rosary and the Soul of Woman,* 1941, id.; *A Light to My Paths,* 1941, id.; *The Priceless Pearl,* 1938, Coldwell, London; excepting the Newman book, these are translations and adaptations; two original books are *Draw Near To Him,* 1942, Pustet; *Praying With the Poverello,* 1943, id.

SARA MAYNARD

MOST PEOPLE have a clear sense of their nationality, but I have not that feeling. In moments of brightness I say to myself: "Well, I have three countries, and so I am luckier than the average"; but at other times there is the unstable feeling that after all I must be a sort of mongrel—for though I may be ready to claim all three countries as mine, yet none of the three may want to receive me wholeheartedly on such terms.

I was born in South Africa, and retain an almost painful love and longing for that country—but my ancestry is entirely Irish—and now I've lived longer in America than anywhere else, and five of my children are born-Americans. Going on a holiday to Canada years ago it was rather startling to hear the customs' official, after examining our passports, call out to another official: "One American citizen and four aliens." I think we treated Paul the baby of the family—the one American citizen—with unusual respect for the remainder of the journey.

Sometimes, when marketing in this small pleasant town of

Westminster, Maryland, where we live, in spirit I am thousands of miles away, walking in the brilliant (yet never too brilliant) sunshine along a wide oak-shaded street in a suburb of Cape Town, where the picturesque Dutch houses stand in gardens full of flowers—and then Clare, who is eleven, will suddenly make some such observation as: "There is no one so Irish as a Casey!" —and instantly the quiet happiness of the Dutch country vanishes, and it is Ireland with its hundreds of years of struggle for freedom, and the tragic part played by my father's family in one of its uprisings, that becomes the visionary land I walk in; and presently I am once more shopping in this friendly American town, glad and grateful to be an American citizen.

My mother did not like South Africa, and so to please her my father took us to live on the outskirts of Dublin, at Glenageary. Near by was Dalkey, and there my sisters and I went to school at Loreto Abbey. The Irish people we loved right away, and our first summer, spent at Rostrevor in the County of Down, was a time of enchantment; but becoming acclimated to the grey skies and wet penetrating cold of the long winters was a terrible trial. We went back to Cape Town, but only once and only for a visit; after that our travelling was confined to Europe.

While my brother was a student at Trinity College he wrote a couple of plays for the Abbey Theatre—and for me that opened a new world. The matinee at the Abbey became something to look forward to every week, in much the same way my children now troop to the movies on a Saturday afternoon. I remember seeing Thomas MacDonagh (who was afterwards executed for his share in the Easter Rebellion) walking in Rathgar, his dark head thrown back, wearing no hat (which was unusual in that climate), reciting as he walked. I used to wonder was he reciting some play of Yeats or Synge that ran in my own head, but which I would not venture to recite aloud in the street, not having his poetic aloofness. Now, I think it was more likely one of his own poems in the making that he was saying to himself.

Because of ill-health I had to leave boarding-school; with lessons cut down to a few special courses I had a good many free hours, and so started writing stories—two at a time, which is hardly the best way.

I never sent the stories to any editor. But when I wrote a play about a Fenian rising, in which the rebels gave the mighty British a glorious beating, I sent it to Yeats; not wanting him to connect the play with the Caseys, on account of my brother, I signed myself John O'Hara, % the local postmistress. Yeats sent the manuscript back, with a very kind letter, suggesting that Mr. O'Hara try a play with a more simple plot. Some years later, when I did have a play done at the Abbey, I put the postmistress into it.

Then I went to school in Germany with my eldest sister. We went to the Ursulines in Cologne. The convent was hundreds of years old. It was situated close to the railroad station and the Cathedral, and so I am afraid there can be little left of it now.

With beginner's luck, I had a novel accepted by the first publisher I sent it to, although it had glaring faults. Walter de la Mare, the reader who accepted it, wanted it lengthened and some changes made. Apart from his good looks, what struck me most about Walter de la Mare was his gentleness. He did not take a blue pencil and slash the manuscript; instead he "ventured to suggest" that a particular passage would be better deleted as it might hurt the feelings of a certain group; and so on.

After that my ambition was to run a children's magazine. I had the financial backing, and a stack of contributions. The profits were to be spent on children who lived in the slums. But it was 1917, the War was on, and there was a shortage of paper. By the time peace came I was married and had a baby, and the pressing problem was to find not paper for a magazine but a place anywhere in London to live in. My plans remained a dream; for soon I had another baby, and my husband had gone to America. A year later, with the two children, Michael and Rosemary, I came to America. Except for brief periods abroad, we have been in America ever since. Yet it remains as a vague disappointment that I was never able to do any of the wonderful things I had planned for the little children born in the slums.

One of my American children fascinates me because of the difference between her childhood and my own. In the middle of a game she will dash upstairs and type out a letter, then dash downstairs again and go on with the game. Her letters, which she leaves lying on my desk, are always addressed to a Mr. Sparrow, and Mr. Sparrow seems to be always in need of a stenographer. Graciously she writes that she will accept the position, and become his "secritry"; and then it is *she* who arranges the terms of salary, and—more important still—the hours. "I will be late the first day," she writes to Mr. Sparrow. When I read her letters I marvel at the change of times since those old-fashioned days when I was a child, and stood in silent awe of every grown-up.

EDITOR'S NOTE: Sara Maynard (Mrs. Theodore Maynard) is the author of *Princess Poverty*, 1941, Longmans; *Here Come the Penguins*, 1942, St. Anthony Guild; *Rose of America*, 1943, Sheed; *Scott and His Men*, 1945.

BENJAMIN FRANCIS MUSSER

ASKED FOR a fifteen hundred word autobiographical sketch, I can give it in one word—Sinner, or, to be more detailed, Miserable Sinner. And this is not rhetorical. Ask my brother, an Episcopalian clergyman; he will agree. But from a "Catholic author" you will expect something else, and here it is.

Born in 1889, the fifth of his name (and guilty of pride in this possession, more so of the fact that one of his sons is Benjamin Musser 6th and of appropriate age to beget Benjamin 7th), mine was a happy childhood though not like yours who were born in the Faith. Three generations of Episcopalians, behind them seven of American Quakers and Mennonites, behind them five generations of English and Welsh and German Protestants, stood between me and the Mystical Body of Christ, and my genealogical love as a boy was shamed to see beyond this wall a very army of canonized saints, direct ancestors. To break a hole through that wall to the truth that makes one free, was my great concern. And following juveniles sallies into several of the arts—choir singer and soloist, three years in an art school, sundry stillborn efforts at creative writing—I did, and this while still a boy, burst that wall wide open and ride into the City of God, with the Holy Name of Mary on my lips.

It has always annoyed me to be referred to as a convert. I am not. I came in at the age of reason. True, that was just past my nineteenth birthday, in April of 1908—I was a little slow becoming reasonable! And reason, plus the grace of faith, might not even then have conquered had I not spent a year in an Episcopalian theological seminary, a Roman kindergarten. May its tribe increase. So life began for me at nineteen. I hope I am still nineteen at heart, childlike not childish.

With the Faith came other things—the three-times struggle to become a Friar Minor, as Priest or Brother, and three times flung back into a world of invalids and pain and resignation, a Via Dolorosa, but with it the solace of being a Tertiary of Saint Francis since October, 1909, and since December, 1940 the unusual honor of being an affiliate of the First Order, by proclamation from Rome (only one other American laic has been so privileged, my friend Paul Martin-Dillon), and now the exceeding great joy of knowing my younger son humbly and holily filling the place I had tried to occupy long ago, the vocation of a Friar Minor; the urge to write and a gradual progression in the field of letters, including, however, a period in which Bohemianism rivaled Catholicism for the field and finally, I pray, forever, fell before the Cross. That "arty" interlude included the editorship of several poetry magazines, on advisory board or co-editorship of six others, the organizing of a "Toy" Theatre, and other flimsy pursuits.

It amused me to become a "jiner" of groups and to give lectures and to declaim execrable verse before audiences who actually paid to hear the juvenilia—and in very rare instances even invited a return engagement! I cannot recall more than a third of the societies to which I belonged and, presumably, still belong; here are a few of them: Poetry Society of America (since 1924), Poetry Society of England (a Vice President since 1937), Empire Poetry League, Academy Member (one of the original thirty) of the Catholic Poetry Society of America, twice former President, now Honorary President, of the Washington Catholic Poetry Society; honorary member of the Poetry Societies of Alabama and of the Southwest, of the Chatterton-Lacy Foundation, of the Press Club of St. Francis' College at Joliet; Life Member of the Order of Bookfellows; perpetual member of the Society for the Propagation of the Faith; member of the Calvert Associates, of the American Catholic Historical Society, of the Liturgical Arts Society since its inception, of the Nocturnal Adoration Society, of the Catholic Unity League, of the Catholic Evidence Guild, of the Catholic Association for International Peace, of the Catholic Alumni Sodality, of the Franciscan Missionary Union, of St. Anthony's Guild, of the Guild of the Cross, one of the original members of the Gallery of Living Catholic Authors, Honorary Citizen of Boystown; local president of our parochial groups in the Confraternity of Christian Doctrine, etc., etc. In 1934, some misguided zealots, backed by the State Governor and ratified by the United States Senate, made me first Poet Laureate of New Jersey. Apparently the post is similar to that of the present occupant of the White House—for life.

I spare you further cataloguing. Nor shall I list the books that poured forth, from that birth at nineteen to these my green and salad days within one inch of fifty-six. There have been, I think, forty-three volumes, maybe forty-five, not counting two in publisher's hands. Nor does this, of course, include, a dozen or more books by others for whom I wrote introductions or saw through the press, including *Of Bitter Grapes,* by the young Detroit priest-poet Emery Petho.

My own wares are divided among verse (politely called poetry), essays, history, biography, philology, lectures and editorials, devotional and mystical studies, Franciscalia, polemics and irenics, liturgical excursions—almost everything except fiction and a catering to popular taste or demand. Consequently, no volume of mine ever came within a mile of choice of any book club. (Anyway, the grapes are sour, said the fox.) None indeed, it is safe to say, has ever been heard of by the vaster reading public, and each little book has had its brief little moment and then died resignedly.

The earliest, published by Benziger Brothers in 1912, was for altar boys; the latest, just completed an hour ago, is called *Don't! A Half-Hundred or More Brotherly Suggestions for Catholics at Mass.* And does it step on your toes! Of these forty odd books, some are very odd indeed. Only two give me any semblance of satisfaction, and this with reservations: the prose study called *Franciscan Poets* and my collected spiritual verse, *The Bird Below the Waves.* Never have I made any bid for popularity, never have I written unless compelled beyond myself, never for sake of emolument. Neither publishers nor writer in this instance ever paid huge income tax because of my books. Publishers could wisely write their contracts with me in red ink!

Finally, let me say this. If my life began when I was just past nineteen, and I became the slave of Mary in the City of Her Son, and have so remained, my Second Spring began in 1921, when the loveliest soul I have ever known took pity on this Miserable Sinner and has since made his path as nearly beautiful as an earthly pilgrimage can be. Four children have blessed our marriage (of these one was recalled immediately to the Nurseries of Heaven), and we have in addition in far Ceylon, at the Papal Seminary, an adopted son, our "Barty," studying for the priesthood. In the family chapel, the Little Oratory of Our Lady of the Angels, where the children gathered with us twice daily, in daily Mass and Communion and visits in our parish church, in their admirable Catholic boarding school education, few children have known a gentler exemplar of the living liturgy, a more patient, a white-souled little mother than have mine—and we are all, they and I, hoping to reach Heaven by clinging to the Amen of one of her prayers! She lives, in the world, the life of a contemplative. And incidentally, she was raised a Presbyterian!

EDITOR'S NOTE: The letters of affiliation give Mr. Musser the right to the initials O.F.M. after his name. He is a resident of Atlantic City, N. J. Restating his preferences, we list his principal books as *Franciscan Poets*, 1933, Macmillan, and *The Bird Below the Waves*, 1938, Magnificat Press.

REVEREND PATRICK O'CONNOR

My father and mother were Irish,
And I am Irish, too;
I bought a wee fiddle for ninepence,
And that was Irish, too . . .

SO GOES AN OLD SONG, and so goes my story.

On St. Patrick's Day, 1899, I was born in Clontarf, Dublin. There was one obvious name to give a baby born on the day, and I am happy indeed that it was given to me. My father was from County Roscommon, my mother from County Galway, God rest their souls. I have much to thank them for—above all, the Faith that they and those who went before them not only kept but treasured. I was the youngest of five children.

A "wee fiddle" is the best I can say of whatever I have written. It is no Stradivarius, vibrant in the supple hand of a master. Still less is it a pealing organ. But even a wee Irish fiddle can carry notes that are true and it may help to speed a good tune on the winds of the world.

I had not long learned to read and write when I nailed my colors to the editorial masthead by bringing out a midget family newspaper. When I was nine, I was already an avid reader, devouring adventure and school stories and some grown-up fiction —*Pickwick Papers,* for instance. Until I was fifteen or sixteen, poetry bored me. It was just an awkward, silly way of saying what could be better said in prose.

When I left the Clontarf school conducted by the Sisters of the Holy Faith in 1909, I went to Belvedere, the Jesuit day school that my brother was already attending. There, a year later, I first wrote for publication, chronicling the junior-house "milestones" for the school annual. I contributed to the *Belvederian* —thanks to indulgent editors—nearly every year thereafter.

Belvedere, its teachers and its boys, did a great deal for me, a shy, skinny youngster. It was good, at the age of ten, to be in an all-man school. Smiling, pleasant Father William Doyle, S.J., was teaching there at the time, but I was not in his class. (And never would be!) I remember gratefully the manly, friendly, invigorating Jesuits whom I knew in Belvedere and who have never ceased to be my friends. The boys had a fine spirit, with a high code of sportsmanship. Rugby football was the major sport, and I longed to be like those who excelled in it. I played, but without distinction. I did, however, have the unforgettable delight of being on the team that won the junior provincial championship in 1914, though two years later I could barely keep my place on the senior team.

During my last year in Belvedere, Dublin crackled and shook and flamed in the dramatic Easter Week Rising. People differed regarding the prudence of the insurrection, but nobody could fail to be stirred by the generous self-sacrifice of its high-minded leaders. "Here's to you, Pearse—your dream, not mine," sang AE in disagreement and frank admiration. "A terrible beauty is born," wrote Yeats, who some years earlier had lamented: "Romantic Ireland's dead and gone."

The example of the men of Easter Week influenced me profoundly in that decisive year of my teens. In my last "Milestones" for the *Belvederian* I wrote my youthful tribute to their "chivalrous heroism." To the everlasting credit of my Jesuit teachers, they let it appear, within four weeks or so of the executions and while a strict British military regime still held sway.

Just then I began to read some letters from China, written by a Father Galvin and printed in the weekly *Irish Catholic*. By July, 1916, I knew what I wanted yet dreaded to be—a missionary. But how? That summer, providentially, Father Galvin came back from China to the United States and Ireland, to launch what has since become St. Columban's Foreign Mission Society. From the moment I heard of his project, I recognized it as the answer to my question. Some time would elapse, however, before he and his comrades could accept student volunteers.

I entered University College, Dublin—constituent college of the National University of Ireland—in the fall of 1916. My English professors were Father George O'Neill, S.J., and the late Robert Donovan. Towards the end of my first year, Father O'Neill gave us an essay assignment, adding dryly that he would accept a poem instead. Some lines of a simple lyric had been singing in my mind. Already I was deep in student activities, and time was precious. It was easier to finish the poem than to write the essay. Rather to my surprise, Father O'Neill praised the lyric and had it printed, under the title, "A Connacht Exile," in the *Irish Monthly*, the review founded by Father Matthew Russell, S.J.

Life at the university became more and more interesting, but I was still watching the development of the new missionary enterprise. Its organ, *The Far East*, was begun in Ireland in January, 1918, and one of the priests asked me to write a poem for it. Hiding behind a pen-name, I contributed "A Prayer of Youth" and "The Splendid Cause." Years later, Father O'Neill, who had gone to Australia for his health, saw "The Splendid Cause" and set it to music. Oscar Deis, organist of St. Thomas the Apostle Church, Chicago, has recently composed choral music for "A Prayer of Youth."

In October, 1919, with a B.A. degree and some misgivings, I

entered St. Columban's, Dalgan Park, Galway, to begin the life
of a seminarian. The missions were what I wanted; this cas-
socked, humdrum preparatory stage did not appeal to me. But
Dalgan, in its second year, with a small student body possessing
all the generous elan of pioneers, soon opened my eyes. I saw
that here was the foundation of the missions, here the first missionary test and task.

I wrote a good deal of poetry for *The Far East* during my
student days, using, as a rule, the pen-name of Benen, the Irish
boy who attached himself to St. Patrick and became his successor
as Archbishop of Armagh. In 1922 I took my master's degree in
English Literature at the university.

The greatest event that can befall any man came for me on
June 10, 1923, when I was ordained a priest. During my last
year in Dalgan the marvelous world of the priesthood and the
Mass was coming nearer to me and clearer. I know that one can
realize these marvels only faintly, at best, and one can never express them adequately. Still the very power of the subject forces
one to attempt some utterance.

The majority of my class went to China that fall. I was de-
tached for service in the United States, where St. Columban's Society was growing and undermanned. *The Far East,* had been
founded here, too, in 1918, and now it became my work. It
still is.

During the past twenty-one years I have had other experiences,
too. For instance, I fell ill and during an extended absence from
my routine work, I saw many phases of life and learned to appreciate the spiritual triumphs—and tragedies—that lie beneath the
surface of everyday existence. For three priceless, crowded years
I served as moderator of the Omaha Conference of the Catholic
Students' Mission Crusade, while editing and writing for *The
Far East* at the same time. This association with those wonderful
people, American Catholic boys and girls, is still refreshing and
inspiring to recall. What I have seen of their candor, enthusiasm
—yes, and simplicity—convinces me that it would be a frightful
mistake to give them no outlet except talk and show or to set

before them no standard higher than merely have-a-good-time-but-see-that-you-stop-short-of-mortal-sin. They have a capacity for generosity; some of them, perhaps many, are capable of heroism. A short article, "Death at Seventeen," which I wrote in 1933 and which appeared in *The Sign* a year later, expresses my outlook after my experiences as Crusade moderator.

At length, in 1937, I sailed for the Far East, though on a round-trip ticket. I went to Manila as spiritual director of St. Columban's Pilgrimage to the Eucharistic Congress. After the Congress I stayed on in the Philippines, later going to China, Korea, Japan, Malaya and Ceylon. This is not the place to sum up all that the missions, so long dreamt of and written about, meant to me, when at last I rode through the rice fields and heard the cadences of Chinese congregations at prayer and saw the springtime of the Faith slowly, painfully and wonderfully supplanting the winter of paganism. I can never forget that year. I know that my experience of the missions could not include the loss of the sense of novelty, the disappointments, the aridity and even distaste that make up the cross of many missionaries. But even supposing all these, one can still recognize the work of the missions as the most glorious and fascinating on earth.

Now in my middle forties I find that I have written little of what I once hoped to write. With a magazine deadline crowding one, month by month, and acting—wisely or unwisely—as staff contributor as well as editor, one must bypass and soon forget the novel, the story, the play, the poem that in some rose-colored hour seemed only waiting to be written down. Probably most of those visions were illusions. Writers are too often their own dupes.

On the other hand, it has been a precious and delightful privilege to write about the missions and to edit a magazine of the missions, reaching many thousands of readers month after month. Joyce Kilmer—I quote from memory—said that he would sooner write tolerably well about the Faith than brilliantly about anything else. I would sooner write for and about the missions than be the author of all the best-sellers of today and all the classics of the past.

My writing has been chiefly articles on everything from the theology of the missions to Catholic life in Singapore. I have also written short stories, verse serious and less serious, and miscellaneous material for "departments." I have used various pennames, including W. O'Malley, Patrick Breheny and Nanky Poo. Around 1924 I wrote some doggerel for the children's pages and signed it the Gilbert-and-Sullivanish Nanky Poo, a name that I kept as I wrote juvenile and light verse through the years. Nothing I have written has traveled farther than some of this unpretentious but apparently "folksy" verse. One piece, "Just For a Minute," has been reprinted many times and in many places, losing all trace of its origin as it made the rounds. Finally people started sending it to me on verse cards, printed by zealous distributors who had taken a fancy to the unidentified lines. "An Editor's Prayer" was reprinted in India and South Africa and came to the U. S. via a Protestant paper.

In 1928 *Songs of Youth,* a selection of poems I had written during the previous eleven years, appeared and went subsequently into three more printings. Sometimes a successor to this book seemed likely, but it has never come. Perhaps a prolonged term in jail or hospital or on shipboard might give me a chance to add to the first lines that have been wandering through my mind for years, waiting to grow into poems.

In 1930 the book entitled *Pudsy Kelly's Gang,* a selection of Nanky Poo verse, came out, and in 1942 *Pudsy Kelly's Follower,* another selection. A few pamphlets, reprints from *The Far East,* have also been published. From time to time I have written for various magazines other than *The Far East,* but my own has claimed most of my writing time.

What advice can I offer to youthful writers?

Begin by writing about what is nearest to you in the medium that is nearest. It is excruciating to try to read a manuscript about Oriental life by a writer whose knowledge of the Orient is restricted to an occasional chop suey dinner on Main Street, U. S. A.

Write immediately when the idea is fresh, the image vivid, the emotion glowing. Write down something there and then, no matter how crudely or hastily. It will hold the vital spark until you have a chance to fan it to full flame. Regretfully I recall the times when I failed to do this—and I have never recaptured the fugitive inspiration.

Read masterly prose and poetry and memorize it. Thus you will develop a sense of rhythm, of structure, of climax. If you mean to write poetry, don't take the easy way of free verse. Those rhymeless, formless, facile lines often lead nowhere, rarely lead to true poetic achievement.

Lately I received a questionnaire from a student of journalism in a State university. It asked what preparation I should suggest for a journalistic career. The first point in my reply was "Become a Catholic." I cannot see how any one can live sanely or write coherently without a satisfactory answer to the great problems of existence. And there is only one such answer. In the same sense I say to the Young Catholic aspirant: Be a good Catholic, well informed and spiritually active.

Your first reference source, your best instruction, your inexhaustible inspiration is in the Tabernacle.

EDITOR'S NOTE: Father O'Connor, who is president of the Catholic Press Association, is the author of *Songs of Youth*, 1928, The Far East, and (under the pseudonym Nanky Poo) *Pudsy Kelly's Gang*, 1930, and *Pudsy Kelly's Follower*, 1942, St. Anthony Guild.

REVEREND LESLIE RUMBLE, M.S.C.

WHEN ONE, born into a most unpropitious environment, finds himself almost miraculously a Catholic, he cannot but find himself also filled with the urge to win as many others as possible to the same great gift of the Catholic Faith. In my case, this experience led to the entirely unforeseen apostolate of the pen; but it was by the long and uphill road.

I was born in 1892, in Sydney, Australia. Both my parents had been born in England, had married there, and had come to Australia where my father thought greater scope awaited him in his profession as a civil engineer.

Religiously, my parents were Anglicans with a conservative low-church outlook, and we children were brought up in a decidedly Protestant tradition, rather neglectful of positive religious duties, but filled with a deep-seated antipathy towards Catholicism.

A purely secular state-school education, which I shared with my brothers and sisters, did nothing to help stimulate any interest in religion; and I left school at the earliest age permissible in order to escape studies for which I had no taste, and the still more irksome restraints of school-discipline.

At the age of fourteen, then, I got a job as a messenger boy, thought only of a commercial career, felt a man at last, and dropped all religion in practice.

Eighteen months later, so far as I was concerned, and I think my brothers and sisters shared my feelings, an announcement fell like a bombshell in our midst. My father, unusually for him, had been going out every night for two weeks running, for the first few days by himself, then taking my mother with him. At the end of that time he told us that he and mother had been attending a mission at a nearby Catholic Church; that he and mother had decided to become Catholics; and that all of us children would have to be instructed and received into the Church also. We looked at one another in silence, stunned. But my father was not one to be resisted. The younger children were taken from the state school and sent to the Catholic school, whilst the three who were working, myself and two elder brothers, were to go to the Catholic rectory one night each week to receive instructions from one of the priests.

I will never forget the misery of those instructions. My eldest brother was nineteen, the second seventeen, myself fifteen and a half. I was not interested in religion, was afraid of the priest, ashamed and humiliated by the thought of the step being forced upon me, and sat through the instructions without paying any attention to them, sullen and resentful. At last, when he had finished explaining the catechism, the priest, taking it for granted that all was well, told us that we three boys would be baptized together, appointed the day, and received us into the Church, shortly after the hurried reception of my father and mother.

So, in 1908, filled with interior rebellion, I was formally received into the Catholic Church, hating it, and dreading only a conflict with my father, of whom I had ever been afraid, did I refuse.

After two years of unwilling and compulsory attendance at a

Mass I did not understand, I defied my parents and began attending the local Anglican Church, saying that that was the Church in which I had been christened, and that I would live and die a member of the Church of England. But no positive love for Anglicanism impelled me to take that step. At heart I was irreligious. I said no prayers. I boasted to my irreligious companions outside the family that I regarded all religion as rubbish. And soon I abandoned the attendance at the Anglican Church which had been due in reality only to a spirit of defiance.

It was in 1911 that my outlook completely changed. A fellow-worker whose decency and integrity were outstanding amongst all the employees with whom I was associated, impressed me deeply by an example that I could not but admire. One day, quite accidentally, I found out that this fellow-worker was a Catholic; and from that moment, try as I would, I could not get the idea out of my mind that all my prejudices against the Catholic religion were unjustified. I determined to study it seriously for myself. I got hold of every book I could on the subject. I became convinced of the truth of the Catholic Church, took up the practice of the Catholic religion in earnest, and within eighteen months felt impelled to offer my life to God as a priest in one of the missionary Orders of the Church.

At the beginning of 1913, therefore, I entered the preparatory seminary of the Missionaries of the Sacred Heart, in Sydney, N. S. W., being then half way through my twenty-first year. There, when I had explained to the rector the circumstances of my reception into the Church, it was deemed necessary to have me re-baptized and re-confirmed owing to my lack of proper dispositions at the time I received those Sacraments; and I commenced a five years' course of secondary studies to supply for my lack of anything beyond a grade school standard, and to fulfil a condition necessary for entrance into the Novitiate.

Within a year my father and mother and brothers and sisters had all abandoned the Catholic religion. As impulsively as he had decided to become a Catholic, my father had decided to be done with all religion. He became a militant agnostic, and suc-

ceeded only too easily in persuading my mother and brothers and
sisters to follow him into what they regarded as comfortable unbelief, though they were little interested in his arguments in justification of his decision.

I, however, was interested in those arguments, and begged my
father to write and tell me just what he had against the Catholic
Church, whether from history or science, philosophy or Scripture.
He did so, and continued doing so intermittently for almost ten
years, the correspondence proving for me a compulsory initiation
into the art of writing, and demanding earnest efforts to be clear
at all costs, to be interesting enough to make him continue the
discussion, and persuasive enough to win him back to the Faith
in the end. There are advantages in having some dominant
interest compelling one to take up one's pen, though one has
no ambition to be a writer, rather than in setting one's heart on
being a writer, and then looking 'round as a kind of afterthought
for something about which to write.

Side by side with this correspondence, I went on with my
studies. During my five preparatory years of literature, history,
and science, I concentrated chiefly on the first, adopting Stevenson's advice to play the "sedulous ape." The attempt to master
and imitate the styles of a hundred authors is a laboratory method
of learning to write English which pays rich dividends in the
end.

However, in 1918, I had to abandon that pursuit in order to
enter the Novitiate, and to become better acquainted with the
principles of the spiritual life, and with something of the vast
treasures of ascetical and mystical writings which are preemi-
nently the glory of the Catholic Church.

Two years of philosophy followed, and four years of theology,
and then, just prior to my ordination as a priest in 1924, came
the conversion of my father and mother and sisters to the Church
from an extreme of militant unbelief which scarcely seemed
credible even to them as they looked back upon it in after years.

After my ordination to the priesthood I applied to my Superiors to be assigned to the Papuan mission-field, only to be sent to Rome for further studies under the care of the Dominican Fathers at the Collegium Angelicum, whence I returned two years later to Australia with the doctorate in theology and an appointment to teach that subject as a professor in the Major Seminary of the Missionaries of the Sacred Heart at Kensington, New South Wales.

It was then that I commenced my writing apostolate in earnest, beginning with Catholic Truth Society pamphlets, and articles in Catholic newspapers and magazines, many of the latter being later collected and published in book form both in Sydney and London. If one has the ambition to carve out a career as a writer, I would certainly recommend beginning with newspapers and magazines. Financially the returns are more assured, and as the demand for books depends to a great extent upon a well-established name, such articles create a field in advance for the sale of more pretentious works.

However, I was not interested in a career as a writer. My duty was the propagation of the Faith under the direction of religious Superiors, and I wrote articles at their request. In 1928, with the advent of the International Eucharistic Congress to Sydney, I was appointed to give a preparatory series of radio talks during several months in advance; and after the event, commenced a weekly Catholic Information Service by radio, the listening public supplying the questions and therefore the subject matter of the session. Each session lasts for one full hour, and it still flourishes from our Catholic Broadcasting Station 2SM in Sydney after sixteen years.

The replies given during the first five years were collected, classified, and published in Sydney in book form under the title *Radio Replies,* towards the end of the year 1933. An American edition of the book was brought out in collaboration with Father Charles Mortimer Carty, Diocesan Missioner at St. Paul, Minnesota, and proved so popular that two additional volumes have since been produced. The complete set of three volumes,

entitled *Radio Replies* by Rumble and Carty, and distributed by
Radio Replies Press, St. Paul, has already run into more than a
half million copies.

For the preparation of the second and third volumes I visited
America, spending the year 1940 in the United States, collaborat-
ing with Father Carty in the production of the books during the
early months, and lecturing throughout the Northwestern and
Eastern States during the latter part of the year. Returning to
Sydney in 1941, I resumed my radio apostolate there, with the
intention of continuing it so long as it retains its public appeal
—and the end is not yet!

EDITOR'S NOTE: Father Rumble's books include *Cobblestones and Catholicity*,
1929, Pellegrini; *Correspondence Course in Catholic Doctrine*, 1929, Sheed,
and 1941, Radio Replies Press; *Radio Replies*, three volumes, 1934–1942,
Radio Replies Press, St. Paul.

REVEREND WILLIAM H. RUSSELL

ONE FEELS a lingering hesitancy about acceding to a request from an editor for an autobiographical article. One is conscious of the tribute, yet he suspects that there may be an obtrusion of the ego in the reply. As I pondered the proposition, that which weighed the scales in favor of expressing in words how I came to be a writer was, first, a sense of obligation to pay tribute to a former fellow student; second, the opportunity to ask why more literary persons do not choose the subject which has kept me close to a typewriter; third, the duty of voicing gratitude for an undeserved blessing and joy at having been led into such a subject.

Practically, my subject has been Jesus Christ. To say that is not to imply that the same might not be true of any priest. But God's providence directs us in different ways. One may not see His guiding hand at the moment of decision, but one is permitted to look back with thankful heart. If one finds that the name of Christ can be omitted from nothing that he writes, need he feel any chagrin?

To write about the Son of God is to be ever conscious of one's own inadequacy, one's own unworthiness and inability to measure up to the subject. Not to him who writes, but to him or her who re-lives the life of the Son of Mary must go primary praise. And into the ears of him who writes there comes across the centuries the echo of the words of the prophet: *nescio loqui*. As one approaches the Carpenter from Nazareth he finds himself inarticulate in the presence of a theme that clamors for expression. The poverty of language, the weakness of mere words, the trembling pen call for an angel to limn the portrait. While I hold that in some respects Jesus differs from other topics in that He Himself is always first, and literary expression secondary, yet here is a field that merits attention from the most spiritual of literary minds.

During my freshman year at Loras College in Dubuque, Iowa, a junior came into my room to read to me his oration for the annual oratorical contest. He had made generous use of the Scripture, and he advised me to spend my leisure hours reading the Bible. His words seemed banal at the time, especially when I tried to interest myself in St. Matthew's Gospel. I realized that no professor ever became enthused over anything which I wrote as verse or as prose composition. Athletics held more inducement for me at the time. Nevertheless the young orator had sown a seed. Then, in my junior year, a friend with whom I was travelling wished to visit the St. Paul Seminary. In the course of our visit Msgr. Humphrey Moynihan picked up his New Testament and showed us the value of reading with full enunciation the first pages of St. John's Gospel. The incident made an impression on me. As a senior in college I began to force myself to peruse the pages of the New Testament. It was a work of drudgery but somehow or other I persevered. Even while following the same procedure in my seminary days at the Grand Seminary in Montreal it was not yet a labor of delight.

After ordination to the priesthood in December, 1919, I was sent to the cathedral in Dubuque. My stay there was short, for I was soon assigned to the college to replace a teacher who had become ill. I was also asked to teach some religion classes in the academy. In the following September I was sent to the Catholic University for a year. Doctor Pace in psychology, Dr. Shields in education and Dr. Parker in biology were high calibre teachers. I cannot recall just why I chose St. Jerome as a dissertation topic for the M.A. in education, but his pungent sentence: "To be ignorant of the Scriptures is to be ignorant of Christ," has never passed from my mind. I had procured a cheap copy of the New Testament shortly after ordination and had begun to carry it with me. I still preserve the muchmarked copy. The livingness and effectiveness of the word of God had now begun to take hold on me.

Upon returning to Dubuque I taught education in the college and religion in the academy. Gradually I began to see the necessity for fulltime teachers in religion. The present Archbishop Howard of Portland, Oregon, who was then president of the college, permitted me to devote full time to the religion classes in the academy. I often noticed a change on the faces of the boys, and likewise on the girls in the Visitation academy where I had begun to teach, when I used Scripture to portray Christ. Thus was confirmed a passage which I had read in Canon Sheehan's *Triumph of Failure*: "Once I commenced to talk about Christ—I mean the Christ of the Gospels, the Christ of the Saints, the Christ of the Martyrs—I held them in the palm of my hand. And what touched them most was what I used to call—I hope without irreverence—the manliness of Christ." Thus did I drift out into that vast ocean of the God-Man. Thus began to unfold His "unfathomable riches." Thus arose the conviction that the proper study of mankind is *the* Man.

In the first articles which I wrote on high school religion in the *Catholic Educational Review* in 1924 I tried to set forth the advantages of teaching religion with and through Christ. In 1926 Herder published my first textbook, *Your Religion*. It never received wide acclaim, although it is still being used and has warm friends because of its theme of Christocentrism. Notre Dame University had begun in 1924 a study of the various high

school religion programs and in the research bulletin No. 2
which it issued in 1925 under the title of *Experimental Courses
in Religion* there was an analysis of the Christocentric plan which
we had elaborated in Dubuque. Notre Dame asked me to present this plan at the University in summer school classes in 1926
and 1929. This experience, together with two summers spent
on the missions in Idaho, with the giving of retreats, and with
membership on the executive committee of the secondary section
of the National Catholic Educational Association provided contact with many fine persons and convinced me of the need for
more literature for the classroom on the historical personality of
Christ. The ancient adage: "To know Christ is to know all,"
had taken on reality.

From the practice of attempting to use the New Testament
as a textbook in the classroom arose the plan for the book *Christ
The Leader*. But there was a delay. In 1931 the Catholic University asked me to become an instructor in the separate department of religion which had been started in 1930. While teaching I continued work for the doctorate. My dissertation was
*The Function of the New Testament in the Formation of the
Catholic High School Teacher,* and was later republished under
the title of *The Bible and Character*. The summer of 1935 was
spent in Syria, Palestine and Egypt. In the same year Ditto Co.
asked me to compose a small *Life of Jesus* for the eighth grade.
Since 1932 I have been active in the Evidence Guild. This
method of talking religion to the street crowds that gather in the
parks of Washington is a sharp test of one's theories of how and
what to teach. All of this formed background for the textbook
Christ The Leader which Bruce Co. published in 1937. It has
steadily increased its sales and is now in use in every State of the
Union.

In 1939 Fr. Cartwright was editor of the Paulist magazine,
The Missionary. He asked me to write for him a monthly infor-
mal column on the qualities of Christ. These were entitled *Chats
With Jesus*. Later Father Cartwright brought them to the atten-

tion of P. J. Kenedy Co. and this accounts for the three volumes of *Chats With Jesus* which have thus far appeared.

New horizons are constantly dawning for the traveller on the ocean of the Son of Man. The psychological aptness, the piercing trueness, and the divine liveliness of the methods of Jesus as a teacher always remain a challenge to the teacher of religion. For the laity likewise there is a spur to Christlikeness and a fascination in observing Jesus live His life among men. To present in a unified view the Person of Jesus in what He taught and how He taught, and to fit this into the American scene, was the aim in *Jesus The Divine Teacher* which Kenedy brought out in 1944.

To those who think that our country, under God, has a destiny to fulfill there must be an inspiration in seeing the connection between the Gospel insistence on the dignity of man and the promulgation of the same principle in the second paragraph of the Declaration of Independence. To show this connection was the purpose of the volume *Democracy: Should It Survive?* which I edited and which Bruce published in 1943 and to which I contributed the essay "Christ and Human Dignity."

"Too late have I known Thee" said an eminent saint. Does the average Catholic layman and woman see in His entirety this challenging, fearless, friendly, unselfish, praying, failing yet winning Christ? To ask that question is to state the need for more persons of literary renown to venture into this inexhaustible subject.

EDITOR'S NOTE: Father Russell's books include *Christ the Leader,* 1937, Bruce; *Your Religion,* 7th ed., 1934, Herder; *Chats With Jesus,* three volumes, 1940–1944, Kenedy; *Jesus the Divine Teacher,* 1944, Kenedy.

ALMA SAVAGE

IT WAS while teaching high school in St. Charles, Missouri, that my efforts at writing emerged from the diary, note-taking stage into attempts at pattern and continuity. I had long wanted to write, but the necessary ingredients—sound material, leisure time, and sufficient maturity of mind—kept eluding me. And although teaching school and trying to be part of the life of the community allowed little free time to pursue so demanding a hobby, something happened that first year which favored my ambition and provided more leisure. I sprained both ankles going down a Halloween shute, thereby literally sliding my way into authorship for the accident provided evenings of leisure. After it had happened I was not too conscious of the outraged muscles, but was delighted that I would now be hospitalized at home evenings and weekends. For though I was able to teach school regularly, I could not continue any outside activities. As a result that year I wrote a number of short stories, two of which were published.

The following summer I took two writing courses at Columbia University, returned for another year of teaching, and then thought I ought to do something about getting better training in writing. So I set out for New York to find a job in publishing. Such a step seems so simple and logical when telling of it afterwards, but actually it involved great strain, for leaving my parents was exceedingly difficult. With the exception of my two years in nearby St. Charles, I had always lived at home in a closely-knit family. My paternal grandparents had come from Cork and settled in Lincoln, Illinois. My mother too was of the first generation, as her parents, both from Germany, had married in Atlanta, Illinois, just after the middle of the nineteenth century. My parents followed the westward course of migration only as far as St. Louis, where our family of four lived.

New York and job-hunting proved much less formidable than I expected. Ten days after I got off the train I found myself publicity director for the Macmillan Company in their Boston office. This meant working with literary editors, booksellers, librarians and Macmillan authors, some of whom have passed into history—Edwin Arlington Robinson, Alice Brown, Rachel Field, William Stearns Davis. I also visited New England from Mount Desert Island to Nantucket.

Then something very important happened to me. In 1933 I went to work for Sheed and Ward, who had that year opened their New York office. From then on my job filled my waking hours. What happens to most people who get publishing jobs because of an interest in writing, happened to me: I was so fascinated by the work that I put aside my four completed novels and short stories. Any writing I did took the form of occasional publicity and promotion letters. Marigold Hunt (with whom I shared an apartment) was assistant editor: I did the selling. Sheed and Ward became our life: we read it, we talked it, we lived it, we breathed it through the pores of our skin.

I have later thought that, when possible, a job should be a postgraduate training in one's chosen field, and neither salary, location, hours of work or demands on free time should be of the

slightest consideration. It was not an understanding of this vo-
cational principle, of course, that brought me into Sheed and
Ward: it could only have been my Guardian Angel. For this
was the most wonderful training in Catholic literature that it was
possible to have.

The following year I began traveling over the country visiting
the bookstores. And since I was the only Sheed and Ward salesman, I varied the route covering different territory on each trip.
Naturally one can hardly travel from the east to the west coast
without sometimes stopping off in Yellowstone Park or the Grand
Canyon. When my vacation ambitions exceeded my pocket-
book, I wrote articles to make up for the cost. This method took
me once to England, once to France, and finally to Alaska, which
again can only be chalked up to my Guardian Angel.

One July day in 1940 I found myself in picturesque Juneau
on the doorstep of Bishop Joseph Raphael Crimont, who proved
so inspiring that I completely forgot all the other articles I had
planned to write on Alaska. Instead, thoughts of a book on His
Excellency began taking form. After this short Alaskan interlude I returned to Seattle for my selling trip and found that in
all the cities I visited, people were treasuring stories about the
life of Bishop Crimont. It seemed that a Bishop-Crimontana
was taking form over the country. It was inevitable then that I
should return the following summer to Alaska to gather all
possible material for such a book.

May of 1941 found me back in Juneau working morning and
afternoon with the Bishop: from there I went by boat, train, and
plane to Holy Cross Mission on the lower Yukon where Father
Crimont and his associates had labored at the turn of the century.
The stream of life flowed deeply there, and the days were free of
the things that we take most for granted. In this hunting and
fishing wilderness of the Indians there were no neighbors (nearer
than thirty miles), no shows, no automobiles, no trains. There
I learned more about these early apostles; the material came in
the form of stories from the lips of the missionaries, from old
natives, and from records and letters of the earlier priests. After
three months I came back to the States and my selling trip and

wrote Dogsled Apostles to record the heroic life of Bishop Crimont and his early associates.

As for learning to write, a process which continues from the
first article to the last book one is always discovering new re-
lationships and methods of work that seem of great moment.
And these differ with each writer, for training in this field is not
a clear-cut thing like that of other professions. After you take
a number of courses in school, you make your living doing something else, and in your spare time you begin to learn to write.
At this point you realize the great amount of hard work that
will be necessary before you are able to record your thoughts
in a form clear and concise enough to make the reader understand
the same thing that you meant when you wrote them. Learning
to make words jump through hoops and do the things you want
them to do comes considerably later.

After allowing for these individual problems, there are two
factors which are true for everyone who attempts any sustained
writing: first, the fact that writing is a tremendously hard job
and must be pursued with much regularity and effort. For you
don't write only when the spirit moves you: you write every day
whether you have a headache, or toothache, or worse, whether
you've temporarily lost entire confidence in the thing you are
doing.

The second trait true of all writers is the continued dislike
of beginning any actual writing. When you have before you a
stretch of free hours in which to write, you invariably choose
something that requires physical energy, like darning stockings,
sharpening pencils, or tidying up your desk. After every excuse
is exhausted, then at last you will tackle your writing. It is only
after much painful experience that you see the highly elaborated
excuses for what they are—mental laziness. This realization first
comes with terrific impact, but it means you have jumped your
first high hurdle. (This is the one I am valiantly trying to jump
now.)

EDITOR'S NOTE: Miss Savage, a member of the Gallery of Living Catholic
Authors, has written Smoozie, 1941, Sheed; Dogsled Apostles, 1942, id.; Eben
the Crane, 1944, id.; Holiday in Alaska, 1945, Heath.

DON SHARKEY

SITTING IN MY UPSTAIRS OFFICE trying to concentrate upon writing this sketch, I am distracted by sounds of laughter coming up from the floor below. My wife is playing with our three little boys, and all four are having a wonderful time. It's fun to have three boys, all below school age. Just listen to them laugh! Even the little fellow who can't talk yet is chuckling so heartily that I can hear distinctly.

But I must stop thinking of what is going on downstairs. I promised to have this sketch ready within a few days, and I'll never get it written at this rate. I'll close the door and see whether that helps. There, that's better.

This is the way I do most of my writing. I put in a full day at the office as editor of *The Young Catholic Messenger* and do my writing at home in my off hours. I come home from the office, eat dinner, and rush upstairs to whatever manuscript I happen to be working on at the time. My hours for this kind of work are so limited that I must make full use of them.

I can scarcely remember a time when I wasn't interested in writing. In school I was always happy when Sister would assign us a composition to do. In cooperation with various friends, I was continually putting out some kind of newspaper. The papers were at first written out by hand. Later we typed them. For a while we used a little hand-operated printing press, but that never worked very well. The next step was a hectograph, and that was followed by a mimeograph.

When I was in high school, a friend and I put out a four-page "humorous" mimeographed publication called *The Weakly Searchlight*. When I see a copy of it now, I cringe and want to get it out of my sight. Our fellow high school seemed to like it, however, and the editor of a local magazine thought enough of it to ask us to make it a regular department in his publication. We thought we had really come up in the world when that happened. Previously we had been the editors of a little paper upon which we had done all the work including cutting the stencils, running mimeograph, and selling the copies. Now we were conducting a department in a regular magazine. Unfortunately, the magazine was forced to suspend publication a few months after we had joined it. There was no connection between the two events. It was the depression that forced the magazine out of business. At least that is what the editor assured us.

At the University of Dayton, I contributed an article every month to the campus literary magazine, *The Exponent*. Most of these articles were of a humorous nature. In my senior year, I became editor of *The Exponent*.

By this time I knew that I wanted a literary or a journalistic career. But such a possibility seemed too much to hope for. The depression still had the country in its grip, and jobs of any kind were very difficult to secure. What chance would I have for a job in the field I loved? Reluctantly, I decided that I had better prepare for something else. Teaching seemed to be the logical choice. My mother had been a teacher, and so had both her parents. My father had taught school in order to earn enough money to put him through medical school. If there is anything in heredity, I thought, I should make a passable teacher. Having arrived at this decision, I proceeded to take courses in education in the evening while taking the regular liberal arts course in the daytime. When I was graduated in 1934, I received a B.A. degree and also a certificate entitling me to teach high school in the State of Ohio.

Getting a job as teacher proved to be impossible. I spoke to many school superintendents and put in applications everywhere, but with no results. Having failed to secure a full-time position, I was fortunate enough to obtain work with my home town paper, *The Middletown Journal,* on a part-time basis. I served as both reporter and feature writer. This work yielded very little in a financial way, but it was a valuable experience.

About six months after my graduation, I met Jim Pflaum, who had been a classmate of mine at the University of Dayton. Jim's uncle and aunt owned the Pflaum Publishing Company, and Jim had just become the first editor of their new publication, *Junior Catholic Messenger.* This was a sister publication to the fifty-year-old *Young Catholic Messenger.*

"Would you like a job?" Jim asked me.

"I sure would!" I exclaimed, the statement making up in enthusiasm what it lacked in grammar. In 1934, anyone so fortunate as to be offered a job accepted it immediately and asked questions about it afterward.

The job, Jim explained, was a temporary one. My duty was to compile an index of the contents of *The Young Catholic Messenger* for the first semester. This would take about three or four weeks.

When the index was completed, a few other little things turned up for me to do, so I stayed on a while longer. Before long, it was time to compile an index for the second semester. I continued to stay on. As a matter of fact, eleven years later, I am still staying on, although I have never been hired on a permanent basis.

I have worked on all three of the Pflaum publications: *Our Little Messenger* for the children of the primary grades, *Junior*

Catholic Messenger for the intermediate grades, and *The Young Catholic Messenger* for the junior high grades. For the past several years, I have been the editor of the last named publication. In this work I have been able to combine my first and secondary interests—writing and teaching,—for the *Messengers* are used in the classrooms of Catholic schools and must conform with the best pedagogical principles.

Nearly every important thing that has happened to me since 1934 has been connected with my work at Pflaum's. The biggest event was meeting my future wife, Miss Martha Shea, who joined the editorial staff a few years after I had. We were married in June, 1939. Martha's editorial experience has proved very valuable to me in my writing. She is an excellent copy reader and critic.

One of my duties at Pflaum's during my first years was to read the manuscripts submitted to *The Young Catholic Messenger*. They were, as a whole, very poor at that time. One day, after reading several serials that were particularly bad, I said to myself, "I could write a better story than these, and I have never written a word of fiction in my life." I startled myself with the suddenness of my reply, "Oh, is that so? Then why don't you do it?"

This was a challenge I could not ignore. I began work on a nineteen-chapter story entitled *The Lost Prince*. After many months I completed it and submitted it to the *Young Catholic Messenger*. To my great delight it was accepted. (No, I didn't accept it myself; I didn't have that much authority.) Later, using tear sheets from the *Messenger* as a manuscript, I submitted the story to Benziger Brothers. They accepted it, too. *The Lost Prince* came out in book form in 1940. There is no thrill like a first book. The day my copies arrived I just stood and stared at them. I just couldn't believe that I had actually written a book.

My first juvenile novel having proved successful, it was perhaps natural that I should write another containing the same characters. The title of the new story was *The Boy King*. By the time I had completed it, however, I had become editor of *The Young*

Catholic Messenger, and I did not wish to be in the position of publishing my own story. Fortunately, I was able to sell it to *The Ave Maria.* The story has appeared serially but as yet has not come out in book form. The Ave Maria Press plans to bring it out in the fall of 1945, possibly under a different title.

The idea for *White Smoke Over the Vatican* was entirely my wife's. While a student at a Catholic college, she was struck by the fact that she and her fellow students knew practically nothing about the Vatican, and yet they were supposed to be well-informed Catholics.

One of her first suggestions when she joined the *Messenger* staff was that we have a series of articles telling the children something about the organization of the Vatican. The editor thought this a good idea and assigned the task to me. I wrote a series of four articles of about a thousand words each. They appeared at the time of the death of Pope Pius XI and the election of Pope Pius XII. The comments we received from the children, the teachers, and the parents indicated that people were very much interested in something that explained the workings of the Vatican in simple everyday language.

I probably should have let the matter rest there, but not Martha. After I had completed *The Boy King* and was wondering what I should write next, she said, "Why don't you send those Vatican articles to the Bruce Publishing Company and ask whether they would be interested in a book along that line?" This I did, and Mr. William C. Bruce said he would be interested. I set to work at once. The amount of research that had to be done was very great. The fact that I had visited the Vatican in 1936 when the International Catholic Press Exposition was held there helped greatly in describing the physical features, but there was a great amount of information that could be unearthed only by the most painstaking research. Much of it came from obscure little items in magazines and newspapers which had never before appeared in book form.

Starting to write the book in December, 1941, I didn't complete

it until June, 1943. By that time things were happening so fast
that I had to make many revisions on the galley and page proofs
in order to keep the book up to date.

By the time the book appeared in March, 1944, Italy had surrendered, the Germans had seized Rome, and the Allies were
slowly advancing toward that city. The eyes of the world were
on the Vatican and on the Holy Father who was virtually a
prisoner of the Nazis. The entire first printing of 6,000 copies
was sold out within two weeks. After the liberation of Rome,
I revised the book to bring it up to date. The third edition
contains new text and new photographs.

All the time I was writing *The Boy King* and *White Smoke* I
was also working for my Master of Arts degree. I received it in
April, 1944. Later in that same year, I was made a member of
the Gallery of Living Catholic Authors.

About the same time that *White Smoke* appeared, Aloysius
Croft, of Bruce wrote to ask me whether I would be interested
in writing a book about Lourdes. *The Song of Bernadette,* he
said, had aroused a great interest in Lourdes, but both the book
and the movie dealt with Lourdes at the time of Bernadette.
He believed that a book dealing with Lourdes *since* the time of
Bernadette would be popular. Naturally I was quick to accept
this invitation. I am putting the finishing touches on the book
now. It is scheduled to come out in 1945.

Between books I have turned out a number of articles for
*Columbia, The Sign, The Catholic Digest, The Catholic School
Editor,* and other magazines.

If I had more time for writing, my record might be more impressive. It is not possible to do much in a few hours each night.
In my best weeks, I get in no more than twenty hours. Usually,
it is much less than that. I'm not complaining, though. I enjoy
being an editor and shouldn't wish to give that up. I'll probably
stick to this plan of being both an editor and a writer till Mr.
George Pflaum, my employer, comes walking into my office some
day and says "Well, Don, back in 1934 we hired you to do an

index. The index has been completed, so I guess we'll not need you any longer."

When that day comes, a lack of time to devote to writing will no longer be one of my problems. Then I shall know what real problems are.

EDITOR'S NOTE: Mr. Sharkey's books include *The Lost Prince*, 1940, Benziger; *White Smoke Over the Vatican*, 1944, Bruce; *The Woman Shall Conquer*, 1945, id.

REVEREND GEORGES SIMARD, O.M.I.

BORN IN 1878, at Baie Saint Paul, one of the oldest French Canadian parishes, I turned my steps towards Quebec when I was fifteen. In that historic City, the characteristics inherited from my ancestors in Charlevoix could not but become stronger. At the age of twenty, I came to the Capital of Canada. This was a most decisive move. Had Providence directed me another way, my career would have been along entirely different lines.

In Ottawa I entered the University conducted by the Oblates of Mary Immaculate. The founder, who had just died, had bequeathed to his successors a very special spirit or mentality, a program of studies and wide prospects of national unity. Around his newly-made grave, we discussed Thomism, a more progressive scientific culture, and plans for a better understanding between the ethnical or religious groups living in Canada.

In such an environment, I began to write on those questions of language and nationality that were stirring all Ontario at the time. Very fortunately I did not become enmeshed in these quarrels. This aloofness I attribute to the fact that my superiors appointed me very early, in 1917, to the chair of Church History in the Faculty of Theology. Already an exceptional circumstance had brought me into contact with the saintly bishop of Hippo. From that time forward I became an ardent reader of the *City of God,* to which I owe the best part of my modest publications. I had noted the magnificent vistas of this "immense and arduous work," and I was influenced by them in my private and public lectures, especially with respect to the social and intellectual life of Christ's Mystical Body. From such an inspiration came *Les Maîtres chrétiens de nos, Pensées et de nos Vies,* and *Maux présents et Foi chrétienne.*

I had also observed that the great African Doctor had studied the causes of the rise and the decadence of Rome. The idea of applying the same criteria to modern Empires led me to write *Les Etats chrétiens et l'Eglise.*

From time to time I narrowed the scope of my thoughts and returned to the object of my first interests. *Les Etudes canadiennes* and many articles in reviews and newspapers are the proof thereof. In these pages, if, without too much apprehension, I have been able to tackle the problems that trouble the minds of my contemporaries, it is because, for me, "there are no burning questions, but only passionate men." The nature and the end of Empires, the evolution of Great Britain and of the United States, the elements of Canadian patriotism, the Christian formation of the future citizen, the relations between the Catholics of different languages, the part that should be allotted to the sciences in our programs of studies—these are a few of the subjects I have dealt with either in lectures or in publications.

It would be a mistake to imagine that the polemist is violent. By temperament and as a result of long practice in his career as a teacher, he visibly strives to be an impassive and objective reasoner. A few critics who think that eloquence and rhetorical devices are arguments have insinuated that his writings are not sufficiently forcible on account of their restraint. To hear them, it

would seem that science and its immediate applications depend
on sensibility and emotion.

In politics, I claim to be neither an Imperialist, nor an Angli-
fier, nor a Separatist, but a Canadian in the full sense of the word
according to our constitutional law. However, one must admit
that patriotism in Canada is very complicated. It has marks that
are specifically French or specifically English; it has others that
are generically Canadian. It divides when it pushes each nationality in its own direction; it unites when it assigns to these
same meditations as identical ideal, namely, territorial integrity,
harmony in a diversity of races, cultures, and beliefs, the liberty,
honour, prosperity, sovereignty and glory of the common land.

On this point and on the matter of the professional and religious qualifications of our elite among the laity, I endeavored to
shed the most salutary light. When the tumult of the war will
have subsided, it is to be hoped that many of the pages devoted
to these themes will contribute towards putting order in the minds
of our rising generations as well as in our public affairs.

A doctrine of Catholic and Canadian education is the sum and
substance of my writings and lectures. At least so it appears to me.

Despite the praises that I have not rarely received, the purifying
fire of criticism has not entirely spared some of my views on Empires or on Canada. Yet, if there is one writer in America who
betrays a reluctance to all forms of imperialism, it is I. Distin-
guishing between the Empire of domination that exploits, and
the Empire of pure might that serves, I liken the first to the
power of a master over a slave, and grant to the second little
more than the right to fulfill the role of a pedagogue among primitive or uncivilized peoples. I can hardly find traces of the latter
in the course of history, which shows that I have a severity of
judgment not met with in certain other writers,—such as Father
Yves de la Briere, S.J.

Before it can be understood that this didactical prose can provoke any adversaries, one must bear in mind that, in Canada, the
word Empire stirs up emotions. Some see in it an attraction to

England, others, a threat to national interests. As a matter of fact, I have never intended to discuss the imperialism that is prevalent in some Canadian centers. I tried to follow the example of the philosopher and the theologian who seek the causes of events and leave to pragmatic politicians the care of daily problems.

One should not conclude, however, that the citizen is indifferent to the building of his country. I have written profusely on what I call the metaphysics of our patriotism. Perhaps the most precise expression of my mind on this matter is an article published in *Le Droit,* Oct. 14, 1940, where we may read this statement: "Canada is not, on the one hand, Ottawa for the English-speaking Canadians, and on the other hand, Quebec for the French Canadians. Canada is made up of two nationalities possessing *in solidum* the same soil, and the same history, pursuing a common good in which the ideals of both cultures are integrated. Canada is a political organization of a particular kind: a federation in which two national elements stand side by side in the pattern of the state, so that Canadianism means political unity and national duality, variety and concord."

For Canadians of whatsoever group the native land means all that, and for each of them patriotism is a compulsory yet devout service to all that. Undoubtedly, the practical applications of such an ideal is most arduous. The writer of these lines, who is conscious of that difficulty, does his best to show how the diverse nationalistic aspirations of our people must respect each other and blend with the exigencies of all Canada. It would be truly unfortunate if a doctrine that involves and fosters national unity should remain misunderstood and ineffective, at a time when so many events clamour for a broader and more generous solution.

In October, 1930, together with some of my fellow professors, I founded *La Revue de l'Universite d'Ottawa,* to which I am one of the most regular contributors. From 1932 to 1938, I occupied the position of Dean of the Faculty of Theology in the same University. During that time, I spent the academic year 1933–1934 in Europe and North Africa in connection with my teaching. From

1939 to 1942 I was the regular lecturer in charge of L'Heure Do-
minicale, which was broadcast from Ottawa. I hold the degrees
of Doctor in Theology from the University of Ottawa, and I am
an honorary Doctor of the University of Montreal. I belong to
several historical associations, to the Royal Society of Canada, and
to the Canadian St. Thomas Aquinas Academy. On May 25,
1929, I received the Apostolic Blessing from Pope Pius XI, for my
pamphlet *La Question Romaine*. On December 2, 1938, the
French Academy awarded me a medal as a mark of appreciation
for services rendered to the French cause in Canada.

EDITOR'S NOTE: Father Simard's books, all available from the University of
Ottawa, include *Etudes canadiennes, Maitres chretiens de nos penées, Maux
presents et foi chretienne, Les etats chretiens et l'eglise,* and *Saint Augustin,
educateur ideal.*

YVES R. SIMON

IT IS ABOUT 1923 that my purpose of devoting my life to work in philosophy became clear and unshakable. I had just passed the examinations that were a pre-requisite to any personal research, and a great deal of adventure was ahead before my career took on its definitive shape.

I was born in 1903 in Cherbourg on the Channel coast. My father was an industrialist. My family environment belonged to the Catholic and conservative middle class. I had two older brothers and one older sister. Until 1910 my family was blessed with great happiness. From then on a series of misfortunes made my childhood a miserable one. My oldest brother died; the other one was gravely ill and had to spend years away from home to recover. At the age of nine I became crippled and was in a cast for several years. When the first World War came my brother was still so sick that the draft rejected him; but in the spring of 1915 he was accepted as a volunteer and was killed in 1917.

Although our city was far from the front lines, the effects of the war were terribly felt all around us. Troops from Normandy had suffered hard blows in the bloody battles of Belgium, and less than two months after the beginning of the war, nearly all the young men whom we knew were dead, wounded, or captured, with a majority of dead. These were years of universal sadness colored with heroism.

Up to the age of twelve I was a very mediocre student. Then I had the privilege of having for a tutor an old teacher of the Lycee of Cherbourg who was a very learned, very saintly, and very sweet man. The loftiness of his soul and the charm of his manners overcame my laziness, and I became sincerely interested in my studies. I enjoyed especially classical literature, and it was decided that I should prepare the section of the baccalaureate which includes Latin and Greek, with a very limited program in mathematics.

In the fall of 1918 my condition had improved enough to permit me to go to school. I attended the classes at the local Catholic school. I passed the first part of the baccalaureat in the summer of 1919. The following school year was for me a decisive experience. As it is known, the upper form of French secondary schools is principally devoted to philosophy. Minor matters are physics, chemistry, biology, history, and geography. I immediately enjoyed the study of philosophy, although I was keeping in mind that I was to be a literary man rather than a philosopher. I used then to write poetry, and I believed in my vocation as a poet with some sort of sincerity.

In 1920 after having quite successfully passed the second part of the baccalaureat, I went to Paris and attended classes at the Lycee Louis le Grand in the form called *rhetorique superieure*. This is where would be students of the *Ecole Normale Superieure* prepare the extremely difficult competitive examination for entrance into the Ecole. This was for me a year of tremendous hardships and almost complete failure. Our program covered Greek and Latin literatures as if we had been majors in classics; French literature as if we had been majors in French; ancient, medieval and modern history as if we had been history majors; plus some philosophy. Not everybody can stand such an over-exacting system with no time for recreation, no time for social life or meditation, and little time for rest. At the end of the school year I still had illusions about my literary calling, but I knew I would never be a classicist. It was then decided that I should leave the Lycee and become a university student in philosophy. Despite all hardships and failures, I am glad I had this year of *rhetorique superieure*. The level of the students was much above that of ordinary university students. It is really the elite of the intellectual youth which gathers there. Many of my classmates have become very distinguished scholars. Also I made there life-long friendships.

Being a university student in philosophy amounted to preparing the licence-en-philosophie. I had this preparation simultaneously at the Catholic University and at the Sorbonne. As soon as I was relieved from the drudgery of the *rhetorique superieure,* my work improved a great deal. I soon forgot all about the Classics. I passed the *licence-en-philosophie* (Sorbonne) in 1922 and the *Diplome d'Etudes Superieures de Philosophie* the following year.

The teachings I was given at the Sorbonne and at the Catholic University were widely divergent from each other. None of the professors of the Sorbonne exercised any doctrinal influence on me, yet I enjoyed some of the topics they treated and I owe them a great deal so far as methods of work and fields of research are concerned.

At the Catholic Institute I had several fascinating teachers, the best of whom was Maritain. He was then in charge of the teaching of modern philosophy. I had courses under him on Descartes and Kant. When I now re-read my class-notes I realized that a beginner such as I was could understand only a very small part of his profound and difficult expositions. But there was in the personality of Maritain a spiritual charm which irresistibly caused the ignorant beginner to love the truth that Maritain loved, and to feel anxious to know more about it. The teaching given at the Sorbonne was completely unsystematic. We could describe it as a combination of positivism and idealistic relativism. I was soon given to realize that one had to make a twofold choice. It was necessary to choose first between practicing philosophy as a mere cultural exercise and looking for a system of philosophical truth; further, when I had made up my mind in favor of the second part of the alternative, it still remained to be decided whether I would resist the enlightenment that the newly re-discovered philosophy of St. Thomas was spreading on us, or welcome it. I shall always be grateful to my masters of the Catholic University for having helped me to understand the problem, and to choose the better solution.

Following 1923 I went through years of uncertainty with regard to my future. The most regular career opened to young scholars, that is teaching in State secondary schools with the hope of obtaining some day a professor-ship in a State university, did not attract me. Like many scholars I entered the civil service through competitive examination, and for a year I did clerical work at the Ministry of Education. This was the happiest year of my youth. My duties as a civil servant were not too exacting. Since the office where I worked was close to the National Library, I could afford to do two or three hours of library work every day. My health was extremely good, and back from my office work, I used to work at home all the evening and part of the night. It was a very solitary life: I had no family relations in Paris, never went to parties, and hardly indulged in spending an evening or a Sunday afternoon from time to time with one of the four or five friends I had. I now realize that this studious life was over-intellectual, gave too little a share to social and human experience.

I was then mostly interested in social philosophy. My attention had been directed at the Sorbonne to the great French social thinkers of the nineteenth century. First I read widely such writers as Saint-Simon and the Saint-Simonians, Fourier, Considerant, Buchez, Louis Blanc. I soon discovered the greatest social thinker of this period, P.-J. Proudhon, and dropped all the others. Indefatigably I read and re-read the forty odd volumes of the works of Proudhon, studied his biography, character, and influence in great detail. My studies on Proudhon brought me in touch with the contemporary sociologists who worked along the Proudhonian line of thought, especially Georges Sorel and Edouard Berth. Sorel had died in 1922; Berth was leading a solitary and almost discouraged life as a civil servant in the administration of a hospital in the outskirts of Paris. He was realizing ever more clearly that the ideas which had inflamed his youth, the doctrines of revolutionary syndicalism, had gone out of fashion. I think it was one of the last joys of his life to be visited from time to time by a young philosopher who loved to spend hours chatting about Proudhon. Berth was not a believer, but he owed to his family life and his philosophical reflections a great interest in religion and especially in the Catholic Church. The fact that I was a Catholic was rather pleasing to this old Proudhonian whose long expected conversion took place on his death bed.

It was surely the first time that a student of Proudhon happened to be a student of St. Thomas. During my daily reading hours most of the time which was not given to social literature was given to St. Thomas and his modern exponents. I had ceased too early attending courses and I had a hard time studying Thomism by myself. My only chance of getting help—this was an invaluable one—was to attend the meetings which took place once a month at Maritain's house.

Some day it will be known that these meetings, compared in historical importance, with the famous Thursday afternoon meetings around Peguy in the narrow shop of the *Cahiers de la Quinzaine*. In a simple and perfectly lovely living room people crowded; there were among them a few students, hardly any teachers, mostly persons without academic connections, cultured men and women with a bent for inward life who knew that St. Thomas would provide them with the principles of the sanctification of the intellect. Maritain read difficult texts of St. Thomas and his commentators, explained them painstakingly without indulging in any of the simplifications that are inevitable in formal teaching. Discussions went on for hours and our research progressed slowly. Whatever may be his ability to understand the technicalities of the problems and demonstrations we were dealing with, anyone could unmistakably grasp the appealing character of a philosophical investigation so conducted: in the hands of Maritain as well as in the hands of St. Thomas, philosophy was an inspiration and perhaps an introduction to spiritual life. Our minds felt irresistibly engaged in a way along which it was impossible to go far without accepting the requirements of moral perfection and the sufferings of the spiritual night.

Besides social philosophy and Thomistic metaphysics, I used to read a great deal in a rather random way without any other guiding principle than the steady purpose of preparing a philosophical interpretation of all fields of knowledge I could get acquainted with. As things were going on, I became increasingly dissatisfied with my background. As mentioned above, my secondary training, owing to the very organization of public programs, had included too little mathematics, and I suffered from a general lack of scientific instruction. I had not felt too badly the seriousness of this deficiency so long as I cherished literary ambitions. But one day came, as I was about twenty, when I suddenly understood that my real calling had nothing to do with literary creation. One evening I happened to read to friends of mine my last two writings: a short story and an article about social philosophy. They found the article very interesting and the short story completely stupid. I agreed they were right, at least so far as the latter was concerned. Immediately I threw away my literary works, very thin indeed, and decided to develop in myself the characteristics of the scientific mind. True to this resolution I became increasingly eager for accuracy, exactness, and systematic orderliness in all fields of knowledge, with the result that the insufficiency of my background in mathematics and positive sciences became intolerable. Also I understood that the way I lived, spending in libraries or in the solitude of my room all the time spared from my office duties, forbade me from acquiring the human and social experience without which a philosopher has a great chance of being an unrealistic and soon sophisticated theorist. It happened that some of my best friends were medical students. Through them I had heard a great deal about the fascinating interest of medical studies and practice. It seemed to me that medicine would compel me to acquire two things I thought I most badly lacked: scientific training and human experience. This is how at the age of twenty three, after several years of philosophic specialization, I went to the pre-medical school and to the college of medicine.

The reasons why I did not complete my medical studies are too personal to be worth mentioning. In 1928 my future was at last clearly outlined: having left school of medicine, I would not resume right away the studies in social philosophy to which I had given so much time during the preceding years. I needed to order and systematize my knowledge. I had to fill up many gaps in my acquaintance with the elements of philosophy. There was only one method: a re-learning of elementary philosophy from beginning to end, beginning with formal logic and ending with politics. I would go again to the Catholic University, attend regular courses, take my degrees in Scholastic philosophy, study exhaustively basic textbooks in all parts of philosophy, read Aristotle, St. Thomas, and his commentators. A year later a great deal of work had been achieved, many gaps had been filled, I had the degree of Lector Philosophiae, and was preparing a doctor's dissertation on the ontology of knowledge which was not to be completed before 1934. It was sufficiently clear that I would some day obtain a professorship in a Catholic university, but I had to wait for a vacancy. This forced leisure was devoted to my dissertation and to the study of German, with a trip to Germany.

It is only in 1930, just ten years after I had begun my higher studies, that I became a teacher. The college of letters of the Catholic University of Lille was creating a new professorship in philosophy. My application was accepted and in the fall of 1930 I started teaching in this school. Simultaneously I obtained a part time employment at the Catholic University of Paris. Each Saturday I went from Lille to Paris to give a lecture to non-academic people who were anxious to know about the doctrine of St.

Thomas Aquinas. And such was my occupational life until I came to the United States.

It was a very busy life with little room for scholarly leisure except during the long summer vacation. I had married in the summer of 1930, and we were blessed with several children. During the school year teaching and family duties took nearly all my time and strength. In summer we used to leave as soon as we could the gloomy city of Lille for some place in the countryside, far away from the industrial plain of northern France. It was comparatively easy to find a house for rent in remote villages where life was pleasant and peaceful, and living quite inexpensive. By the end of the summer of 1933 my doctor's dissertation was finished. It appeared in the spring of 1934, almost simultaneously with a little book on the *Critique of Moral Knowledge,* which was the summary of a course delivered at a school of Carmelite priests in Lille.

For several years I had given up writing any magazine articles in order to concentrate upon my philosophical research and the composition of my doctor's dissertation. Once I had obtained my doctor's degree, it became possible for me to turn again to current events and timely problems. I had made a long retreat from the life of action, even from the study of social philosophy, in order to ascertain my theoretical basis; I thought the time had come to play my part in the field of human relations through an application of philosophical principles to the burning problems of the day. An immensely sad event gave me a chance to come out as a political writer. As the Ethiopian war was being prepared, in 1935, we witnessed a furious development of the worship of force, a wild campaign against the principles of law and the worth of pledged faith, a ruthless exploitation of all wicked instincts in favor of the crimes which were under way. My protest took shape in a booklet entitled *The Ethiopian War and Political Thought in France.* I now realize that I made a serious mistake as I preserved in the writing of this book and in some publications about similar topics the serenity of expression, the abstractness, and the exquisite politeness which become a philosopher under normal circumstances. Circumstances were no longer normal; total war had begun. The time had come when philosophers also had to fight and to assume all the responsibilities of men of action engaged in a deadly struggle.

In the spring of 1938 a letter from the University of Notre Dame most kindly invited me to come over to this school in order to teach the philosophy of St. Thomas. My mind was soon made up. We landed in New York at the beginning of September, 1938, with our four children. The magnificent welcome we were given by our guests gave us invaluable encouragement as we were starting our new life.

This happened just a few weeks before the Munich Agreement. Ever since then, catastrophes unfolded with ruthless logic. Only recently, in the midst of universal suffering, did a better future come in sight. Most of the boys I had the privilege of teaching during the last four years, are now in the armed forces. To them my gratitude goes: they have been marvellous friends to me as we were studying together; their enthusiastic interest in philosophy, their candid search for truth, have kept alive in me the flame of our theoretical ideal, and have saved me from despair. Today their spirit of sacrifice exemplifies the unity of the love for truth and of the love for justice—which shall ever remain indissoluble in the soul of the philosopher worthy of his task.

EDITOR'S NOTE: Professor Simon's books include *Introduction à l'Ontologie du Connaitre*, 1934, Paris; *Critique de la Connaissance morale*, 1934, id.; *La Campagne d'Ethiopie et la Pensée politique Francaise*, 1936, id.; *Trois lecons sur le Travail*, 1938, id.; *Nature and Functions of Authority*, 1940, Marquette Univ. Press; *The Road to Vichy 1918–1938*, 1942, Sheed; *The March to Liberation*, 1942, Tower Press, Milwaukee.

A. M. SULLIVAN
Poet

SOME POETS get into print by well-ordered academic life and some degree of indicated talent. Usually a sprig of Shelley is detected on the sapling, and unless promptly pruned the teen-aged poet begins his imitative verses to the well-thumbed catalog of the emotions. I had no such introduction to belles lettres and the relation after twenty years is pretty much touch and go as I make my living writing and editing in the business field and serving the muse with the left-overs of the week. In this way I have elbowed into print with poetry of the modern scene and quarreled myself into the critical corner with current arbiters of verse standards.

As a matter of vital statistics, I was born in Harrison, New Jersey, August 9, 1896, reared at Oxford Furnace, New Jersey, educated at St. Benedict's Preparatory College, Newark, New Jersey. That was the end of formal schooling. I failed consistently in English, partly for lack of grammar and mostly for an atrocious handwriting which discouraged my teachers.

Being the eldest of twelve children, I went to work at sixteen.

I had written a piece of pious doggerel for the graduation number of the school magazine, and that was the end of poetry for ten years. Meanwhile, I wrote and sold a story to the venerable Jesuit, Father John Henry O'Rourke, editor of the *Sacred Heart Messenger,* and he gave me some good advice on prose composition. For a few years I wrote many stories and sold a few of them, enough to keep my fingers beating the typewriter through the middle hours of darkness. During this period, I wrote one story called "Wings for an Eagle," which was remembered and was later made into a radio play.

Sent back from Fort Slocum in 1917 because of a severe heart murmur, I edited a house organ for the Submarine Boat Corporation, and gradually got into advertising and public relations activity. From the shipways at Port Newark, I watched a hundred and fifty cargo ships slide into Newark Bay, and went out on trips on some of them during their shakedown trials. After the war, I made several trips in these "tramps" along the coast, and began to write some prose sketches and an occasional jingle about the sea.

In 1924, I joined an advertising agency in New York, and began writing industrial copy covering tugboats, diesel engines, automobile trucks, lubricating oils, and, eventually, airplanes. One evening at dinner, a facile friend produced a poem he had written for a birthday occasion and said importantly, "This is a sonnet, a Petrarchian sonnet; they're more difficult than the Shakespearean." "Indeed, everyone knows that," said I. And that night I searched back through Father Coppens' textbooks of English literature to find out what the difference was. Then, for personal punishment, I set out to write a hundred Petrarchian sonnets, most of which were workshop samples. I then made the mistake of publishing them under the title of *Sonnets of a Simpleton,* a volume which arises to plague me on the second-hand book shelves.

In 1926, a short lyric entitled "Shadows are Black" won the Edward Coate Pinckney one-hundred-dollar prize, and with that incentive I began taking a serious attitude toward poetry. Aware of how little I knew of the traditions of great English poetry, and the techniques of the classic and modern poets, I began to catch up on some reading. All the furor over the imagists, and the debates of the rhymers versus the verse libre writers had passed me unnoticed. In 1928, I published *Progression,* a pamphlet which contained one long philosophical poem and a few lyrics. It received some favorable comment, in fact, more than *Elbows of the Wind,* my first serious volume, which was published in 1932. The poems were praised for their "challenging subject matter," "original imagery," and blamed for their "boisterous attitude toward life," "cobble-stone rhythms" and "lack of technical grace"; to quote a few critics pro and con.

The beauty of the spoken poem has always appealed to me, and I saw in radio an opportunity to recapture for the bard some of the eloquence lost in cold type. In 1926, I appeared on a poetry forum over WJZ at New York, and at every other opportunity that presented itself. The larger opportunity came on January 1, 1932, when WOR invited me to conduct "The New Poetry Hour" each Sunday morning. Later on, the program joined the Mutual Network, with a reasonably alert audience throughout the country. During the eight years on WOR, I presented some three hundred poets, representing every shade of talent and technique. The program was followed by many schools and colleges as an educational accessory, but no one benefited more by the consistent discussions of poetic ideas, definitions, sources, and techniques than the conductor of the program. Some of these programs were recorded, and the text of the dialogues with important American and foreign poets have been preserved for future reference. Among the poets were Stephen Vincent Benet, Anna Hempstead Branch, Joseph Campbell, R. P. Tristram Coffin, Padraic Colum, Mark VanDoren, Father Leonard Feeney, S.J., Edwin Markham, Edgar Lee Masters, David Morton, Harriet Monroe, Lennox Robinson, Jesse Stuart, Ridgely Torrence, John Hall Wheelock, and Margaret Widdemer; to select a few.

This program carried with it a large management problem. Nothing is so welcome in radio as a good mail response, but when every letter requires an answer to special questions, it becomes a problem in time, energy and postage stamps. I answered more than ten thousand letters, introduced a hundred new books of verse, and never got fully extricated from arguments with left-wing poets, many of whom shared the forum with me. In all, it was a trying, exciting and rewarding adventure, that ended when Sunday morning became too important as a news period for the war commentators.

My radio work led me into office in the Poetry Society of America where I served as president in 1939, 1940, 1941. This society was founded in 1910, survived and, I believe, profited by the excitement of the poetic revolt of 1912–1913. Poets are highly individual people, and a poetry society is almost a contradiction in terms, but the Poetry Society of America, despite many faults has given a focus to the achievement of poets in this country. It was my privilege to preside when the medals of the society were given to Robert Frost, Edgar Lee Masters, and Edna St. Vincent Millay.

During my radio work I developed a larger appreciation for the poetic chorus, and began to write and adapt some poems for this purpose. The first of these, "Transcontinental," a chant of the trains moving westward was produced by Norman Corwin over the Columbia network. Later he also produced "Midnight Caravan" a story of the trucks on Highway Number I. A longer work, "Day in Manhattan," was produced by the Columbia Workshop under the direction of Earle McGill. These chorals and several others produced in part by myself over the Mutual Network were published by E. P. Dutton under the title of *Day in Manhattan*. The war, with its demands for radio time, has interferred with the experiment with modern chorals, but there ought to be a fine chance for the poets to bring the majesty of great poetry in massed voices when peace descends and shares a little of the precious radio hours. Great poetry is only half-enjoyed unless it is heard as well as seen.

The nature of poetry is a subject for long discussion and debate. Even definition. To me, a poem is a group of words, walking on tiptoe to the rhythm of the senses. It is the awareness of the senses that finds the newness of the world about us, and takes the poet out of the intramural atmosphere of the classics. In my own work I have attempted to interpret some of the feeling of industry and science in our time without dealing in equations, but rather by looking upon the machine as a fruit of man's conquest of nature. I have discussed this point of view in an essay entitled "Horsepower and Pegasus," and my collection of poems in this category is called *This Day and Age,* some sixty poems dealing with a long catalog of machinery and scientific items.

If I have any preference to a poetic form it is for the old ballad meter. Practically every device we have in English poetry is inherited from the Greeks and Romans—except the ballad where roots go through Anglo-Saxon poetry to the Icelandic and earlier. Where the ballad first started no authority is certain, but they agree it belongs to Northern Europe. I have written a number of long ballads on Irish, folk, and American Revolutionary incidents. *The Ballad of a Man Named Smith* and *The Ballad of John Castner* have been published as separate small volumes. Another small volume of semi-narrative interest is *New Jersey Hills,* written in devotion to a historic area ignored by novelists and poets. It is the hilly country around the Delaware Water Gap where I spent most of my childhood and not far from the farm on the Muscontecong where I spend my summers now.

As current work for publication, I have completed a long poem interpreting the sea in its political and economic influence on the lives of men. It is called "The Bottom of the Sea" and is written in iambic quatrains. As for future plans, I can only suggest that my interest is likely to swing more and more toward radio and the theatre through the vehicle of verse drama. I believe that poetry and the theatre in particular is in for a thorough regeneration through the younger poets with a rekindled faith in the purposes of God and the works of man. The cycle of frustration and denial has spent itself, and there is no other way to go but back.

EDITOR'S NOTE: Mr. Aloysius Michael Sullivan lives in St. Albans, N. Y., with his wife (née Catherine V. McNamee) and daughters, Catherine and Mary Rose. He is associate editor of *Dun's Review* and advertising manager of Dun & Bradstreet, Inc., in New York City. His books include *Elbows of the Wind,* 1933, Kingsley Press; *A Day in Manhattan,* 1941, Dutton; *The Ballad of John Castner,* 1943, Fine Editions Press.

SISTER M. THÉRÈSE,
SOR.D.S.

(Florence Mae Lentfoehr)

HOWEVER DISCONCERTING the thought of writing an "informal, anecdotal biography" might be to the nun-writer, the added request that it be written to "appeal to the high school student," at once levels her defenses and stimulates her to note down without apology whatever might be of interest to these most delightful of God's children. As I write I see a group of lovely young creatures, very precisely though uncomfortably seated in the stiff-backed chairs of an austere convent parlor. It is Catholic Book Week and the High School journalists have come for an interview. I am met with the most disarming questions—"Francis Thompson wrote 'look for me in the nurseries of heaven,' where shall we look for you?" "With the early Christians," I may answer, leaving them a little shocked though fascinated, and ready for a spiritual adventure into the real meaning of my words. It is for such "innocents abroad" that I write these simple biographical details, using no other method than that of giving answers to the eager questions asked by these inimitable, irresistible young lovers of wisdom.

If this be not sufficient reason for writing a biography I can give another. In every life God speaks a *word* to us. If in each atom of His creation some aspect of His divinity is reflected, surely in man created "a little less than the angels" that spark of His infinite beauty must burn with a peculiar clarity. Is it too much to say that each created soul reflects in its own induplicable way some facet of the beauty of God? Each has its own unique preciousness, its own revelation of God to others. Who can say that he knows his own secret? Perhaps we were never meant to know it. But some other may discover it; indeed, it may be there precisely for that other, whom we may never know, of the great family of God. This may partly account for the element of wonder and fascination we experience in reading the lives of others, or in knowing intimately some unspeakably precious soul. The child playing in the street, the beggar at the gate—through each God speaks His *word* to us.

But to return to my young and utterly lovable interviewers with their soul-searching questions:

"Your ancestry?"—It is complicated. I am a fusion of three bloods, which has left me with a friend once neatly described as a "thoroughly French temperament, with a dash of English conservatism, and the profundity of a German mind." The remark was not meant to be complimentary. To be precise: my maternal great-grandmother who came from France to Quebec, was of the old French family Beaufort, with titles as picturesque as those in any medieval tale of knights and noble ladies; my maternal great-grandfather left England to build a home on the sea-buffeted coast of Maine, later moving with his family down to Boston, and my childhood was thrilled by strange and harrowing tales of one of his sons who for half a century was captain of a merchant ship that sailed the stormy Atlantic. Portraits of great-aunts, stiff, starched, and formal, hung in massive gold and ivory frames in the living room of my mother's home, and their names, Abigail, Cora, and Ida Mae, the latter of whom was the wife of the American composer, George Whitfield Chadwick, were enchanted ones in childhood's wonder book. When she was yet a little girl my paternal grandmother came with her parents from her home on the Rhine and settled in Waukesha, Wisconsin. Only she knows how frequently she was harassed with questions of "fair Bingen on the Rhine" and its famous mouse-tower, which constituted my sole knowledge of that lovely far away land. My paternal grandfather came from Schleswig-Holstein on the North Sea. They met and married in Wisconsin. A staunch American, my grandfather became an officer in the Civil War; his youngest son, a volunteer in the Spanish-American, was killed in the Philippines, and I still recall stories and pictures of flag-draped grey steel casket in which his body was sent back to the States after the war and given military burial in the small cemetary at Gillett, Wisconsin.

My father's family, though devout Christians, were of the Lutheran faith, my father becoming a Catholic at his marriage. My English grandfather, a Congregational, received baptism on his deathbed. So it is through the French strain in my blood alone that the Catholic Faith came down to me, and when four years ago I stepped from the small Channel boat at Dieppe to the soil of France for the first time, it was with a song of gratitude in my heart for that glorious faith which my French forefathers had passed down beautiful and untarnished to all their children. At Notre Dame of Paris I knelt and gave thanks.

"Your childhood?"—It was a simple one. My earliest memories are of lovely and holy things: walking under the sharp winter stars to midnight Mass; being lifted to the top of a high trunk in my mother's bedroom together with my next younger sister, to say our new rosaries, while a baby sister prowled beneath, striving vainly to snatch at the brightly colored beads which dangled from our fingers as we prayed blissfully on; or my mother's taking me to see the new statue of Our Lady in the small parish church at Wabeno, and how kneeling before it she told me of the beauty and loveliness of this heavenly Lady who was

my mother as well as God's. This Lady has dominated my life
ever since and been the inspiration of a great number of my
poems. As all young children do, I thought deep thoughts of all
that I saw and heard. The mystery of death entranced me, and I
remember standing motionless for long moments at a time trying
to capture the meaning of the word "eternity," and "world without end," fearing to move lest the loveliness of the thought escape
me. When I heard of the mystery of One God in Three Persons, I
immediately set out in my childish way to fathom that thought by
sheer intensity of concentration. I was terribly disappointed,
though not at all embarrassed, when told that what I had foolishly
tried to do could never be done by any human mind. I was a
presumptuous child, indeed.

"What did you wish to be when you grew up?"—"An artist like
mother!" was, I am told, my invariable answer. I crept and
played beneath her easels. Whenever she opened the large mysterious box with its twisted tubes of color, I was there at once
with little fingers clutching the table edge as I peered over, sa-
credly promising "not to touch anything." The promise was not
always kept however, and there were several disastrous skirmishes
with the brush. Not till I was fully eight did my sister and I sit
in state for our first painting lesson. After the experience of being "accepted" as an art-student, I often returned from school
with my tablet covered with drawings done from memory of the
paintings that hung from our parlor walls. At my mother's death
—I was but thirteen—her magic paint-box fell to me, and I have
kept it as a treasure. Two years ago I opened tubes of oil which
she had closed some twenty years before, and with their color,
bright and fresh as ever, painted tabernacle curtains for the altar
of a little chapel dear to me—the nearest to its fulfillment that I
have yet come of that far away childish wish to be an "artist like
mother." Yet I like to think it was a fulfillment which more than
any other would have pleased her—that her precious colors
should be placed so close to the Eucharistic Christ.

My mother planned for me a musical career and set me to studying piano at the age of six. I loved it intensely and continued my training to graduation from the conservatory, yet it was neither music nor art that ultimately claimed my heart.

"It was writing!"—Yes. When four years ago from the deck of an ocean liner anchored in her incomparable bay I looked out on Naples, and Vesuvius with its dark veil of smoke flattening out against the sky, I thought of a little girl who, on an afternoon long ago, came home from school with the first pages of her new copy-book scribbled close with rigid little quatrains. In metrical lines she had told the tragic tale of this threatening mountain that she had seen come to mysterious life upon her mother's canvases. Had the child stood where she was to stand some twenty years later I am sure that the sight of Vesuvius in all its dark majesty could never have been so present, so soul-stirring, as it was that long ago. This was my first poem. A thanksgiving verse followed close upon it, and my father, fond and proud, would have taken them to press at once had my mother not restrained him. Though she appreciated my lyrical efforts she was far from allowing me to feel important because of them, which was wise and well. Her wisdom and encouragement guided all my early work, and since she was musically gifted, a litterateur as well as an artist, but most of all a mother, her influence upon my writing was invaluable. At that ripe age of nine I also attempted a novel, but beyond a few frequently revised pages of rapid dialogue it seems to have progressed no further.

Though it was beauty made real to me upon my mother's easels that first moved me to write, it was not the only influence. Among her books I early found Shakespeare, the Brownings, Shelley and Keats, and without grasping half of what I read, through frequent reading, I memorized long portions of poems, captivated by their sheer music alone. The lyricism of the Book of Psalms won me at once, and I can still recite long excerpts learned in those early years. Whether or not my mother ever wrote poetry I do not know, but it is significant to me now to remember that her gift-books, beautifully bound and inscribed, were almost invariably books of verse.

"But were you interested only in writing?"—Oh, no. Despite the strong artistic influence on my early years I was by no means the proverbially cloistered child. Rather the opposite was true. I delighted to swim, boat, skate and toboggan, and go on long excursions into the country to gather wild flowers. For one glorious week each summer we went to my aunt's farm at Kelley Brook, where I was known for being most adept at climbing the highest apple-trees where I would hide away in the branches and read a book. As most children are, I was also a searcher of attics. In my father's long grey chest I came upon exquisite lettering and stencils which with the aid of my sisters and a bucket of bright red paint I used to make garish borders on the walls of the attic. A search into mother's old trunks brought to light volumes of classical and modern drama which we immediately set about staging in the family living room. Gowns from the gay nineties were also unearthed and fearlessly cut apart to suit our purposes. Days when my mother would be sure to attend church socials were booked long in advance for our dramatic performances. My younger brother, now a priest, and professor of philosophy at Divine Savior Seminary, Lanham, Maryland, rightfully resented his being used indiscriminately for the roles of romantic or tragic hero, or villain, as the script might demand, but he served patiently and well. Each grand finale was illuminated by red tableau fire, also discovered in the trunk, which we burned on a small fire shovel according to directions. When my mother eventually heard of our dangerous escapades we were duly reprehended, and though allowed to continue our dramatic activities, all stage-illumination ceased. Our guardian angels must have been on constant alert or we had burned the house down on a number of occasions. In many of these plays I remember to have enlivened what we considered a dull script with insertions of original dialogue and verse.

"How did you decide to become a nun?"—The answer is easy. *I* didn't. *God* did. One day when I was a very little child my mother called me from play to see two nuns who were passing our home. I responded by running not to the window but into my

mother's bedroom and promptly hid under her bed. What my
concept of a nun was at that age I do not know, but it must have
been a somewhat ominous one of something tall and black, and
frightening to little girls. There were no Sisters in our town and
I was thirteen years old when I saw one for the first time. Though
my mother was devout to them—she had been educated by the
Sisters of Notre Dame—I was awe-stricken at the first encounter,
and thought them quite ethereal beings. I certainly had no intention of becoming one. But not so many years later, God had
very much His own way in the matter, and on September 31, 1923,
I entered the convent of the Sisters of the Divine Savior in Milwaukee. To enter an order so young in the Church was to me a
great spiritual adventure. On July 14, 1924, I was clothed in the
habit; on July 15, 1925, I was professed. In Rome, years later, I
had the joy of holding in my hands the little statue of Our Lady
before which the first Sister of the Divine Savior, Mother Mary of
the Apostles, whose cause for beatification has recently been introduced, took her first vows.

My higher education was received at Marquette University, Milwaukee, with bachelor's and master's degrees in English and
philosophy. During the summer session of 1929, Father Louis
Forrey, my professor of English, urged me to submit to the editor
of the *Commonweal* a short poem, "Dolor," which I had written
for a class assignment. I finally sent the manuscript to Michael
Williams who replied with a gracious letter of acceptance, and
"Dolor" appeared in the *Commonweal,* October 16, 1929. Soon
after, my verses found publication in the *New York Times, Catholic World, American Mercury, Saturday Review of Literature,
Spirit,* and *The Savior's Call.* My Alma Mater, after giving me
two golden keys for scholarship, gave me the Laureate in June,
1933. At its foundation, I became a charter member of the
Catholic Poetry Society of America, and later one of the founders
of its Milwaukee Unit.

During my graudate years at Marquette, I was allowed to submit a collection of thirty-five unpublished poems to fulfill the re-
quirement of a master's thesis. These poems formed the nucleus

of my first book, *Now There is Beauty*. A second volume, *Give Joan a Sword,* was the lyrical fruit of a trip abroad in the summer of 1939. Perhaps nothing will influence my future writing quite so much as this experience of travel through England, France and Italy. London, Oxford, Stratford-on-Avon, Paris, Lisieux, the Italian Tyrol, Florence, Naples, Rome, were on my itinerary. In Rome I was favored with witnessing a First Mass (my brother's) in the Catacombs of St. Callixtus, and an audience with Pope Pius XII.

"What things moved you most to write?"—Almost always, simple and casual things; for instance, the small room in Littlemore where Newman prayed, studied and suffered before the great Light came; the sight of a child's face among the vested choir-boys singing Vespers in Christ's Church, Oxford; a small boy climbing to kiss the statue of Our Lady in a Roman basilica. "Salute" in *Give Joan a Sword* tells the story of this little boy and Our Lady. The solemn opening of the new basilica of St. Therese at Lisieux did not move me nearly so much as the sight of a poor beggar signing himself at her shrine. And Rome! Were I to give my impression of Rome in a single breath I would say that there one feels like a child in its father's house. Everything is yours to see, to touch, to love, and to carry away in your heart. It is as if the early Christians walked beside you—Cecilia, Lawrence, Agnes, and the rest. I lived in Rome for two months at our Motherhouse on the very summit of Monte Verde. Whenever I lifted my eyes from my desk I could see the triple towers of St. Mary Major, etched against the blue and gold of the Sabine mountains. My brother, for three years a student of theology at the Gregorian University, was an expert guide; each day we went out together on a new spiritual adventure.

Then there was that rare and precious grace of looking up into the face of the Vicar of Christ, Pope Pius XII. I saw him on a number of occasions and twice had the privilege of speaking to him. I asked for and obtained the Apostolic Blessing for the officers and members of the Catholic Poetry Society of America. I likewise presented to His Holiness the manuscript of my poem

"Prayer for the Pontiff." Through a touching coincidence, I received from him the gift of his silver pencil. "I will look for something appropriate," he had said, and gave me his pencil.

"Your favorite authors?"—Of many, let me name two: Cardinal Newman, scholar and saint, and the distinguished French philosopher, Jacques Maritain, whose luminous writings have been a grace to me. Dr. Maritain honored me with a preface to *Give Joan a Sword*.

"Your favorite theme?"—Perhaps I should say my most persistent and absorbing theme—the human soul, and that soul as a revelation of God's infinite beauty. Many of my poems have been inspired by contacts with certain rare souls, friendships, if you will. Next to a prayerful union with God, nothing so enriches, deepens, and spiritualizes one as closeness to a beautiful soul.

"Your message to young writers?"—A friend, a scholar with depth of spiritual vision, recently quoted me a motto he had come upon in his reading, *"Porta patet, sed magis cor,"* and remarked that apart from the pertinence of its application to the molding of character, it would make a fine inscription over any door. It undoubtedly would. "Open is the door, but more so the heart." With a nuance of interpretation this text lends itself well to my message. Before the young writer dare open the door of his thought and place the word on paper for all the world to see, he must first make deep and rich and wide the gateways of his heart, whence the beauty and truth of his thought proceed. He must first *be* the beautiful thing that he would write! He must escape from the boundaries of his little self and enter the spaciousness of the true world of God where, sensitively aware of the beauty that surrounds him—the beauty of heavenly things and the loveliness of human things, each one of which speaks to him its own *sursum corda*—he may become a channel of the Word to others.

On the side of technique, from an intensive and careful reading of the literary masters he must acquire faultless writing habits, and a discriminating taste. He should be his own most exacting critic.

Then, let him write! If you say, "I cannot," have you tried?
Only when you have honestly given yourself a chance can you
really tell. It may take years to arrive; a lifetime is not too long.
And if at the end, your finished work, though as near perfection
as you can bring it, still does not measure up to the vision in
your mind, the creative idea you set out to enshrine in words, you
need not be cast down. You are sharing the lot of all literary
artists.

> "For words are human only, taking their measure
>   By a sun or a star—
>   Infinities beneath the things that are."

But most of all, remember that what *you* are, so will be your
song!

EDITOR'S NOTE: Macmillan issued Sister's *Now There Is Beauty*, 1940, and
Give Joan a Sword, 1944.

VERA MARIE TRACY

(1891–1940)

By Reverend Martin A. Kraff, C.PP.S.

THE SUCCESSFUL WRITER confines his work to the field he knows best. Assuming that he possesses natural ability and adequate training, the range of his knowledge and of his personal and vicarious experience indicates his potential power and prescribes his choice of themes, be they fact or fiction. The reader, on the contrary, wants the unfamiliar—that of which he has not heard or of which he knows only enough to arouse his curiosity.

We are so busy learning of things afar that the greater number of us know little of what lies nearest and should be dearest: the realm of the soul, the supernatural. Possibly this is because few authors have the warmth of sympathy and the absence of egoism which enables them to chart The High Adventure. A literary saint would be best qualified for the self exposition of a character devoid of self. St. Therese of Lisieux, St. Teresa of Avila and St. John of the Cross have demonstrated its possibility. So did David and Paul. So do some of our contemporaries. On a plane less exalted than that of the canonized saints, they have enriched us by sharing the intimate experiences of their own souls—and this without violation of any canon of good taste or delicate feeling.

Such a contemporary is our own American Vera Marie Tracy. She utilized recognized forms of poetry and a delicately fanciful form of fiction for this intimate revelation. Her problems were always spiritual. Their intensity suggests that at one time or another each of them was personal. It is the reality, resonant in each bit of prose or poetry which fascinates the reader. The author is less concerned with the purely human aspects of circumstances than with the part played in each character's life by the living personal God.

This resonant spiritual reality, peculiarly characteristic of Vera Marie Tracy, is the trait which insures her success. Her literary expression has intensely personal charm. The paralysis of her body enhanced the intellectual and emotional sensitiveness characteristic of invalids, accentuating her freedom in her spiritual flights. Her fiction is the projection of her personal experience. We find this again and again in *Burnished Chalices, The Blue Portfolio,* and *Break Thou My Heart.* It is because she visualized death as "The dear embrace of the lover, God," that she can transfer her spiritual life to the printed page. Her readers are able to visualize them with as much clarity as if they were happening to a self other than that which experienced them. Fiction, then, became for her an imaginative projection of this "experiencing self" upon the pages of her "hospital sketches," *Burnished Chalices,* 1931, and of her more deliberately fictionized tales in two other prose volumes *Blue Portfolio,* 1933, and *Break Thou My Heart,* 1936.

Break Thou My Heart is really a misleading title to Miss Tracy's most mature prose work. Far from being morbid, as certain critics have asserted, it contains the gem of all the sunny stories,—the one in which the little adventuress enjoys a delightful tea party with hosts who, she discovers many years later, had been dead for more than seven years. Several of the stories end in death, but for the character involved death is the happy solution of the spiritual problem,—"the dear embrace of the Lover, God."

The influence of Francis Thompson is evident in all Miss Tracy's work. Some lines in *The Mistress of Vision* illustrates the method by which her spiritual life was transferred to the printed page;

> Pierce thy heart to find the key;
> With thee take
> Only what none else would keep;
> Learn to dream when thou dost wake,
> Learn to wake when thou dost sleep;
> Learn from fears to vanquish fears, . . .
> Die, for none other way canst live . . .
> When thy seeing blindeth thee
> To what thy fellow-mortals see . . .
> Search no more . . .

Miss Tracy's heart had been pierced indeed before she found "the key." In addition to the personal tragedy of her 'teens, when a Denver specialist frankly told her of the incurable nature of the creeping muscular paralysis which had begun in her infancy, thus substituting the wheel-chair and the bed in lifelong prospect for the natural fulfillment of buoyant youth's fresh hopes, next misfortune struck at her two "most beloveds" at the same time. Her aunt's health began to fail (her parents had died when she was about three years old), and one August day her grandmother fell and sustained injuries which resulted in her death two weeks afterwards.

Other lines from the same poem describe with almost startling exactitude the "Persean conquest,"—a victory in defeat, and vast gain in spiritual vision.

> When to the new eyes of thee
> All things by immortal power,
> Near or far,
> Hiddenly
> To each other linked are,
> That thou canst not stir a flower
> Without troubling of a star;
> When thy song is shield and mirror
> To the fair snake-curled Pain,
> Where thou dar'st affront her terror
> That on her thou mayst attain
> Persean conquest; seek no more."

The Catholic faith, whose outward forms she had desultorily continued for the previous few years only to save her loved ones from added grief, gave her no solace in this final blow. During nearly four years, the only real companionship her young girlhood had known was with this darling grandmother. Her loss was irreparable. That night she went to bed numb, exhausted, completely dispirited, feeling as did Francis Thompson:

> "Naked I wait Thy love's uplifted stroke!
> My harness piece by piece Thou hast hewn from me
> And smitten me to my knee;
> I am defenceless utterly.
> I slept, methinks, and woke,
> And, slowly gazing, find me stripped in sleep.
> In the rash lustihead of my young powers,
> I shook the pillaring hours
> And pulled my life upon me; grimed with smears,
> I stand amid the dust o' the mounded years—
> My mangled youth lies dead beneath the heap.
> My days have crackled and gone up in smoke,
> Have puffed and burst as sunstarts on a stream.
> Yea, faileth now even dream
> The dreamer, . . ."

"Slowly gazing!" Though she hardly realized it, she was ready to fall into the yawning emptiness of practical atheism and despair. Many years later she was to write of those years in "When It Was Morning" (*Burnished Chalices*): "In your blind pride you spurned His hand and essayed to walk alone! How you stumbled on and on bewildered. . . . Dear God, the horror of it! But why has He been so sweet and patient with you?"

"Yea, faileth now even dream the dreamer!" She had dreamed of being a great writer, one whom the world would acclaim. She would show God. She had thought to stand in her own strength. The results were like those of Samson: "I shook the pillaring hours and pulled my life upon me; grimed with smears!" In her private Autobiography, she noted that her stories "came back in such posthaste it made me dizzy."

Her writing was a failure, complete and absolute. Everything she loved was blighted—her aunt with illness, her grandmother with death, her work with defeat, her life with incurable paralysis.

In very fact, she was "stripped in sleep," that is, in her helpless-
ness, of everything that the world, that youth, held dear. Then
occurred what she called her conversion.

In the private Autobiography, she told it simply. "The night
she (her grandmother) died I fell into a deep dreamless sleep. . . .
I had wondered how I could bear to awaken and realize she was
gone. But with the dawn light Christ Himself was there beside
my bed, holding my hand, comforting. . . . It was no mere
fancy. He was there. I knew it as certainly as if my eyes beheld
Him. There was no reproach, only infinite tenderness and sympathy." Her grandmother's first plea, she believes, had been for
her need. "And so He had come Himself. I was given strength
and courage in that one day to face the loneliness ahead. . . . I
began to hunger for the Sacraments. . . .

Not only was her Catholic faith "re-born!" She was given the
courage to "accept His Cross." Again she discovered with the
soul sought by "The Hound of Heaven":

> "All which I took from thee I did but take,
>   Not for thy harms,
>   But just that thou might'st seek it in My arms."

A volume of the poems of St. Therese, the Little Flower of
Jesus, fell into her hands during these days: "They thrilled me
through and through and charged me with a great longing to pour
out my heart to God likewise in lovely verse. . . . I could scarcely
write down fast enough all the inspirations that came to me. The
very first one I wrote, "For Thy Shall Be Comforted," (*Incense,*
1926) was published in the Catholic magazine, *Truth,* and others
were accepted."

In 1926, a year and a half after she had entered Glockner Sana-
torium permanently for 'ordinary care,' because of her increasingly inability to help herself, her first volume was printed. The
final lines of that first poem demonstrate that experience, intimately realized, is the source of all worthwhile literature.

> "Broken at last, I lay with grief-marred face,
>   The lonely years ahead were guised in fear;
>   I could not guess the measure of His grace,

Nor that He stood so near,
Until He stooped and pressed me to His heart—
Dear God, Thy tenderness to one who mourned!"

A friend, wondering how it was that Vera Tracy had come to write these beautiful books, asked,

"Did you think, perhaps, to help others—to give them some of the strength and comfort God had given you?"

"Yes," she replied, "but that came later. You see, I fell in love with Him—with God. And I wanted to tell Him how I loved Him, as the Little Flower had done. It was all I could do. So I asked Him to help me, and He did. Then I thought it would be so nice if I could maybe make a little book, with just His name on every page, and something beautiful to go with it!"

When *Incense* had created a mild furore in Catholic literary circles, Miss Tracy tried her hand once more at prose,—this time, following the theme she had adopted for her poetry, stories with Christ as the Hero, the Prince Charming to all the little maiden souls in their various and ingenious forms of distress. Some critics praised them with a great deal of sentimentality; others read deeper and found a great deal more than the outward narratives. *Burnished Chalices* has gone through four editions. Readers of the tales, either in magazines or in book form, took Miss Tracy to their hearts. She became (in 1931) an Academy Member of the Catholic Poetry Society of America, an honor given to only thirty living poets. In 1933, because of her "outstanding contribution to poetry," she was named member of The International Mark Twain Society. Hundreds of personal letters came to her.

These honors pleased and delighted her; her human heart had been nearly starved for some sort of approbation. But, sterling Catholic woman with a heart touched by the Heart of God and a cross laid on her by His hand, she never forgot Who had given her this power to move men's hearts, in spite of apparently insuperable obstacles: physically inept muscles, and an almost unceasing tremendous, torturing lassitude. In 1934 she wrote in the Autobiography: "I sit propped up in bed . . . and type with one finger. . . . The paralysis has crept into my hands until I can no longer use a pen." At the time of this writing, she has become too weak even to press down a typewriter key, though says, "I still have two more books in my head!" Of the happy days, she writes in "Joy" (*Gold-Dusty 1937*): "I loose . . . a winged aerial of prayer . . . to tell Him gratefully how glad I fare."

The years brought fruition, both in personal spirituality and in literary power. Two poems, frankly concerned with her crippled condition, in both of which the fact is accepted uncomplainingly, illustrate this mental and moral broadening of her horizons. The first one, "Broken Wings," (*Incense*) seems (at least to this writer) ever so faintly to intimate the hurt which even noble youth could hardly be expected not to feel. Despite the sympathy of the second stanza, there is an implication of what one might call at least heartlessness in the first. Ten years later, in "Broken Things," (*Gold-Dusty*) occur the exquisitely tender, understanding lines of the sestet of the sonnet:

> "I perched upon the threshold of the world,
> Proud, poising carelessly for lofty flight,
> When lo! from His unerring Hand was hurled
> The stone reducing me to sorry plight.
>
> But now I know that I would rather be,
> In His cupped Hand, a maimed and helpless thing,
> Held to His Heart in closest sympathy,
> Then soar, a joyous songster, fleet of wing!"

The lines beautifully express Christian resignation.
Now read the sestet already described:

> "Full well I know God loves His broken things!
> If my cold heart is torn, how must His Heart
> Yearn o'er the hurt of all this writhing world,
> Gather it in His arms and soothe its smart!
> Yea, I who languish here with maimed wings,
> Look up and know—God loves His broken things!"

Her horizon has broadened: her own hurt is least considered, and then only as one instance of the hurt of "all this writhing world." Now there is not only resignation; she has learned contentment with pain and futility. Pain has ceased to be a problem.

Though the lover-lines of "Eucharistic," (*Incense*) seem faintly

reminiscent of Sister Madeleva, they have a throbbing intensity
all their own.

> "As the moth to the flame, my Jesus,
>   My soul to Thee . . .
>
> My heart is a winged whisper,
>   My love is a flame . . .
>
> Sweet are Thy eyes, my lover,
>   As all the garnered sweetness of spring.
>
> White, ethereal, remote, as winter moon at full,
>   Yet kindling to strange fires, Thy fingers round my heart.
>
> Climbing the stars, importuning with soft prayer,
>   My hand in Thy hand, Dearest, homeward bound."

Now read the second stanza of "Whisper," (*Gold-Dusty*). And
note, not the difference in spiritual attitude only, but also the
growth in poetic power, in observation (the almost unnoticeable
mastery by which she makes the night-sounds which immediately
precede dawn subserve her purpose), in technique, and in the im-
plicitness of expression, so much stronger than explicit statement:

> "I say: 'He is coming! Ah! listen!
>   O heart of me quicken and throb!
> The stars swing low in their courses,
>   The dark trees tremble and sob.
>
> Alone in the night I gather
>   One ravishing thought to my breast—
> 'He will come to me in the morning'—
>   And slip back to sleep and rest.

Behind and beneath the never-broken passion of her loving
came the immeasurable gift, tranquility,—"the Peace of Christ
that passeth all understanding," peace which remained unbroken
in the midst of pain, of uncontrollable heart-ache—peace of soul
which no earthly storm can ever disturb. Read the lines in
"Apology," (*Gold-Dusty*):

> "Dearest, forgive these slow hot tears of mine;
>   This is poor welcome for a royal Guest . . .
> Then bear with one who cannot stay her tears
> For that her foolish heart broke in the night;
> Thou too hadst bitter hurt and thorn-crowned years,
> And Thou didst die to set my own aright!"

The disturbing phenomenon of "slow hot tears," most frequently devoid of any emotional accompaniment, is one peculiar to frequent night-time sufferers, especially if the night has been also sleepless. I have been told that it is an automatic nerve release, a relief from a strain which might otherwise have serious physical or mental consequences. As to the poems, it would be presumptuous to state that this is the "heart-break" referred to—but there is no doubt of her frequent nocturnal misery.

One could give repeated instances of the spiritual, mental and artistic growth of Vera Marie Tracy in a short period of crippled years—"thorn-crowned years" as Christ's were! In *Incense* the poems about the Blessed Virgin are chiefly concerned with her youth, her joy in the small Christ, though they touch, too, upon her sorrows. But the feeling is still immature. In the later books, especially the second collection of poems, her own grown-up woman's heart thrills and grieves and grasps some of the cutting human hurt that lingered ever in the heart of Mary after she had said: "Be it done to me according to Thy word."

Growing closer to Christ did not lessen Vera Tracy's physical suffering; yet one who met her was impressed by the simplicity of the heroism with which she accepted the difficulties of her condition. She had steadier, more difficult patience than in the early years when, apart from the grace of God, youth's natural buoyancy gifted her with an easy gayety which drew friends innumerable to her side.

One dare not conclude from these lines that she was unbelievably superhuman. She was and remained every inch—there aren't many inches, really!—a simple, humble, unassuming Catholic woman. Neither would it be legitimate to conclude that she was either old or saddened. Still a young woman, she looked even younger than her years. (The vital data in the Introduction to *Incense* is erroneous.) She was a joyous companion, a glad, fresh, vital personality, with whom it was a rare pleasure to spend a too-swiftly flying hour. Despite the seeming impossibility, she faced the grave problem of how to achieve expression for the beautiful things still unsaid which she would have liked to get on paper for "her Lover."   Of course, quoting her own words spoken to a friend:

"He knows them, but I'd so like to say them!"

EDITOR'S NOTE: Miss Tracy's prose works, *Blue Portfolio, Break Thou My Heart,* and *Burnished Chalices,* and her poems, *Gold Dusty,* and *Incense,* are all out of print; but selected stories and sketches from the three prose works were published by Bruce under the title *All the Aprils,* in 1944.   Miss Tracy's chapter is included in *The Book of Catholic Authors* through the courtesy of *The Magnificat.*

DOM HUBERT VAN ZELLER, O.S.B.

WHEN A MAN IS ASKED to say how he came to take writing books about the Bible he is tempted to lie. I can think of numberless reasons why I *might* have started writing Biblical biographies—to fulfil a vow made in early youth, for instance, or in obedience to an inner voice—but if I am to be honest with myself I can admit to only one: Scripture was the single subject about which the general public seemed to know even less than I did.

From my nursery days I had always been interested in the Bible, and, not wanting to keep a good thing altogether to myself, I suppose I grew up wishing I could somehow or other get other people to share my discovery. Whether the initial interest owed its origin to the fact that I was born in the land which for a time sheltered Abraham, Joseph, Moses and Jeremias I do not know; certainly the rustle of Egypt's river-bank reeds was in my boyhood's ears, and the dry smell of the desert reaches my nostrils still. But whatever the sources of my Biblical tendency, the motive which urged me to follow it up was the desire to get

Catholics to read the Bible. I know that while at school here at
Downside (where I am now a monk) the only subject which made
me want to get up upon the house-top and shout was the subject
of Old Testament History. That was due to the inspiring quality
of the text together with the inspiring quality of the teaching (I
was taught by Dom Rupert Brace-Hall, now Headmaster of Ealing
Priory School), and not to any merit of mine, is quite certain. Because I never did get up upon the house-top and shout.

Now without asking anyone who reads these lines to buy my
books and study them, I would venture, by way of introduction to
what follows, to summarize the conclusions of those brave men
and women who have. I write, my reviewers state, for a threefold
public. First for the young people (these are in the class-room
and lecture-hall, and so cannot decently escape); second for the
layfolk (the men-in-the-street who read a book of mine for what
they can get out of it, and because their wives have given it to
them, and in the hopes that it will get more amusing later on . . .
in spite of the fact that there's a lot of Scripture mixed up in it);
third for monks and nuns (who find problems of mystical theology
and prayer treated in an idiom which is for once not the language
of translation, and who can at the same time enjoy the feeling
that they are keeping up their study of Holy Scripture). It is,
then, equally the interest of the student, the layman, and the religious, which I am out to foster. So far my reviewers. I welcome
this direction which is given to my work because it happens to be
correct. Let me illustrate the above with three stories, each of
them true.

The first incident belongs to the time when I was at school. A
travelling salesman had motored over from Swindon one summer
afternoon in the hopes of interesting the authorities in a new
kind of fire-extinguisher. Applying a restricted sense to the word
"interesting," the hope was fully justified: the authorities were
interested, and vastly more so were the boys. It was the practical
demonstration which gripped us. The Headmaster and one or
two others were invited into the quadrangle to watch the little
man first of all setting fire to his car and then extinguishing it

with the preparation which he was trying to sell. I was witnessing the operation from my room where another student and I were engaged upon a Latin translation. The salesman's act was so successful that the Headmaster called upon him to repeat it. He obligingly complied. "Do it again," cried the Headmaster. The car blazed anew. "And again," shouted the Headmaster when the conflagration was put out. "Once more," came the enthusiastic but imperious command. At this point, recalling a similar incident in the pages of Kings where a Prophet of the Lord is heard to challenge the priests of Baal, I turned to my companion and quoted: "And he said: Fill four buckets and pour it upon the holocaust . . . and he said: Do the same a second time. And when they had done the same a third time." True, the salesman was reversing the order of Elias's commands, but even so the reference was not recognized by my fellow student. Scholars, I reflected, did not know their Bible.

The second story has nothing to do with me; it has, however, a Downside connection. Abbot Trafford, during the period when he was Headmaster before becoming Abbot, was on one occasion showing the school to a lady who was thinking of sending her boy to us. Admiration was expressed at all that she saw, but never did her appreciation reach such a height as when this somewhat worldly-minded woman allowed herself to dwell upon the thought that her little boy would be able to attend classes in the company of other little boys whose parents were of the highest nobility. "I had heard so much about Downside," she said as she took her leave, "but it has exceeded my wildest hopes." "Which is much what the Queen of Sheba said, if you remember," replied Father Trafford, "Oh, did *she* send her boy here too?" is the reputed rejoinder. When I heard this story I decided that students were not the only people who needed Biblical instruction.

My last story refers to a time which I spent in a Carthusian novitiate. I must explain that in the Charterhouse there is but one clock, visible to all within the enclosure and loud enough in its chime to tell the hour to the surrounding countryside. When the ordinary time is changed to summer time, the clock is so adjusted as to proclaim the adopted hour in its striking capacity while with its hands it indicates "God's time"—the time by which the monks' day continues to be regulated. This arrangement was explained to me by a fellow member of the novitiate on the day when the outside world began its observance of summer time. "I see," I said, "the voice indeed is the voice of Jacob, but the hands are the hands of Esau." My informant looked puzzled. "It's all one clock, if that's what you mean," he said, "the community brought it over from France at the Suppression." Religious, I thought, as well as laymen and schoolboys, could do with a little more Scripture. (In fairness I should add that the novice left the Carthusians, as I did, before taking vows.)

Now though I cannot claim that I would never have written about the Bible had these incidents not taken place, I do very definitely say that their significance confirmed in me the desire to write. The next thing was to start on the books themselves. In the summer of 1935 I wrote *Prophets and Princes, Watch and Pray* and *Sackcloth and Ashes*—the two books covering the twelve Minor Prophets—came out in 1937. After this I got ill, and wrote in bed *Isaias: Man of Ideas.* This book was meant to be a "feeler" to see if the public was ready to take full length biographies instead of, as hitherto, snapshot impressions of people and periods. The reviews seemed to justify the belief that it was. So I set out and wrote *Daniel: Man of Desires, Jeremias: Man of Tears* (which came out in 1942 and which was chosen as the book of the month by The Catholic Book Club), and *Ezechiel: Man of Signs,* which should be out by the time this sketch is printed. *Daniel* was held up for some months because I sent it to the wrong address and it was lost in the post. Dovetailed into the above list come *Lord God,* a prayer book for boys, and *Come Lord,* a companion volume for girls. *Liturgical Asides* is a prayer book for anybody who cares to read it. I have never seen it quoted, so perhaps nobody has read it. I am, however, often being reminded of the dedication. Why do people always want one to be funny?

From Creation to Christmas, which was published in 1943, is the

story of the Old Testament and is meant for young people between the ages of twelve to fifteen. The first draft of this work
was being set up in type when the whole thing was destroyed in
an air-raid. I had taken no carbon copy and so had to begin all
over again—without notes. I know now what Lawrence, Carlyle,
and Jeremias must have felt when they learned that their manuscripts had perished. The experience has at last persuaded me
to make use of carbon paper.

In addition to the above list there have been various minor
publications: a pamphlet, a number of poems, an article or two,
and an occasional essay. I have also written two plays (memorials
to Father Bede Jarrett, O.P., who was my friend and master for the
last fifteen years of his life and for the most formative years of
mine) which are at the moment going the rounds of publishing
houses. (So if any enterprising American publisher is looking for
a play with a moral and with no sex, I hope he will send me a
cable. He might also like to look at a detective story, a Victorian
romance, and some fifty unpublished poems.)

And that's not all. The photograph which accompanies these
pages is a kind one: I am not as good as that. I was born in 1906.
I have no degrees attaching to my name. I began my studies in
Munich but got ill and had to come home. I became a Headmaster for a little while but again I got ill. I am now a House-
master, and so far no one has thought me ill enough to justify my
removal. When not writing or teaching or being ill, I paint
pictures and carve stone. Photographs of my sculpture have appeared from time to time in art periodicals at home and abroad,
but I have never had an exhibition. Once, after some months at
an art school, I managed to get together enough paintings for a
one-man show but in bringing them by train from the studios to
my monastery I unfortunately left them on the rack and never saw
them again. A week went by before I remembered where I had
last seen them, and then it was too late. The canvases were un-
signed, and I am still expecting to come upon them in some not
very front rank gallery.

To end on a sententious note may I make an appeal to the aspiring Catholic writer? *Do please approach the business in an apostolic spirit.* We of the True Faith should be able to create a demand for things true and Catholic. We should be able to establish a Catholic press, a Catholic drama, a Catholic school of art, a Catholic literature—a Catholic way of looking at life. We should aim at turning men's gaze towards Truth and Beauty at their Source. The danger is ever—and I say this with my eyes open after writing a chapter which is of necessity all about myself —to draw men's gaze towards ourselves. We have to remember that we are lighthouse-keepers only, tending the flame and showing it to others, and that we have nothing of our own which is in any way worthy of attracting the admiration of mankind.

EDITOR'S NOTE: Dom Van Zeller's books, all published by Burns, Oates & Washbourne, include *Isaias, Liturgical Asides, Prophets and Princes, Sackcloth and Ashes, Watch and Pray, Daniel,* and *From Creation to Christmas.* He also compiled and edited a prayer book for young men (*Lord God*) and one for young women (*Come Lord*).

DR. JAMES JOSEPH WALSH
(1865–1942)
By Ella Marie Flick

JAMES J. WALSH was born April 12, 1865, at Archbald, Pa., son of Martin J. and Bridget (Golden) Walsh. He used jokingly to say that two days after his birth his parents put a black band on his arm for the death of Lincoln. He was a grandson of an Irish schoolmaster of Killala, County Mayo, Ireland, from whom he received his first lessons. He attended primary classes in the Wilkes-Barre, Pa., parish school conducted by the Sisters of Mercy. At fifteen he was sent to St. John's College, Fordham, where he graduated at nineteen years of age (A.B., 1884; A.M., 1885; Ph.D., 1895; LL.D., 1900).

His childhood must have been an extraordinarily free and happy one. As a member of a huge family consisting of grandparents (two sets), aunts, uncles, and ten sisters and brothers, he grew up in an interesting world. The Walshs were one of the few families in Parsons (where the family grew up) who took both *The Irish World* and *The Pilot*. The children in the family read everything in both of them. Young James' first interest in literature came through the columns of *The Pilot,* the "Ant Column," conducted by the wife of John Boyle O'Reilly.

Any account of Dr. Walsh begins with the story of his Irish grandmother who at sixteen took her elder sister's place when she was afraid to cross the Atlantic, spent 93 days in crossing, saw half the passenger list die off from typhus, landed at Quebec, and took two years to get to her brother who was down at Honesdale, Pa. This grandmother, whom Dr. Walsh loved to quote, made so great an impression upon him that he had in manuscript form her biography entitled "Peggy Sees Life."

Dr. Walsh would often tell of the part his mother played in building the family fortune in their general store. How she would make a yearly trip to New York City to lay in supplies and always brought the newest baby with her. Mrs. Walsh died at the age of fifty-five, just two months after Joseph and James graduated from the University of Pennsylvania.

At Fordham he played center on the college football team. He was 19 at that time and had to train down from 220 pounds to 205. Between 1884, the year of his graduation from Fordham, and his graduation as a doctor of medicine from the University of Pennsylvania in 1895, he spent six years with the Jesuits in the study of philosophy preparatory to entering the Order. Illness ended that dream. The Jesuits forever after held a special place in his heart. He used to say affectionately: "I was associated with them in nine communities and was a member of their Order for six years."

After receiving his M.D. in 1895, he went abroad for special studies at the Universities of Paris, Vienna, and Berlin. In speaking of those days, he said of course one of the reasons why he went to Europe immediately after graduation was in order that he might know something about Europe and be able to talk about it.

His whole life was taken up with teaching and writing. He was dean of the Fordham University School of Medicine until its closing in 1913. His first job upon returning from abroad in 1900 was as instructor in medicine at the University of New York Polyclinic School of Medicine. In 1904 he became dean and professor of neurology at the Medical School of Fordham and professor of physiological psychology at Cathedral College. He thus provided for many years an introduction for young ecclesiastical students to analytical psychology. During these same years he was professor of nervous diseases and the history of medicine at St. Francis Xavier College in New York.

For many years he was medical editor of the New York *Herald* in the days when it was an eight-page paper, carried a lot of ship news and devoted much space to Wall Street. To Dr. Walsh it seemed immense.

He began to write shortly after graduation with the publication of several articles on orthopedic subjects. While still a student he' became a great lover of history, especially Catholic history. In a letter he once stated: "A favorite expression of mine (I think that I am the inventor of it) is, Facts are truth, but facts are not truth unless you have all the facts."

He wrote sketches of many of his contemporaries: Martin Glynn, John Quinn, Joseph O'Dwyer, Gilmary Shea, Sir William Hingston. He jokingly remarked: "I have written so many sketches of my contemporaries that I shall probably be known as the man in whose bibliography will be found nearly everyone else." This sort of work paid him only a dollar a page; but he liked doing it.

Because he wrote so fast, he had extensive experience with publishers. He brought out one book a year for forty years. He estimated each book netted him at the most a thousand dollars. All his books were turned down at least once and some of them three to six times. He said he could not get anyone to take *The Thirteenth, Greatest of Centuries,* and many of his friends told him he was foolish to think it would ever be published. And then when all the publishers had finished with it, except a Catholic one who proposed to bring it out in a cheap edition, he concluded his friends were right. But he decided to get it into print anyway. Yet later he estimated that it had probably meant more than $40,000.00 to him in the years up to 1933.

Dr. Austin O'Malley, M.D., summed up the big idea in the

teachings of Dr. Walsh when he said: "Despite the wide compre-
hension of the material he has handled, there is unity in his aims.
He says 'I do not think man has ever made a bit of progress; his
mind is today just the same as it ever was, excepting that now it
is occupied mainly with trifles.' "

Dr. O'Malley also said: "The immutability of man was the
fundamental thought in most of Dr. Walsh's books: *Education*:
*How Old the New; Old Time Makers of Medicine; Modern Prog-
ress and History; The Thirteenth, Greatest of Centuries; Medieval
Medicine; The Century of Columbus.*" Most of these books ran
into third and fourth editions.

Dr. Walsh was very generous with his pen and firmly believed
every Catholic had certain responsibilities toward the Catholic
Press. He did not care about money himself. He thought money
dangerous.

Over many years it was our pleasure to call for Dr. Walsh after
his Monday afternoon lecture at Chestnut Hill College, his last of
five lectures given on that day between New York and Philadelphia. We would call for him and bring him home for dinner.
He asked so many questions on subjects hard to answer that in our
younger days we were always glad to have him go to sleep and
snore until we got home. He always carried a bag suitable to his
size and the bag was always filled with heavy books. When my
father and he were settled on the sofa before the fireplace with
their after dinner cigars he would call for the bag, bid us open it,
and delight in showing us what he had found in the way of
treasures at some old bookstore or stand. When thoughtlessly
we would admire a book, he would say "I will give it to you, it
cost only a penny." With that he would take out one of his find-
ings, write something on the fly leaf and bestow it upon one of us.
His bag was a treasure trove to all of us. Also a magician's hat.
We never knew just what would come out of that huge black
satchel.

He was full of poetry, tender thoughts of God, ecclesiastical
gossip, and wide-world news. He had a very tender sympathy
with any form of trouble, but he did not believe in making one

soft. At times when I knew he was quite broken-hearted over a situation, he tried his hardest to rouse my fighting blood and generally succeeded.

Dr. Walsh had lectured all over the world and spent months out of every year in travel. On his first trip abroad, while in Rome with his father and uncle, they received a letter telling them that they were to receive Holy Communion at the hands of the Pope. His father wept. "That's the way an Irishman expresses joy," said Dr. Jim.

In 1904, again in Europe, he visited Canon Sheehan in his garden at Doneraile and spent two hours with him. That same summer he hunted out the cliffs of Moher and the beach of Kilkee and Lisdoonvarna. He used to tell of the brakeman on the narrow gauge railroad which ran through Kerry and up to Ennis who came along and opened the doors and announced loudly, "If there's anybody for here there, let him get out."

Dr. Walsh had a childlike simplicity about him for all his greatness. In March, 1910, he asked my father to give a short series of lectures at Fordham covering one afternoon and two nights. "We shall be ready to receive you at Fordham the night before and to give you a little touch of community life during the evening and morning." In describing the location of the room reserved, he added: "The Blessed Sacrament will not be far away from you."

He talked to liberal clubs at half a dozen colleges and universities, and the students thought to have fun poking questions at him. But he had more fun answering them.

In 1932, Dr. Walsh went to Ireland to attend the Eucharistic Congress. With his wife and two children he attended another in Buenos Aires in 1934. During the 1934 session he talked over a world-wide radio hook-up about the Congress.

As late as 1936 he was still giving lectures at four separate stop-offs between New York and Philadelphia. But he was weary. "Sister death of the body is gently picking us up," he wrote Dr. Flick in that year.

His letters were always full of clippings. Bits of news, funny

items, unusual accounts of events. He went to endless trouble
to send one clippings he thought one might be interested in.

In 1934 he was chosen to preside at a meeting of the book division of the National Arts Club to introduce four or five new
authors. He had very distinct likes and dislikes in a literary
way. And so set were his opinions that they sometimes worried
him. He did not like Whitman. "Walt Whitman is one of the
men whose poetry I do not appreciate or even understand," he
wrote me upon a literary occasion. And again on the Nobel
Prize, "I can not see why Pirandello should receive the Nobel
Prize. Neither can I understand why Bunin got the Prize in
1933. . . . I don't even see any reason why Bernard Shaw got the
Nobel Prize."

He helped to organize the Catholic Writers' Guild in the long
ago and for a few years he was very active in it. He was also an
Academy member of the Gallery of Living Catholic Authors.

He was a marvelous correspondent. He loved to write letters
and he loved to get them. No one could outdo him. His letters
were treasures in literary information, political chit-chat and
general world information. Once while on vacation he scribbled
across a post card: "No secretary here to let me pour myself out."
I have no doubt it was a real privation.

Dr. Walsh was the recipient of many honors, notably that of
Knight Commander of St. Gregory the Great, with Cross, and
Knighthood in the Order of Malta. In 1916, Notre Dame University conferred the Laetare Medal on him. Notre Dame also
awarded him the honorary degree of Doctor of Science in 1908,
while in 1915 the Catholic University of America bestowed upon
him the degree of Doctor of Literature and Georgetown the same
degree. In 1940 he received the gold medal of the American
Irish Historical Society in recognition of "eminence in cultural
leadership."

He was universally beloved. Among his closest friends he
counted Cardinal Farley and Cardinal Hayes. He made friends
easily and he had the talent of keeping them. His popularity
with all classes was partly due to his humility and partly to his

good nature. He was one of the most humorous men I ever heard talk, and it was a kindly humor.

In his last years he thought and wrote much on suffering and the mystery of pain. "The mystery of suffering has touched man very deeply and his response has been deep," he said. He used to name in one of his most famous talks on suffering and evil the five greatest dramas ever written as being: Job in the Old Testament, Aeschylus' Prometheus, Shakespeare's Hamlet, Calderon's El Magico Prodigioso, and Goethe's Faust.

"I feel so well now for some days when it is not raining or when the barometer is not dropping that I think I might be willing to go on for half a dozen years more," he wrote us in 1938. And again that same year: "It is rather hard to give up the things that seemed so much a matter of course just a few years ago, but nature is gradually teaching me the lesson that it must be done. . . . It is the hardest thing in the world to be turned out to grass without the harness."

On the death of his dear friend, my father, in July, 1938, he sent me a very beautiful little memorial "Magnificat," with the query: "I wonder whether that isn't the greatest poem ever written. That and her intervention at the wedding in Cana represent Mary as we know her best, but I have always thought that the Magnificat was never fully appreciated."

Dr. Walsh went to bring his testimony in person to Our Lady's paean of praise on February 28, 1942.

EDITOR'S NOTE: Miss Flick wrote a sketch of Dr. Walsh for the *Catholic World;* the above is a revision of that sketch, made for this book. We express our thanks to the *Catholic World* as well as to Miss Flick. Dr. Walsh's books include *The Thirteenth, Greatest of Centuries,* 1907, 1937, Fordham University Press; *American Jesuits,* 1934, Macmillan; *The Catholic Church and Healing,* 1928, Macmillan; *A Catholic Looks at Life,* 1928, Stratford; *High Points of Medieval Culture,* 1937, Bruce; *Our American Cardinals,* 1926, Appleton; *The World's Debt to the Catholic Church,* 1924, Statford; *Sex Instruction,* 1931, J. F. Wagner.

LENORA MATTINGLY WEBER

I WAS BORN in Dawn, Missouri, October 1, 1895. After a childhood in a small town in Ohio, my parents, with their six children, came west and took up a homestead on our Colorado plains. The plains at that time were mostly given over to big cattle and sheep ranches, but we never encountered any of the animosity which history and fiction claim the old timers felt for the "nesters."

It is this plains background that I like to use in my teen-age stories and books. For when I'm writing about raising motherless lambs on bottles, hurrying to chop wood and carry in water before a blizzard strikes, herding sheep on windy spring days, or breaking shaggy, stubborn broncos, I'm on my own stamping ground.

When I was sixteen, I rode in the "Frontier Days" at Cheyenne, Wyoming, still known as the Daddy of 'em All. I won the Ladies' Relay Championship. In a relay race the rider starts on a saddled horse, rides around the half-mile track and changes the saddle to a second horse; another half-mile lap and changes to the finishing horse. I note the time engraved on the cup is three minutes and forty seconds. This silver cup, with stag-horn handles, has been a handy recepticle all these years for the children to stache away their best "shooters," their bicycle licenses, and other valuables.

There was no high school near our small ranch so I came up to Denver to high school. My senior year I was captain of the girls' basketball team, and the young coach, Al Weber, by name, used to come home with me after games to carry the basketball and other paraphernalia. So that after graduation I decided against higher education and became Mrs. Weber. I've taken extra courses at the University of Denver. The first years of married life were a jumble of psychology courses, baby tending, football games, when my husband's team played, contemporary literature courses, nursing children through measles, and writing stories.

We have six children, five boys and a girl: Harry, William, Rosemary, David, Lawrence and Thomas. Lawrence and Thomas are attending St. Francis de Sales school here in Denver.

I have been writing for some twenty years now. I started writing stories and books for teen age readers but now, although I still write for them, I write magazine stories and novelettes. I try to do a teen age book every other year besides magazine stories. I like to write for a young audience. Perhaps because when I do, the years between now and my own youth fold together like an accordion, and I am one with my readers and long to make them get the thrill out of the things I loved to do.

Most of the writers I know are the kind who don't worry a great deal about the lesser details, or I should say the worrying small details of living. Writers live so much in an imaginary world. Writing is a nice shock-absorber for the lesser bumps. As one writer put it, we have to worry so much about helping our fictional characters lift the mortgage off the old homestead, that we forget about the one perched on our own roof.

People often ask me if I get my stories from happenings in real life. Yes, and no. Often a story or book springs into being from a certain incident we hear about or read about. My book, *Sing for Your Supper*, which is about an early-day theatrical troupe, came about after I read of a family troupe who, with a loaded wagon drawn by mules, toured through our mining towns and put on Shakespearean plays. The line which started me thinking about the whole story was "Madame Waverly had four daughters." I began imagining how tough the going would be over muddy mountain roads in April, and how the meager scenery and costumes would have to be worked over for different plays. I remember a mystery story writer telling me once that he got the thread of a long story from a tiny item he read in a newspaper. It told of a man who had been murdered but who, before he died, tried to write a message by dipping his fingers in his blood and scrawling an unfinished word.

Again, a writer may write a story to put over one of his favorite themes. For instance, in my girls' book, *Meet the Malones*. The theme of that came from two quotations from Emerson; one, "What wilt thou? quoth God; take it and pay for it," and the other, closely aligned in thought, "The highest price you can pay for a thing is to get it for nothing." The Malone family (Beanie was my favorite) came into being to prove that Emerson was right.

Occasionally an interesting relationship will start a train of thought and, with weaving back and forth and filling in, a story emerges. Such was the case of a story of mine in a recent *Saturday Evening Post,* "My Uncles O'More." My first picture of that story was of two unmarried brothers and their sister, who was trying to get wives for them so as to take some of the burden off her own shoulders. And because I love the Irish and their strutting and their loud talk ('gulderin,' is the Irish word for it) I made them that.

Writing isn't as easy as some people think. I find that a great many people think a writer gets an inspiration, writes it at white-heat, sends it off to an editor and presto, comes the acceptance. There's a great deal of drudgery in between that first inspiration and the final copy. A great deal of thinking and rethinking, writing and rewriting. More pages are carried out in the waste-basket than ever are mailed out.

Our home is in Denver and, like all parents, we are praying that the war will be over before too many months go by, so that our family, and all families, may be united again. Our three oldest sons are in service—Harry, in armored engineers; William —Bill, to all who know him—was on Bataan when it fell, and is a Japanese prisoner. David is in radio in the navy.

There are times when family and writing don't mix well together. But on the whole they dovetail together to form a crammed full schedule. Each brings its own happiness, so that I am often reminded of my Irish grandmother murmuring as she doused the churn-dasher up and down, "Ah, God is good—and life is sweet."

EDITOR'S NOTE: Mrs. Weber's books include *Mr. Gold and Her Neighborhood House*, 1933, Little; *Wish in the Dark*, 1932, id.; *Sing for Your Supper*, 1941, Crowell; *Meet the Malones*, 1943, id.

HELEN CONSTANCE WHITE

MY LIFE IS THE QUIET but far from dull life of an academic person. Born November 26, 1896, in New Haven, Connecticut, I am the daughter of John and Mary King White. I am the eldest of four children, another of whom, Olive B. White, is also a professor of English and a novelist. Our family moved from New Haven to Boston and there we children grew up and were educated. I went to Girls High School in Boston, the oldest of American high schools for girls, with a fine tradition of devotion to New England standards of education and to awareness of community responsibility and public service. At that time the student body represented a wide variety of national backgrounds, many of the students being themselves recent immigrants. It was a very stimulating and valuable social atmosphere for a child from the suburbs. From there I went to Radcliffe College to receive the B.A. degree with a major in English and a minor in History in 1916, and a Master's degree in English and Education in 1917.

Although I had very early wanted to write I had always known that I wanted to be an English teacher—a choice of vocation which still seems to me the best of all choices even after more than twenty-five years of teaching. Radcliffe brought the stimulus of contact with first-class mature minds among the faculty and first class promising minds among the students. From there I went to teach at Smith College—four sections of Freshman English for two years. The freedom of organization of that teaching gave scope both for all the mistakes of and the enthusiasm of a beginner. And I emerged from that experience with a sense which I have never lost of the infinite complexity and challenge as well as delight of the art of teaching. Those two years gave a chance, too, to begin to get acquainted with some of the movements of current literature, especially among the novelists and poets, and with the help of a generous French colleague, to make real progress in acquaintance with French literature. At the end of the two years older colleagues convinced me of the desirability of trying a year in another part of the country with the opportunity for a combination of further graduate work and teaching that a university might provide.

So in 1919 this young New Englander came out to the University of Wisconsin for a year and has been there, except for leaves of absence, ever since. I arrived in time to welcome the last Army back to the University, an unforgettable experience which I hope to turn to the advantage of the returning veterans of this war. At the present moment I am not sure which was the greater problem—the young man who had been through the hardships of war or the younger man who had struggled up to the University through the distractions and dislocations of war-time home society. I am still inclined to think that the less publicized problem may well prove the more urgent. With my major in English and a minor in philosophy and the doctor's thesis on the mysticism of William Blake I received my Ph.D. degree from the University of Wisconsin in 1924. A promotion to the rank of assistant professor in 1925, with increasing opportunities in advanced work opened up a future which brought in turn the associate professorship in 1934, and the full professorship in 1937. It has been a very rich and interesting experience not only of teaching but of a good deal of committee and organization work both with individuals and groups of students and very stimulating opportunities for work on university and community problems. The "joiner" probably wastes a lot of time and energy, but there is no question of the human experience which she wins from its distractions, and that work is of even more importance than efficiency to the writer.

One of the most fruitful of these ventures was the leading of student parties under the Open Road of New York and the International Student Hospitality Association of Paris to Europe in the summers of 1926 and 1927. England, Holland, Germany, France, were tasted the first summer with a much more concentrated experience for six weeks of literary England and part of France and Italy in the summer of 1927. The opportunities which these summers brought for contact with students of other countries and the current problems of their lives as well as with the cultural past that is so important to the American proved of lasting influence.

The Guggenheim fellowship gave the opportunity for a year's research in seventeenth century literature in the year 1928–29 and the summer of 1930. Most of this year was spent at work in the British Museum in London, but six weeks of the summer were spent with Olive at the Bodleian Library in Oxford. An April holiday in the company of a sculptor friend gave a chance for a more prolonged visit to Florence and Rome in Italy and a very exciting first visit to Assisi and Venice. Ultimately the experiences of this year were to lead to *A Watch in the Night*. Out of the research came more immediately the book, *English Devotional Literature* (Prose), 1600–1640, and later, when a grant from the University of Wisconsin made possible a return to London in 1935, *The Metaphysical Poets, a Study in Religious Experience*, in 1936. *A Watch in the Night*, published in 1933 made use both of studies in Franciscan history and mysticism and the traveler's acquaintance with medieval architectural monuments in Italy and other countries. This was followed by the story of the eleventh century *Not Built with Hands,* published in 1935, and a study of the French Revolution, *To the End of the World,* published in 1939. A fellowship at the Huntington Library in San Marino, California, for the year 1939–40 made it possible to push on with studies in the sixteenth-century religious background as it affected literature which partly, at least, culminated in the *Social Criticism in Popular Religious Literature of the Sixteenth Century* published in 1944, and it made possible a more immediate acquaintance with the background of the Franciscan missions in California which is the basis for the novel in progress at the present moment.

EDITOR'S NOTE: Dr. White is president of the American Association of University Women. She received honorary doctorates from St. Scholastica College, Kansas, and Mount St. Mary College, Milwaukee, and in 1942 the Laetare Medal from the University of Notre Dame. Her books, published by Macmillan, include *The Metaphysical Poets,* 1936; *Not Built With Hands,* 1935; *A Watch in the Night,* 1933; and *To the End of the World,* 1939.